# FEMINISM AND ANTI-FEMINISM
# IN EARLY ECONOMIC THOUGHT

*For Joe and for Naomi*

# Feminism and Anti-Feminism in Early Economic Thought

Michèle A. Pujol
*Women's Studies Program*
*University of Victoria*
*Canada*

Edward Elgar

Published by
Edward Elgar Publishing Limited
Gower House
Croft Road
Aldershot
Hants GU11 3HR
England

Edward Elgar Publishing Limited
Distributed in the United States
by Ashgate Publishing Co.
Old Post Road
Brookfield
Vermont 05036
USA

CIP records for this book
are available from the British Library
and the US Library of Congress

TP

ISBN 1 85278 456 3

Printed and bound in Great Britain by
Billing and Sons Ltd, Worcester

# Contents

*v*

# Acknowledgements

This book would not have seen the light without the initial impetus provided by the faculty and students of the Simon Fraser University Women's Studies Program in the late 1970s. Over the years, it benefited tremendously from the exciting intellectual and practical challenge and nourishment provided by the feminist movement in Canada and worldwide and by the ongoing growth of woman-centred knowledge and feminist theory. The writings of Mary O'Brien, Heidi Hartmann, Nancy Folbre, Nancy Hartsock and Louise Vandelac have been particularly challenging and inspiring.

I am indebted to Mike Lebowitz, teacher and friend, who has contributed enormously to shaping my theoretical understanding. I am grateful to Joe Dolecki, Keith Fulton, Naomi Guilbert and John Loxley for the invaluable criticisms, the encouragement and the friendly support they have offered all these years. Useful comments, suggestions and criticisms were also received on various parts of the book from Anthony Waterman, Robert Dimand and anonymous referees. Extracts from *The Economics of Welfare* © A.C. Pigou, 1932, are reproduced with the kind permission of Macmillan Ltd.

Efficient secretarial help, as well as comments and encouragement were provided by Lynne Slobodian, Betty McGregor and Jean Wilson. Patricia Steele offered proof-reading and support at a much-needed time. Val Hemminger helped with final editing. The Economics Department at Brandon University graciously gave me some work-space. Val Paape, through her yoga teaching, and Winnipeg's Hinode Taiko, kept me sane through the final months of writing.

Finally, I must thank my former 'colleagues' at the University of Manitoba who have provided me with the practical experience of what it means to be a feminist in a male-dominated discipline, experience which has contributed to the theoretical elaboration of this book.

# Introduction

Women do not figure prominently in the writings of economists. They are often not mentioned at all, or only in the odd example or footnote. It is not clear whether the 'economic laws', declared universal, apply to them. A scrutiny of economics texts shows, however, that women are not the object of complete neglect, rather they are construed, explicitly or implicitly, as exceptions to the rules developed, as belonging 'elsewhere' than in the economic sphere, and as participating only marginally if at all in the nation's economic activity. They are denied the status of economic agents in their own right, and as a consequence, normative decisions are made on their behalf regarding the place they should hold in the economy and in society.

My intent in this study is to trace back to the origins of the neoclassical school of thought the particular biases in methodology and discourse which characterize the school's treatment of women and their place in a capitalist economy. I will investigate the extent of the presence of women and of issues specific to them in early neoclassical writing, the nature of the theoretical developments focusing on women and their economic activity, and the positions taken by economists towards feminist demands for equality.

Feminist critics of the discipline have questioned its neglect of women and have attempted to effect changes. In the early days of feminist scrutiny of the traditional disciplines, Janice Madden wrote:

> if the subjects discussed in traditional economic publications are an index of the concerns of economists, there has been an evident lack of professional interest in the [woman] problem. Therefore, a history of economic thought on women has to be pieced together from comments in feminist writings, from implicit and explicit references to sex discrimination in the discussions of the economics of race discrimination and social class exploitation, and from political debates on equal pay legislation. (1972: 21)

Since then, although still small in volume, the economic literature on women has grown due in part to the increased visibility of women in the labour market and to feminist pressure on the discipline. Analyses of women's work, in the labour force and in the home, and of the economic inequality of the sexes, have appeared in the various paradigms (neoclassical, institutional, Marxian). Yet these analyses

*1*

have proven limited and fraught with the male perspective and ideological biases of the paradigms in which they were developed.

Fifteen years after Madden's initial review of the history of economic thought on women, Barbara Bergmann noted a polarization emerging between a tentative feminist economics[1] and a boisterous anti-feminist component of the neoclassical school:

> Currently, most economists are probably in the nonfeminist camp, which continues hostile to any suggestion that the economic position of women needs improvement. The profession continues to be overwhelmingly male. Women economists are still under pressure to conform to traditional male attitudes. (Bergmann, 1987: 132)

Economics has been more impervious to women's realities and women's concerns and more resistant to change than other social sciences. The feminist challenges which have swept the academy in the past twenty years have barely troubled the discipline. This can be attributed to a number of reasons.

First, as documented by Ferber and Teiman (1981), economics is the most male dominated of the social sciences. Women, historically and to this day, have been virtually absent from the profession. This situation is worse within the confines of the dominant neoclassical school. The alternative paradigms (post-Keynesian, neo-Ricardian, institutional, Marxian and radical) fare slightly better, but the women in their midst can be doubly marginalized.

Secondly, to a greater extent than other social sciences, economics is under the hegemonic control of one paradigm, the conservative, apologetic, pro-capitalist neoclassical school of thought. Martha Mac Donald has stated that this hegemony 'has made it extremely difficult to get answers to the questions in which feminists are interested' (1982: 169). Bergmann further comments:

> most economists have an ideological commitment to the free enterprise system and spend their professional lives trying to disprove assertions that it does not function well. These economists are predisposed to give short shrift to women's complaints that the market system treats them unfairly, and to oppose women's demands that the government should interfere in the market place on women's behalf. (1987: 132)

Issues relevant to women are, therefore, not addressed, or, when they are, it is within a framework which redefines them in a blatantly anti-feminist fashion. This is the case with the whole of the 'new home economics'. Bergmann states: 'The major statement from the non-feminist camp is Gary Becker's *Treatise on the Family* (1981). Becker explains, justifies and even glorifies role differentiation by sex' (ibid.).[2]

Thirdly, in the neoclassical paradigm, and to a similar but possibly lesser extent in the others, the scope/subject matter of economics has been defined in a narrow and exclusionary fashion. Neoclassical economics has traditionally focused on exchange relations, excluding non-monetary/non-market economic activity.[3] This has partly been remedied, more recently, in some of the 'new home economics' where the neoclassical framework is applied to allocation of time between market and domestic work, to reproductive work and to marriage contracts. These attempts are flawed because they use concepts and methodologies developed for market activities to analyse non-market phenomena (McCrate, 1987, 1988). This bias is sexist in that economic activity, both productive and reproductive, which is central to women's life, is ignored: 'economics has evolved a methodology which for the most part cannot "see" women's economic behaviour' (Cohen, 1982: 90). This results in major gaps in theory which have severe policy consequences.[4]

The other paradigms, in part because they developed as critiques of the 'orthodox' approach, also tend to limit themselves to market activity.[5] Yet they have a scope wider than the neoclassical paradigm, analysing the structure and the social and class relations of capitalism. Nevertheless, they have been traditionally silent on gender relations and have only recently attempted to integrate a study of economic inequalities and non-market economic activity in their analysis. In sum, the narrow focus of the discipline makes it overall irrelevant to women's lives and concerns.[6]

Fourthly, in its assumptions, neoclassical economics simplifies and stereotypes the nature of women's lives, social relations and economic motivations. For instance, women tend to be seen as wives and mothers, members of a nuclear family household where they are economically dependent on a male breadwinner, and the family is consistently depicted as a harmonious and consensual entity.[7] By assuming the prevalence of the social relations it wants to perpetuate, neoclassical economics derives theoretical approaches and policies which tend towards the replication of such social relations. For instance, the standard neoclassical assumption of the prevalence of a perfectly competitive market serves to obfuscate the nature of the problems women encounter in the labour market. It also serves to 'predict' that such problems (in so far as they exist at all in the minds of neoclassical economists) will wither away as a result of competition. Such is the case with Becker's (1971) prediction that discrimination on the basis of race or sex will disappear over time as the discriminatory employers suffer from competition.

Biases and assumptions lead to caricatural, inadequate and false representations of women's economic realities. Neoclassical assumptions have proven frustrating for feminists: they engineer avoidance of women's concerns and simply leave important questions unanswered as they 'take[] us around the vicious circle that we want to have explained'.[8]

Fifth, the alienation of women by the neoclassical paradigm happens at the methodological level with the use of abstractions, tools such as mathematical models and econometrics, distance from primary economic actors, and the lack of empirical tests (Driscoll and McFarland, 1989).

Finally, economics has traditionally been sexist because of its androcentrism. Individuals are assumed to be men and the male point of view is the only one considered. In the neoclassical paradigm, the 'new home economics' has systematically construed women as mere parameters of the 'joint' household[9] or male utility functions. Women's time and human capital are seen as factors that affect their husband's (or their children's) utility, income, and human capital.[10] This perspective is never reversed.[11] Having been methodologically excluded from the field of inquiry, women were reintroduced in the 'new home economics' as an incidental object of study with very specific and overdetermined characteristics which only depict, at best, a phallocentric fantasy of women's 'nature' and activities.

Further, the discipline's androcentrism is augmented by classism and racism:[12] in Beckerian discrimination theory what is analysed is the impact of discrimination on the male/white employer, rather than its impact on the female/black employee (Becker, 1971). This is accompanied by assertions that any attempt by women or people of colour to eliminate the effects of discrimination will cause a decrease in 'general' welfare (Edgeworth, 1922, 1923; Pigou, 1952; Killingsworth, 1985). These biases can only lead to theoretical conclusions which reinforce and justify the patriarchal and racial capitalist status quo.[13]

As pointed out by MacDonald (1984) and McFarland (1976), the conjunction of methodological limitations and outright ideological controls on the content and nature of economic theorizing has meant that economic issues of concern to women have only been addressed outside the discipline, mostly by sociologists who escape the consequences of neoclassical hegemony. The flipside of this situation, denounced by Louise Vandelac, is that women economists are forced to adopt the dominant discourse. Ignored as economic subjects, women are colonized within the field.[14] This in turn legitimizes the discipline and 'contributes paradoxically to maintaining the illusion of the neutrality of its discourse' (1986: 17; my translation).

MacDonald has remarked that, in contrast to the other social sciences, economics lacks 'even a recognizable fringe field . . . devoted to the study of women' (1984: 152). The one development which could claim to qualify as such a fringe field, the 'new home economics', is more devoted to the maintenance and the rationalization of the patriarchal status quo than to a bona fide economic study of women. Beyond its ideological and policy-making consequences, the 'new home economics' has filled a theoretical void, and, as Bergmann notes, 'has somewhat retarded the development of feminist economics by seeming to preempt large areas of relevant subject matter and attacking the issues with what looked to be a sophisticated methodology' (1986: 133). This is only one example illustrating Margaret White's assessment that 'the theory can be viewed as inhibiting the development of theories that would allow us to progress towards a more equitable society' (1984: 20).

Feminist economists thus face a particularly difficult task, a task which is both intellectual and political, and which is fraught with the dangers of academic censorship, collegial ostracism and professional demise.[15] Yet, in spite of the adverse conditions presented by the methodological nature and the ideological construct of the discipline, a feminist critique of economics and the building of a feminist economics are under way. This, at first, took the shape of attempts to integrate an analysis of women and their economic activity within the existing paradigms. But, such attempts have led to the realization that 'fitting [women] in the existing analysis now does not work' (Cohen, 1982: 99). Feminists working within the confines of a particular paradigm must be prepared to recognize its epistemological limitations. They must be ready for the imperative theoretical leap beyond its restricting boundaries. A feminist economics must necessarily lead to a re-visioning, if not a revolutioning of the existing male-constructed frameworks. Vandelac notes, for instance, that a feminist reconstruction of economic categories, such as labour, must necessarily operate an epistemological transcendence of the existing disciplinary boundaries (1986: 18).

This study will investigate some of the epistemological bases for the biases that characterize the neoclassical economics discourse on women, their behaviour, their economic activities and their place within the modern capitalist economy. The book will focus on the early days of neoclassical economic theory and on the development of approaches to the questions of equal pay for women and men, the determination of women's wages, women's role within the family and as reproducers, their place in early human capital theories, and the proposals relating to women in early welfare economics.

It is essential to situate this study within the setting of the first feminist movement, which was contemporary with the birth of the school. Ideas develop within specific social and political contexts, and the economists reviewed here were all involved, in one way or another, in the intellectual and social interactions prompted by feminist activism. An analysis of the development of neoclassical thought on women as part of and within the context of these interactions is highly relevant. It helps to determine how theories are influenced by their authors' positions with respect to sex, class, and race, and by their personal/practical stake in the issues. What transpires is the economists' adherence to sexist bias and their defence of patriarchal values, as revealed in the contrast between the actuality and logic of feminists' concerns and the silence/obfuscation/apology with which the discipline has met them.

The birth of the neoclassical school was signified by a radical shift from a labour-based to a utility-based theory of value. This paradigmatic shift is significant to our subject matter because it involved a new approach to the issue of wage determination, and the determination of women's wages seems to be the recurrent issue dealt with by early neoclassical economists in their writings on women. Wage theories based on subsistence requirements, on the wage fund doctrine, and more generally on the cost of reproduction of labour were discarded by the neoclassics, to be replaced by the marginal productivity theory. Yet, as we will see, when it comes to women's wages the old theories resurface as last resort justifications of inequalities.

In the neoclassical paradigm the market provides the central mechanism for resource allocation, production decisions and income distribution. By assuming perfectly competitive conditions, utility maximization (for individuals) and profit maximization (for firms), the market mechanism is shown to provide the most economically efficient, maximizing outcome. In this perfect fiction there is no room for discriminatory situations where women, or other minorities, receive salaries below their productive contribution.

Critics of the paradigm's methodology have pointed out that its assumptions are unrealistic (perfect competition seldom obtains in real life) and unverifiable (how does one test whether individuals actually maximize their utility?). They state that it is prone to circular reasoning and leads to tautological conclusions, already implied in the premisses.[16] Neoclassical economists have retorted that these criticisms are inconsequent as long as the model yields accurate predictions.[17]

Another set of criticisms concerns the political and ideological characteristics of neoclassical economics. The paradigm has been used over time to extol the wonders of capitalism and the market system and to defeat its opponents (for instance, marginal productivity theory is used to deny the possibility of exploitation of labour). Neoclassical economists have time and again used the model, disregarding the limiting nature of its assumptions, to 'prove' that market mechanisms, their outcome, the distribution of income and so on, are fair and optimal, turning the abstract nature of the model into an ideological mystification and justification of reality. Further, the model has been used to argue against any economic policy which could be depicted as potentially tampering with the working of a 'free market'.

Undaunted by methodological criticism, some neoclassical economists have, in the last two decades, proclaimed the universality of their paradigm, asserting its applicability to non-market and non-economic human interactions. This move, spearheaded by Gary Becker,[18] was based on the application of the market-based choice-theoretic model to all aspects of human life. Besides the question of the applicability of a methodologically flawed model, this move raises that of the applicability of an epistemological approach which assumes that all human behaviour can be seen as exchange interactions, all motives can be reduced to the balancing of costs and benefits, and money or a money equivalent can be taken as the common measure of everything. The Beckerian expansion of the paradigm is a development in bourgeois economic thought congruent with the increased fetishization of human relations in capitalism, whereby people see themselves as capital, households become firms, human intercourse becomes monetary exchange.[19]

Neoclassical theory has consistently denied the existence of social or economic power relations between classes, races or sexes. In a theoretical approach where everything is reduced to exchange dynamics, freedom of interaction and equality of the actors are assumptions essential to the predicted outcome of harmony in the free market. With the Beckerian paradigmatic expansion, this ideology is applied to all individual, non-market decisions. This has particularly significant implications given the 'new home economics' presumption to provide a theoretical framework to explain human relations in the household and the family. Whereas the presence of power as a factor in class relations in the public/market sphere was denied in traditional neoclassical economics, it is now also being ignored as a factor in the relations between the sexes in the private/family sphere (Sawhill, 1980; Hartmann, 1981; Folbre, 1988; McCrate, 1988).

In this paradigmatic expansion, another dimension is therefore added to the traditionally apologetic character of neoclassical economics. The obfuscation of patriarchal relations and the concurrent strengthening of patriarchal ideology explicitly complement the bourgeois character of the paradigm. The theoretical inadequacy of neoclassical economics therefore lies, not only in its methodology and in its traditionally bourgeois ideological bias, but also in its sexist bias, which manifests itself both methodologically and ideologically.[20]

The pro-patriarchal nature of mainstream economics is not something new. The purpose of this study is to document that this aspect has been present all along, although not necessarily as explicitly as in the 'new home economics'. Two specific issues concerning women's place in the economy allow us to scrutinize the theoretical purity of the paradigm.

First, women's wages and the conditions of women's employment permit us to test the universality of the marginal productivity theory of wages and of neoclassical approaches to the labour market. It becomes apparent both that the theory fails to explain the wage inequalities encountered by women and that there is a refusal by neoclassical economists to reckon with the consequences of this failure, by admitting to the limits of their approach or by advocating corrective measures which could allow women access to the ideal conditions where the doctrine applies. Faced with an embarrassing problem, the economists choose the strategy of flight, alleging the excuse of intervening extra-economic elements.

The ideological positions defended in this matter are best evidenced by the glib dismissal of more cogent approaches tentatively developed by the feminists of the time (for example crowding theory, segregated labour markets) or resulting from the continued use of a subsistence theory of wages. The naked reassertion of biased beliefs resorted to by neoclassical economists to counter these theoretical attempts generates a most awesome exercise in apologetics whereby the internal consistency of the neoclassical model is thrown overboard.

Secondly, in the development of early welfare economics, the treatment given to women allows us to test the extent of the economists' adherence to the dogmas of freedom of the market and of individual utility maximization. Here again these principles are overridden for reasons which are at best vague and which resort to an imperious extra-economic order. The study of the elaboration of welfare economics and of early human capital theory also gives us some insight into the theoretical and policy consequences of the extant denial of the economic nature of women's reproductive activity.

The present study therefore uncovers the *double* ideological role (bourgeois and patriarchal) of early neoclassical economists and the *double* nature of their apologetic model-building and policy prescriptions. It also shows that this double bias generates serious contradictions within the model and leads to the breakdown of its internal consistency.

A feminist critique of neoclassical economics thus furthers the methodological and ideological questioning of the paradigm. The radical critique of the paradigm has been limited because it has been one-sided, itself marred by the blindness inherent in the male bias of the critics. A feminist critique strengthens the criticism of inadequacy and unrealism of the model's assumptions, and further exposes the tautological nature of neoclassical theorizing. It adds to these critiques the more serious ones of the internal inconsistency in the model and of the deficiency of its claim to universality.[21]

This book is organized into one preliminary chapter and two main sections. Chapter 1 investigates some of the approaches to the status of women in the pre-neoclassical period. The roots of women's invisibility and of the neglect of non-market activity in economic theory are sought in the writings of Adam Smith. The work of John Stuart Mill and the influence on his approach by Harriet Taylor permit us to evaluate a specific attempt to integrate a feminist analysis into economic theory. The limits present in Mill's position relative to Taylor's are further highlighted by the more radical ideas of one of their contemporaries, Barbara Bodichon.

Part II examines the debate which went on for over a third of a century on the question of equal pay for men and women. The debate was sparked by feminist demands for equal pay and features economic writings by feminists printed in economic journals. The section is divided into three chapters, along with an Introduction and a Conclusion. Chapter 3 looks at the early, pre-World War I debate, which produced innovative theoretical formulations by feminists and pro-feminist positions by some of the male economists. Chapter 4 analyses the approaches developed by three notable feminists, Millicent Fawcett, Eleanor Rathbone and Beatrice Webb, during the war. It shows that there was not a single, cohesive feminist position on the issue. Differences involved both priorities and strategic approaches to the issue. Chapter 5 assesses the two articles written by Edgeworth on the equal pay question in the early 1920s, which can be taken as an enunciation of neoclassical thought on the issue. They close the debate without resolving the question.

Part III focuses more closely on two of the main builders of the neoclassical paradigm: Marshall and Pigou. Chapter 8 critically analyses the construction of women's role in Marshall's 'human capital' theory. In Chapters 9 and 10 Pigou's theory of exploitation is contrasted with his treatment of women's wages while Chapter 10 appraises his vision of the place of women in his original blueprint for a welfare state. This section reveals the ideological position which informs neoclassical theorizing on women's place in the economy and the contradictions this position creates.

## Notes

1. A feminist economics should not be seen as a homogeneous concept; there are diverse theoretical positions and tendencies within feminism itself. In Bergmann's reformist and liberal vision, feminist economists are 'attempting to develop the outlines of what they claim will be a more equitable future, and are trying to formulate policy proposals that might bring us closer to a workable yet equitable system' (1987, 131). A more radical approach is provided by Leghorn and Parker: 'when we look at women's place in the economy, we cannot begin from traditional male concepts of what is valuable and productive, and what are commodities. We must begin from women's perspectives. We must question and reevaluate all the institutions and concepts with which men have defined, measured and understood the economy, and develop a woman-centered perspective for attempting to understand women's lives cross-culturally' (1981: 4).
2. See Becker (1981b). See also, for instance, Mincer and Polachek (1974); Lloyd (1975); Schultz (1974).
3. For an ironic treatment of the ideological biases of the scope of economics, see Marsden (1981).
4. See McFarland (1976) and Cohen (1982).
5. A number of feminist critics have noted that male radical or institutional economists are still reluctant to expand their approach to include women, and often dismiss, distort or ignore feminist theories and criticisms. See, for instance, Hartmann and Markusen (1980), MacDonald (1984), Folbre and Hartmann (1988). MacDonald has remarked that 'the disagreements between paradigms are for the most part disagreements among men' (1984: 154).
6. See Leghorn and Parker (1981); Cohen (1982); Markusen (1977); Waring (1988).
7. See Hartmann (1981); Folbre (1984); Folbre and Hartmann (1988). Note that these assumptions are also present in the Marxian paradigm.
8. MacDonald (1984: 172). See also Cohen (1982) and Isabel Sawhill: 'we have come full circle. We have seen that women earn less than men because of their special role within the family, but that their special role within the family – and indeed the desirability of marriage and children – are importantly related to the economic status of women' (1980: 133).
9. A 'joint utility function' is a contradiction in terms; see Arrow (1963) and Galbraith (1973: Ch. 4).
10. See Leibowitz (1974); Mincer and Polachek (1974); Benham (1974); Gronau (1973).
11. Louise Vandelac describes the 'variable femme' (the woman variable) as a 'lapsus significatif de l'omniprésence du référent masculin' (a significant sign of the ever-present masculine referee) and calls for its replacement by the more balanced 'variable sexe' (sex variable) which would allow economic inquiry to recentre away from women, construed as the anomaly, the problem, the marginal element, to the more central problematic of relations between the sexes in the economy (1986: 17).
12. It is also characterized by heterosexism.
13. Capitalism cannot be dissociated from the social and economic structures which create and reinforce the power of men and male-dominated institutions over women,

the oppression of people of colour, and the imperialist domination of colonies and non culunih s (Innes, 1986).

14. Vandelac, a sociologist herself, writes. 'les femmes économistes se retrouvent dans l'incomfortable position d'adhérer à un discours qui, non seulement les ignore comme sujets, mais qui s'est élaboré sur leur mise à l'ombre' (Women economists find themselves in the awkward position of having to subscribe to a discourse which not only ignores them as subjects, but which also was developed on the basis of their overshadowing) (1986: 16; my translation).

15. Vandelac notes that feminist economists risk 'd'être accusées d'impertinence, et aussitôt renvoyées hors-champ économique et mises hors-jeu . . .' (to be accused of impertinence and immediately driven out of the discipline, driven out of the game). She characterizes the censoring response of mainstream economists as 'un mécanisme classique d'auto-défense disciplinaire et professionelle, où la scientificité s'autoproclame sur la base d'un jeu complexe d'interdits, renvoyant la critique épistémologique à des préoccupations hors-discipline et donc hors-science permettant du même coup de minimiser la critique et de dénigrer les esprits, dits non-scientifiques, qui la porte . . .' (a classical mechanism of disciplinary and professional defensiveness, where scientificity is self-proclaimed on the basis of a complex game of prohibitions, throwing out all epistemological criticism to a sphere of extra-disciplinary, and hence extra-scientific concerns, consequently allowing the criticisms to be minimized and the alleged non-scientificity of its authors to be disparaged) (1986: 16–17, my translation).

16. See for instance Boland (1979); Dolecki (1984); Godelier (1972); Hunt and Schwartz (1972); Lebowitz (1973–4); Mini (1974); Rowthorn (1974), and Salama (1975).

17. This response is based on Friedman (1953). According to this criterion, Becker's 1957 theory of discrimination should have been discarded by now.

18. 'In recent years, economists have used economic theory more boldly to explain behavior outside the monetary market sector, and increasing numbers of noneconomists have been following their example. As a result, racial discrimination, fertility, politics, crime, education, statistical decision making, adversary situations, labor-force participation, the uses of "leisure" time, and other behavior are much better understood. Indeed, economic theory may well be on its way to providing a unified framework for *all* behavior involving scarce resources, nonmarket as well as market, nonmonetary as well as monetary, small group as well as competitive' (1973: 813–14).

19. According to Nancy Hartsock (1985), such developments in economic thought have had an influence in other social sciences, leading to the development of exchange-based theories of social interaction and human behaviour.

20. Patriarchal relations are not new or specific to capitalism. They are present, although in different forms, in all economic systems, except possibly those which predate man-made history. The absence of analyses of these relations in most malestream writing is an illustration of their sexist bias. The term 'malestream' was coined by Mary O'Brien (1981).

21. For discussions of feminist method, methodology or epistemology, see Harding (1987).

# PART I

# SOME APPROACHES TO THE ECONOMIC STATUS OF WOMEN BEFORE 1890

# 1 Adam Smith, John Stuart Mill, Harriet Taylor and Barbara Bodichon

An analysis of the treatment of women and women's work by the classical economists could be the object of a study of its own. This chapter does not attempt an exhaustive survey of the classical school. It merely reviews the approaches of two of the classical economists: Adam Smith and John Stuart Mill. It also examines the early insights of Harriet Taylor and Barbara Bodichon.

Smith was the founder of the classical school and the 'father' of modern economics.[1] He wrote the first comprehensive economic treatise and also dwelt on issues of law and society, at a time of major economic, political and societal transformations. His writings give an indication of the initial treatment women received from the pen of an economist who set out to develop a theory of the workings of the nascent capitalist system. They thus offer an invaluable perspective on the origins of contemporary economic approaches to women and of the failure of Smith's 'sons' to analyse the characteristics and role of the sexual division of labour (productive and reproductive) in the capitalist system.

John Stuart Mill, like Adam Smith, also wrote on philosophy and political theory. The relevance of Mill's thought to this study lies in his subscription to the feminist causes of his days. His feminist convictions appear in his economic writings and are fully expressed in *The Subjection of Women* (Mill, 1970a).

Yet, although influential in the politics of his day, Mill's lead into alternative approaches to the economic situation of women and his insight into the patriarchal economic relations which determine their place in capitalist society were confined to a dead end by subsequent economists. Mill remains to this day a remarkable exception to the mainstream/malestream tradition of economic theorists: it is notable that the profession has failed to produce a modern counterpart to Mill among its luminaries.

A study of Mill's feminist approach to the economic issues concerning women necessarily requires an acknowledgement of the role Harriet Taylor played in the elaboration of his thought. We will see that her understanding of the economic consequences of patriarchy are more far-reaching than Mill's. So is Barbara Bodichon's. A contemporary of Mill and Taylor, she wrote the first coherent feminist treatment of women's work.

**Adam Smith**

It is possible to trace some of the roots of most current economic concepts and approaches to Adam Smith's *The Wealth of Nations* (1976; hereafter referred to as *WN*). Among these is the tendency to pay scant attention to women's work and to women's place in and contribution to the capitalist economy.

Unlike some of his contemporaries, Smith does not even mention the epistemological link between political economy and *Oeconomia*, the management of a household.[2] As argued by Jane Rendall, Smith was writing at a time of transition and restructuring of social reality 'in which both public and private spheres received new definitions, dividing the commercial world of the market economy, from the domestic morality of the family' (1987: 45). This transition was of course linked to the capitalist industrial revolution which made industry and the market the only legitimate *loci* of economic activity. The economic activity taking place in the household, and carried out in great part by women, was relegated to a trivial status, if not made altogether non-existent in the minds of the theoreticians of capitalism. At the same time, the participation of women in market or industrial activity was made invisible.[3]

Yet Smith was aware of the importance of women's employment to the family's economic viability. In his chapter 'Of The Wages of Labour' (*WN*: I.viii) he discusses the minimum wage requirements of wage workers and, interestingly, switches abruptly from the needs of 'workmen' as individuals in the labour market, to the needs of the family attached to the male worker.[4]

> A man must always live by his work, and his wages must at least be sufficient to maintain him. They must even upon most occasions be somewhat more; otherwise it would be impossible for him to bring up a family, and the race of such workmen could not last beyond the first generation. (*WN*: I.viii.15)

Speculating on rates of infant mortality, he elaborates that workers 'must every where earn at least double their own maintenance, in order that one with another they may be enabled to bring up two children'. Women are matter-of-factly assumed to work for wages as well as raising a family: 'the labour of the wife, on account of her necessary attendance on the children, being supposed no more than sufficient to provide for herself', establishing that this must have been the common practice. Later, Smith recapitulates:

Thus far at least seems certain, that, in order to bring up a family, the labour of the husband and wife together must, even in the lowest species of common labour, be able to earn something more than what is precisely necessary for their own maintenance. *(WN: I.viii.15)*

This single passage recognizes the commonality of married women's employment, the limitations to their wage-earning capacity stemming from their reproductive role and the necessity of their wage-earning and of their reproductive unpaid work to the economic survival and generational reproduction of the working class.

The only other explicit reference to women's work for wages is a passing comment on the low wages of women spinners and knitters in Scotland, attributed to their deriving 'the principal part of their subsistence from some other employment', such as domestic service *(WN: I.x.b.49,50)*. The point made here will be taken up by the next generations of economists who attribute wages below subsistence levels to alternative income, such as the Poor Rates, or the support of male family members.

Women spinners 'who return to their parents, and commonly spin in order to make cloaths for themselves and their families' in the 'cheap years', or years of decreasing wealth, are also mentioned as an example of work 'which never enters the publick registers of manufactures' *(WN: I.viii.51)*. This point prefigures future economists' taxonomy of production which should or should not be included in national income accounts. It should have led Smith to a reflection on the shifty nature of commodities production, and on the role of women workers in the transition that was taking place from home to manufacturing production.

In short, except for all of one page in the two-volume *Wealth of Nations*, and in spite of Smith's own acknowledgement of the common and necessary nature of their employment, women are conspicuously absent from his seminal discussion of the nature, organization and operations of capitalist production.

Women are nowhere mentioned in the groundbreaking treatise on the division of labour *(WN: I.i–iii)*, denoting utter blindness on Smith's part to the specific place women held in his day in industrial as well as agricultural production, not to mention the provision of domestic services. He is also blind to the use and manipulation of female workers in the transformation of the labour process and the introduction of technology which were taking place in manufacturing.[5] The connections between the sexual division of labour within the labour market and in society as a whole and the social division of labour are completely bypassed.[6] Could all the needs of 'man' be satisfied in the absence of productive or reproductive labour by women? And what, in Smith's eyes, would have been the relative influence of 'habit, custom and education' as opposed to 'nature' on the origins of the female sex's place in the social division of labour?

There is no discussion of women's access to occupations. Similarly, there is no documentation of the general level of women's wages[7] and of whether the five 'circumstances' which affect the relative level of wages in different employments (*WN*: I.x.b) apply evenly across the sexes. Although a large proportion of paid domestic service was provided by women in Smith's day, the actual extent of the presence of the female sex in this, or any other, field of employment, classified as productive or unproductive, is not documented. Were women present in larger numbers in the productive or the unproductive occupations? What was the nature of their unpaid work in the home? Was their labour in the home which resulted in 'some particular subject or vendible commodity' (*WN*: II.iii.1) to be considered productive?

Smith's definition of productive and unproductive work would normally point to the unproductive nature of all reproductive work (performed mostly by women, but also by male servants, teachers and tutors). Yet, if productive labour is that labour which replaces or augments capital (*WN*: II.iii.16ff), and given Smith's inclusion in the category of 'fixed capital' of the 'acquired and useful abilities of all the inhabitants or members of the society' (*WN*: II.i.17), what is the status of labour which does not produce a physical good but which reproduces or augments the fixed capital embodied in workers' productive capacity?

Smith is very explicit on the 'human' portion of 'fixed capital':

> The acquisition of such talents, by the maintenance of the acquirer during his education, study, or apprenticeship, always costs a real expence, which is a capital fixed and realized, as it were in his person. Those talents, as they are made part of his fortune, so do they likewise of that of the society to which he belongs. The improved dexterity of a workman may be considered in the same light as a machine or instrument of trade which facilitates and abridges labour. (*WN*: II.i.17)

Income spent on education or training is clearly seen as a contribution to capital. The work of educating and nurturing the productive abilities of people should, by Smith's definition, be seen as productive labour.

While not addressing this question Smith deals at length with the necessity of an appropriate system of education for both the upper classes and the working class. In *The Theory of Moral Sentiments* (*TMS*) Smith advocates domestic education over 'the education of boys at distant great schools, of young men at distant colleges, of young ladies in distant nunneries and boarding schools' (*TMS*: VI.ii.1.10) which, in his view, fail to inculcate ethical values (that is, duty towards parents, and the nation). He adds: 'Domestic education is the institution of nature; public education, the contrivance of man. It is surely unnecessary to say, which is likely to be the wisest.'

In *The Wealth of Nations* the more specific point is made that travel abroad makes a young man 'more conceited, more unprincipled, more dissipated, and more incapable of any serious application either to study or to business, than he could well have become in so short a time, had he lived at home' (V.i.f.36). Smith contrasts this with the down-to-earth, domestic-based education of young women in the upper classes:

> There are no publick institutions for the education of women, and there is accordingly nothing useless, absurd, or fantastical in the common course of their education. They are taught what their parents or guardians judge it necessary or useful for them to learn; and they are taught nothing else. (*WN*: V.i.f.47)[8]

But, whereas Smith advocates that young men educated at home 'may, with propriety and advantage, go out every day to attend public schools' (*TMS*: VI.ii.1.10), no such suggestion is made for young women.

The domestic education of women is sufficient to prepare them for everything that will be required of them:

> Every part of their education tends evidently to some useful purpose; either to improve the natural attractions of their person, or to form their mind to reserve, to modesty, to chastity, and to oeconomy: to render them both likely to become the mistresses of a family, and to behave properly when they have become such. In every part of her life a woman feels some conveniency or advantage from every part of her education. (*WN*: V.i.f.47)

This passage reveals Smith's view of women in the bourgeois and upper classes, women who are presumed to never be or need to be employed, women who only have one vocation: that of wife and housewife, and who must make themselves attractive to a husband to attain it.

In the *Theory of Moral Sentiments*, Smith expands on this view. Chastity and modesty are essential virtues for women (*TMS*: VII.iv). A wife must be 'careful, officious, faithful and sincere' towards her husband (*TMS*: III.5.1). She should not be motivated solely by 'duty' but also by love (*TMS*: III.6.4). The husband is not given similar duties or obligations; there is more discussion of the proper behaviour of one man towards another than of a husband's towards his wife. In marriage, the man has rights, which include the right to the love and obedience

of his wife, and property rights over her and their offspring. The woman
has no equivalent rights (*TMS*: III.5.1; III.6.4; VI.ii.1.14).[9]

Both *The Wealth of Nations* and *The Theory of Moral Sentiments*
emphasize the importance of the family environment, 'where every
thing presents us with the idea of peace, cheerfulness, harmony, and
contentment', in the education of children (*TMS*: I.ii.4.2). The building
and day-to-day maintenance of such an environment is the work of
women, a 'moral' component of 'oeconomy', but Smith does not
elaborate on this element of women's role.[10]

The passage where Smith recommends that the workers, who are
made 'stupid and ignorant' by the division of labour, have access to
public education as compensation is well known (*WN*: V.i.f.50). But
nothing indicates that working-class women are included in this recommendation. Would they have time for education between the hours
spent in employment and those spent in 'attendance of the children'?
Are they receiving a domestic education in the same manner as
bourgeois women? Are they responsible to the same extent for maintaining harmony in the home and nurturing the future generation?

Although sketchy, Smith's views deny women across the classes
access to public education while assigning them an educative role within
the household, a role essential to the development of an appropriate
social fabric. Besides the charge of forming its 'morals', women have
the primary reproductive role of bringing the next generation into the
world. Women's fertility, in relation to the standard of living of
working-class families, and as a resource in the building of a nation's
population stock, is the object of repeated discussions in the *Wealth of
Nations*. Smith remarks that there seems to be an inverse relation
between women's fertility and their standard of living.

> Poverty, though it no doubt discourages, does not always prevent marriage.
> It seems even to be favourable to generation. A half-starved highland woman
> frequently bears more than twenty children, while a pampered fine lady is
> often incapable of bearing any, and is generally exhausted by two or three.
> Barrenness, so frequent among women of fashion, is very rare among those
> of inferior station. (*WN*: I.viii.37)

But fertility is not all; the survival of children depends on the material
conditions of the families they are born into. Poverty 'is extremely
unfavourable to the rearing of children'. Of the twenty born to the
highland woman, only two will survive (*WN*: I.viii.38).

Income level is not the only factor responsible for child mortality
rates. The care the children receive, presumably from their mother, has
crucial importance: 'This great mortality . . . will everywhere be found

chiefly among the children of the common people, who cannot afford to tend them with the same care as those of better station' (ibid.). This point is made more explicitly in the *Lectures on Jurisprudence*:

> The better sort, who can afford attendance and attention to their children, seldom lose near so many. Few women of middling rank who have borne 8 children have lost 4 by the time they are 5 years old, and frequently none of them at all. It is therefore neglect alone that is the cause for this great mortality.[11] (Quoted in *WN*: I.viii.38n.)

This belief is also expressed in Smith's distinction between the 'sober and industrious' and the 'dissolute and disorderly' poor.

> It is the sober and industrious poor who generally bring up the most numerous families, and who principally supply the demand for useful labour. . . . the dissolute and disorderly . . . seldom rear up numerous families; their children generally perish from neglect, mismanagement, and the scantiness or unwholesomeness of their food. (*WN*: V.ii.k.7)

The skills in 'oeconomy' of the mothers, as well as their 'morals' are essential to 'their ability to bring up families, in consequence of this forced frugality'.[12] The children who happen to survive in the latter case will have suffered the bad influence of their parents and will turn out as 'publick nuisances' rather than 'useful to society by their industry'.

Women's reproductive capacities and labour are seen as even more valuable in an economy where a labour shortage exists. Taking the example of North America, Smith comments that labour is 'so well rewarded that a numerous family of children, instead of being a burthen is a source of opulence and prosperity to the parents'. Women there seem to be in high demand for their reproductive abilities, 'the value of children is the greatest of all encouragements to marriage', and a 'widow with four or five children . . . is there frequently courted as a sort of fortune' (*WN*: I.viii.23).

In summary, it is clear that women's reproductive work, not just in bearing children but also in rearing them in an appropriate environment and in fashioning them into productive workers and loyal citizens, is an essential contribution to the 'wealth of nations'. This element does not, however, figure prominently in Smith's economic writings. Neither does women's overall contribution, productive and reproductive. Women are as invisible in Smith's work as in the work of the succeeding economists, with the exception of that of J. S. Mill. Their economic contribution through participation in wage work is ignored, and their fundamental role in reproducing the nation's 'human capital' is taken for granted.

Smith was writing at a time of major changes in the modern western economies and in the history of ideas, in both economic and political thought. As Jane Rendall (1987) shows, he participated in the formalization of the division between the public (market, capitalist) sphere and the private (moral, personal) sphere. This formalization, constructed by the political philosophers of his time, contributed enormously to the delineation of sex roles. Smith's writings provide the link between the development of a modern political theory which rationalizes gender roles in society,[13] and a modern economic theory which rationalizes the operations of the capitalist market. Yet the fact that these themes are treated in two separate works has divided the attention of modern theorists or historians of thought to their subject matter. An overall understanding of Smith's analysis of the transformations taking place in his time and of the subsequent influence of his theories can be reached only by a comprehensive, global study of his work.

A pertinent question, for instance, is whether the doctrine of the 'invisible hand' developed in *The Wealth of Nations* can be reconciled with the candid, patriarchal beliefs informing Smith's discourse on women in *The Theory of Moral Sentiments* and, to some extent, in *The Wealth of Nations*. Does it matter to the relevance of his doctrine that at least half of the human race is not allowed to be freely guided by self-interest?[14]

In Smith's *Lectures on Jurisprudence* he acknowledges that 'the laws of most countries being made by men generally are very severe on the women, who can have no remedy for this oppression'.[15] This denotes greater awareness than most of his successors have had on the subject. Yet his own discussion of women's role and appropriate behaviour indicates his application of the very same bias to the sex.[16] Furthermore, he is not known to have argued for the abrogation of these laws, freeing women from oppression being, in his mind, a much less urgent necessity than freeing the capitalist market from anything that might impede its operations. Or is it implied that confining women to the private and moral sphere, to provide men with a nurturing and ethical environment in a world increasingly impersonal and unethical, and denying them self-interest and self-determination in the exercise of their productive and reproductive activities, in a world increasingly ruled by selfishness and individualism, are the necessary result of the agency of some invisible patriarchal hand?

The divisions emerging in the times and works of Adam Smith appear to have become finalized by the time his followers undertook to write their own treatises of political economy. As the divisions between the public and the private sphere, between the market and the home, between production and reproduction, are perfected, economic writings come to focus exclusively upon the first elements in these dichotomies.

Women, the domestic sphere and reproductive activities are nowhere mentioned in Ricardo's *Principles of Political Economy and Taxation* (1962) and in Malthus's *Principles of Political Economy* (1964). The obliteration of the female half of the population would be difficult in the *Principles of Population* (1970), yet Malthus manages to consider women only as mechanical reproducers, relegating their existence to an animalistic, natural state. His treatment of the arithmetics of maximum fertility ('prolifickness') and of the 'checks' to population growth (late marriages, widowhood, famines . . .) is based on a vision where women are not considered as human (and even less as economic) beings.

James Mill does draw a parallel between 'Political Economy' and 'domestic economy' in the first pages of his *Elements of Political Economy*,[17] but it seems to be only for the purpose of helping the reader who enters the arcane world of economics by providing a comparison with a more familiar concept. The domestic economy is not referred to again beyond this introductory parallel.

It took John Stuart Mill's feminism and progressive liberalism to break (albeit momentarily) the tradition started by Smith and to introduce women, their economic activities and the oppressive conditions they face in society in an economic theory text.

## John Stuart Mill and Harriet Taylor
In contrast to Smith, and his followers, John Stuart Mill had developed an acute awareness of the contradictions within liberal capitalist society emanating from its patriarchal structure and institutions (which he saw as remnants of the obsolete feudal order).[18] Instead of ignoring the problem by relegating women and their work to a separate sphere and to economic marginality, he set out to advocate egalitarian reforms to salvage capitalism and liberal society. This is the main theme of his essay, *The Subjection of Women*:

> the principle which regulates the existing social relations between the two sexes – the legal subordination of one sex to the other – is wrong in itself, and now one of the chief hindrances to human improvement; . . . it ought to be replaced by a principle of perfect equality, admitting no power or priviledge on the one side, nor disability on the other. (1970a: 125)

The same ideas are also present in Mill's *Principles* (1965).

Mill took position early for the rights of women, opposing his father's view that their interests were fairly represented by men and that consequently they did not need access to suffrage.[19] Harriet Taylor, whom he met in 1830 and eventually married in 1851, was to have a profound influence on his convictions, on his political involvement in the cause of women and on his writings.[20] Given the nature of Mill and Taylor's partnership and Mill's own attribution of authorship of ideas to Taylor, I will here consider that the *Principles* was jointly authored by them.[21]

Taylor's acquaintance with early socialist thought also influenced Mill. He recognized that the class nature of capitalism made it a less than perfect economic system. Unlike the previous classical economists he did not try to hide the problematic reality of capitalism behind a Panglossian harmony model such as that of the invisible hand. Yet he did not espouse socialist ideas and reject capitalism altogether. He saw it instead as perfectible, as attested by his statement that 'the principle of private property has never yet had a fair trial in any country' (1965: 207).

Mill stands out among liberal philosophers and classical economists for his feminist ideas.[22] This added a distinctive touch to his critique of society and to his reformism. It also made him into an invaluable ally of the feminist movement of his times.[23] The *Principles* is the first text in political economy which gives more than passing consideration to economic matters affecting women and which considers them as autonomous economic agents.[24]

Mill and Taylor insisted that women should have the same claim as men to property, to the ownership of their own earnings and to inheritance.[25] They argued that women should be freed from moral and economic dependence on men, that they should be treated as adult, autonomous human beings, that they should have unhindered access to employment and free decision-making. They opposed the restrictions to women's work set out in the Factory Acts and saw these as mere window-dressing, aggravating the situation by creating further restrictions on women's economic autonomy: 'it is the great error of reformers and philanthropists in our time, to nibble at the consequences of unjust power, instead of redressing the injustice itself' (1965: 953).

They denounced the condescending attitude of those who wanted to 'protect' working women. Women should not be treated like children, 'children below a certain age *cannot* judge or act by themselves . . . but women are as capable as men of appreciating and managing their own concerns' (1965: 953). They very perceptively identified the real motive behind the Acts: ensuring women's continued availability as dependent servants in the home:

> If women had as absolute a control as men have over their own persons and their own patrimony or acquisitions, there would be no plea for limiting their

hours of labouring for themselves, in order that they might have time to labour for the husband, in what is called, by the advocates of restriction, *his* home. Women employed in factories are the only women in the labouring rank of life whose position is not that of slaves and drudges. (1965: 953)

Chivalry is exposed for what it is, the obfuscation of power relations between the sexes and the bolstering of coercion under the disguise of protection. Chivalry is an obsolete sentiment: 'we have had the morality of submission, and the morality of chivalry and generosity; the time is now come for the morality of justice' (Mill, 1970a: 173) and protection is no longer needed for a 'woman who either possesses or is able to earn an independent livelihood' (1965: 761).[26]

In fact, it is women's 'protectors' who are their oppressors: 'The so-called protectors are now the only persons against whom, in any ordinary circumstances, protection is needed. The brutality and tyranny with which every police report is filled, are those of husbands to wives, of parents to children' (1965: 761).[27] In this striking argument, Mill and Taylor link women's economic and social dependence to patriarchal power relations within the home and to their social, ideological and especially legal reinforcement.

Mill and Taylor do not believe that women should be confined to domesticity. They deplore the lack of choice women face, and condemn as 'unnecessary' their resulting economic dependence on men:

the least which justice requires is that law and custom should not enforce dependence . . . by ordaining that a woman, who does not happen to have a provision by inheritance, shall have scarcely any means open to her of gaining a livelihood, except as a wife and mother. (1965: 765)

Under the guise of being protected, women are kept away from economic autonomy. This is reinforced by their situation in the labour force: 'that there should be no option, no *carrière* possible for the great majority of women except in the humbler departments of life, is a flagrant social injustice (1965: 765). The solutions proposed are 'the opening of industrial occupations freely to both sexes' and allowing women an unconstrained choice: 'Let women who prefer that occupation [wife and mother], adopt it' (1965: 765).

In the jobs available to them, women receive wages that are 'generally lower, and very much lower than those of men' (1965: 394). Wage equality for equal efficiency is exceptional. Three concurrent explanations of wage inequity are given.

First there is 'custom; grounded either in a prejudice, or in the present constitution of society, which, making almost every woman, socially speaking an appendage of some man, enables men to take systematically the lion's share of whatever belongs to both' (1965: 395). Here two sources of the customary discrimination suffered by women are identified: outright prejudice and their dependent status.

Secondly are 'the peculiar employments of women', which are 'comparatively so few'. Crowding is identified: 'the employments are overstocked: that although so much smaller a number of women, than of men, support themselves by wages, the occupations which law and usage make accessible to them are comparatively so few, that the field of their employment is still more overcrowded'. Both custom and the Factory legislation are at fault. As a result, the remuneration women receive is 'greatly below that of employments of equal skill and equal disagreeableness, carried on by men' (1965: 395).

Yet these observations are not pushed as far as they could go. In the same chapter Mill and Taylor developed the theory of non-competing groups, remarking that certain employments (unskilled) are generally overstocked while others enjoy high wages due to a limited supply. In the latter case they surmise that the high wages are a rent resulting from a monopoly of the 'caste' of skilled workers over these occupations. A similar reasoning could have been applied to the wage difference between men and women. This application would have to wait for Millicent Garrett Fawcett.[28] What makes this oversight more surprising is Mill's mention elsewhere of 'all the functions and occupations hitherto retained as the monopoly of the stronger sex' (1970a: 181). Taylor also refers, in the *Enfranchisement*, to male monopoly over employment: 'in the exercise of industry, almost all employments which task the higher faculties in an important field, which lead to distinction, riches, or even pecuniary independence, are fenced around as the exclusive domain of the predominant section [sex]'. She also deals with the argument that opening these employments to women would increase competition and lower their remuneration by saying that this would be akin to 'the breaking down of other monopolies' (Taylor, 1970: 97, 104).

In the third explanation, the dichotomy between 'family wages' for men and subsistence wages for women is explored. 'The wages, at least of single women, must be equal to their support, but need not be more than equal to it; the minimum, in their case, is the pittance absolutely requisite for the sustenance of one human being', to which level women's wages are easily kept by the crowding condition (Mill, 1965: 395). A man's wages cannot descend to that level, even under severest competition, because they must 'be at least sufficient to support himself, a wife, and a number of children adequate to keep up the population' (1965: 396).

In this perceptive, albeit incomplete, analysis Mill and Taylor are able to integrate into their theorizing on women's wages an understanding of the economic consequences of the specific social relations which affect women's economic status. However, no specific remedies are suggested: the passage on women's wages is part of the chapter on 'Differences of Wages in Different Employments', which follows two full chapters on 'Remedies for Low Wages' where no consideration is given to women's wages. The discussion of remedies – in particular that of 'legal or customary minimum wages, with a guarantee of employment', to be administered by Boards of Trade – is silent on the question of whether a minimum wage, with guarantee of employment, should be considered for women. The main remedy advocated for low wages, inspired by the wages fund doctrine, is population control, in itself and as a necessary complement to a minimum wage policy. This approach concerns women only in so far as they are reproducers (1965: II.xii).

Mill and Taylor, unlike most economists, do not think that women are less productive than men. This is expressed in the following commonsense argument: 'Women are not found less efficient than men for the uniformity of factory work, or they would not so generally be employed for it' (1965: 128).

They draw on their observation of the work processes of women to take issue with Smith's proposition that specialization of tasks is a more efficient organization of work than varied occupations:

> Women are usually . . . of far greater versatility than men; . . . There are few women who would not reject the idea that work is made vigorous by being protracted, and is inefficient for some time after changing to a new thing. Even in this case, habit, I believe, much more than nature, is the cause of the difference. The occupations of nine out of every ten men are special, those of nine out of every ten women general, embracing a multitude of details each of which requires very little time. Women are in the constant practice of passing quickly from one manual, and still more from one mental operation to another, which therefore rarely costs them either effort or loss of time . . . (1965: 127–8)

Harriet Taylor made a similar observation in 1851: 'the varied though petty details which compose the occupation of most women, call forth probably as much of mental ability, as the uniform routine of the pursuits which are the habitual occupation of a large majority of men' (1970: 111). Both Mill and Taylor rejected the absolute nature of Smith's axiom on the division of labour and instead stressed that efficiency is not related so much to the nature of the work process as to the 'habit' or training developed by the worker in handling particular work processes.

The argument is remarkable because it counters part of the received Smithian doctrine on the division of labour. Mill and Taylor comment on the origin of this analysis and on the epistemological necessity of not limiting scientific inquiry to the experiences of the male sex: 'the present topic is an instance among multitudes, how little the ideas and experience of women have yet counted for, in forming the opinions of mankind' (Mill, 1965: 127).[29]

It is further remarkable that women's ability to handle efficiently a varied set of tasks is not attributed to their 'nature'. This type of efficiency is thus a specific skill which women acquire. This skill, consistently ignored or devalued by most economists,[30] is here given an honest and respectful assessment. But, while these particular skills of women are recognized, what is lacking in the *Principles* is an overall judgement of women's ability to participate equally in industrial production. If they are efficient at what they do now, could they be efficient in the occupations monopolized by the men? If they are freely to gain access to all occupations, should they also have free access to the education and training required? When Mill later addresses these questions in *The Subjection of Women* his argument seems more rhetorical than practical (1970a: 181–4).

Similarly, the analysis of the sexual division of labour, both in the market and in society as a whole, is at best vague in the *Principles*. While the original division of production within the household between men and women in agrarian societies is mentioned (1965: 118), there is no attempt to follow it up in subsequent history.

By contrast, in *The Subjection of Women*, Mill links restrictions to women's employment to women's economic dependence, to their role as wife and mother, and to the enforcement of patriarchal power over them:

> On . . . their admissibility to all the functions and occupations hitherto retained as the monopoly of the stronger sex . . . I believe that their disabilities elsewhere are only clung to in order to maintain their subordination in domestic life; because the generality of the male sex cannot yet tolerate the idea of living with an equal. (1970a: 181)

In other words, men use market power to keep women out of employment, the better to assert their power over them at home and in society in general.

Women's responsibilities in the domestic sphere are thus connected to their overall economic and social status. Mill also passes judgement on the nature of women's tasks in the home and the family and their overall effect on women's ability to participate equally in the public realm. He gives us a description, unprecedented on the part of a male philosopher and economist, of the constant demands made on women's time, faculties and appearance in the middle and upper classes.

> The time and thoughts of every woman have to satisfy great previous demands on them for things practical. . . . The superintendence of a household, even when not in other respects laborious, is extremely onerous to the thoughts; it requires incessant vigilance, an eye which no detail escapes, and presents questions for consideration and solution, foreseen and unforeseen, at every hour of the day, from which the person responsible for them can hardly ever shake herself free. . . . All this is over and above the engrossing duty which society imposes exclusively on women, of making themselves charming. (1970a: 209–10)

He further observes that beyond these duties, women are 'expected to have [their] time and faculties always at the disposal of everybody' (1970a: 211). All this does not leave women 'either much leisure, or much energy and freedom of mind' to engage in productive or creative activities (1970a: 210).

Having noted the impact of the socially determined assignment of women to domesticity and of the nature of their duties on their overall standing in society and on their ability to claim economic and social equality with men, Mill does not propose specific solutions. His approach is more idealist than materialist: what has to change is men's and society's views of women. Taylor's position differs significantly from Mill's.

Mill felt that women could accede to equality merely by being given the option of employment: 'The *power* of earning is essential to the dignity of a woman if she has no independent property', and by making marriage 'an equal contract' (1970a: 179–81). Under such conditions, women would not need to use the option of employment, their mere potential to do so being a sufficient guarantee of their equality. Once a woman decides to marry, however, she has once and for all chosen her vocation, and 'renounces, not all objects and occupations, but all which are not consistent with the requirements' of marriage (1970a: 179). This 'choice' would be a definitive one as divorce appears to be an allowable option only in extreme cases.[31] Mill definitely saw marriage and employment as incompatible pursuits for women.

Expressing his Victorian and class biases, he opposed in the *Principles* the idea that married working-class women should contribute to the income of their families:

> It cannot, however, be considered desirable as a *permanent* element in the condition of the labouring classes, that the mother of the family (the case of

a single woman is totally different) should be under the necessity of working for subsistence, at least elsewhere than in their place of abode. (1965: 394).[32]

If women had to work, they could only do it in the home, notwithstanding the greater exploitation they might suffer in such cases. Mill's espousal of traditional sex roles is also evidenced by his support of the concept of a family wage for men. The same Victorian bias is applied to middle-class women in *The Subjection of Women*:

> When the support of the family depends, not on property, but on earnings, the common arrangement, by which the man earns the income and the wife superintends the domestic expenditure, seems to me in general the most suitable division of labour between the two persons. (1970a: 178)

Mill details that 'the wife' is responsible for 'the physical suffering of bearing children', their 'care and education in the early years' and 'the careful and economical application of the husband's earnings to the general comfort of the family'. This constitutes 'not only her fair share, but usually the larger share, of the bodily and mental exertion required by their joint existence'. Taking on paid work 'seldom relieves her from this, but only prevents her from performing it properly' (1970a: 178). A married woman's domestic duties and the double workday she would face if she took paid work are used as arguments against her employment.

Mill does not look for alternatives to this entrenched sexual division of labour. It never occurs to him that domestic duties could be shared between husband and wife, allowing her the time and energy to engage in paid work and a real choice of that option. He also never takes a serious look at alternative social arrangements, where some of the reproductive work performed individually by women could be socialized. Yet proposals for such arrangements were already being developed in Mill's day. For instance, in the *Principles* he mentions the Fourierists' scheme that 'all the members of the association should reside in the same pile of buildings; for saving of labour and expense, not only in building, but in every branch of domestic economy' (1965: 212). He must also have been aware of some of the proposals for communal housekeeping made by the Unitarian Radicals whom he frequented in the 1830s (Rossi, 1970: 37). It seems that Mill had a very traditional view of sex roles.

By contrast, Harriet Taylor's ideas on sex roles are more revolutionary. She unwaveringly insists that a married woman's earning of her own income is essential to her access to equality: 'a woman who contributes materially to the support of the family, cannot be treated in the same contemptuously tyrannical manner as one who, however she may toil as a domestic drudge, is a dependent on the man for subsistence' (1970: 105). Her analysis of the status of women is rooted in a materialist understanding beyond Mill's grasp.

Economists traditionally ignore women's domestic and reproductive work. This work is refreshingly the object of descriptions in both the *Principles* and *The Subjection of Women*, yet Mill and Taylor fail to recognize the economic value of women's work. It is clear that they see it as part of economic activity and as productive of utilities, but they do not classify it as productive labour, which is defined as labour productive of 'utilities embodied in material objects' (Mill, 1965: 49).

Mill and Taylor hesitate, however, to classify as unproductive all labour 'of which the subject is human beings' (1965: 40). Such labour is recognized as essential to procuring the conditions for production:

> Every human being has been brought up from infancy at the expense of much labour to some person or persons, and if this labour . . . had not been bestowed, the child would never have attained the age and strength which enable him to become a labourer in his turn. To the community at large, the labour and expense of rearing its infant population form a part of the outlay which is a condition of production. (1965: 40–1)

In spite of this, the reproductive labour which constitutes women's major activity is not given productive status. As part of a rather confused definition, two criteria are used to determine which type of labour is productive: the labour expanded must 'terminate in creation of material wealth' (1965: 50) and its very purpose, as it is being performed, must be production, or the 'returns arising from it' (1965: 41).

Under the first criterion, Mill and Taylor classify as productive the 'labour expended in the acquisition of manufacturing skill' and 'the labour of officers of government in affording the protection which . . . is indispensable to the prosperity of industry' (1965: 49). To this they add 'the labour of saving a friend's life [if] the friend is a productive labourer, and produces more than he consumes' (1965: 50). Under the second criterion they retain as productive only the labour consciously performed to increase human productive capacity: 'the labour employed in learning and in teaching the arts of production, in acquiring and communicating skill in those arts', which is 'really, and in general solely undergone for the sake of the greater or more valuable produce thereby attained' (1965: 41).

The reproductive work women perform when bearing or raising children and when caring for their families is not recognized as productive, because it is 'usually incurred from other motives than to obtain such ultimate return'. Mill and Taylor add that 'for most purposes of political economy, [it] need not be taken into account as expenses of production' (1965: 41).[33] Thus the established criteria exclude women's reproductive work while including men's; in Mill and Taylor's day this meant 'all concerned in education; not only school-masters, tutors, and professors, . . . governments, . . . moralists, and clergymen; . . . physicians' (1965: 47).[34]

Women's reproductive work is deemed unproductive because their intention, when they have children and raise them, is not to increase production or productive capacity.[35] We can contrast this with Mill and Taylor's treatment of the 'labour of invention and discovery'. Its 'material fruits, though the result, are seldom the direct purpose of the pursuits of savants, nor is their remuneration in general derived from the increased production [caused . . .] by their discoveries' (1965: 43). Under the same criteria such work should be considered unproductive, but they rationalize otherwise:

> when (as in political economy one should always be prepared to do) we shift our point of view, and consider not individual acts, and the motives by which they are determined, but national and universal results, intellectual specula- tion must be looked upon as a most influential part of the productive labour of society, and the portion of its resources employed in carrying on and in remunerating such labour, as a highly productive part of its expenditure. (1965: 43)

Somehow Mill and Taylor were not prepared to apply the same shift in point of view to women's reproductive work.

These juxtapositions blatantly show the arbitrariness of their criteria and the double standard applied to men's and women's work. They expose their flawed definition of productive labour, the shortcomings of their analysis of the sexual division of labour, and their subconscious acceptance of the ideology of the day which served to deny the economic nature of women's reproductive work.

In the *Principles* Mill and Taylor elaborate a human capital theory similar to Smith's. They state that the 'skill, and the energy and perseverance, of the artisans of a country, are reckoned part of its wealth, no less than their tools and machinery' (1965: 48). This constitutes part of their rationale for considering some reproductive work as productive. They argue that expenses on education should be considered as investment (1965: 48–9). Yet they are willing to consider as such only the formal education processes, and not the formation of human resources that is carried on by women in the private sphere.

For Mill and Taylor, building the quality of the workforce – through the work of male educators – is seen as a contribution to the accumulation of wealth and must be treated as investment. Population growth, by comparison, is treated as a phenomenon to be contained, and women's contribution to human capital, whether quantitative or qualitative, is not recognized as productive. This position can be linked to their views on the stationary state and to their adherence to the wage fund doctrine.[36]

Mill and Taylor present population control as beneficial to women:

> It is seldom by the choice of the wife that families are too numerous; on her devolves (along with all the physical suffering and at least a full share of the privations) the whole of the intolerable domestic drudgery resulting from the excess. To be relieved from it would be hailed as a blessing by multitudes of women. (1965: 372)

They use their analysis of patriarchal structures and ideologies to draw connections between the subjection of women and unbridled population growth. They advocate education on birth control methods and eloquently condemn the religious and social ideologies which promote large families (1965: 368–9). They also observe that the emancipation of women would foster a decrease in fertility. They foresee as one of 'the probable consequences of the industrial and social independence of women, a great diminution of the evil of over-population' (1965: 765–6).[37]

It is notable that Mill's feminist awareness and Harriet Taylor's influence led him to publish pertinent and pathbreaking observations on the economic and social status of women. The *Principles* went much further than most economic texts in giving women economic status and in attempting to apply to them equally the methods of political economy.

By the time the *Principles* was written, the mutations in the social and economic order incipient in Smith's days had come to fruition. The failures of capitalism and political liberalism to generate a more harmonious and fair society could no longer be ignored. Social and political thinkers had become either stubborn apologists of the capitalist system and its brand of patriarchal and political despotism or idealist or practical social reformers (such as the socialists and feminists). Mill and Taylor equivocally placed themselves in between these two tendencies, refusing to reject capitalism and political liberalism while espousing feminism and some of the criticisms and ideals of socialism.

Their inconsistencies and their insufficient questioning of the patriarchal and capitalist economic order should come as no surprise.

In the final instance, these shortcomings can be attributed to Mill and
Taylor's liberal ideas, to their class position, and to Mill's attachment
to a romantic view of women and the family.[38]

Mill and Taylor's awareness of the inequalities created and reproduced by the capitalist system led them to denounce 'all its sufferings
and injustices', the prevalent situation where

> the produce of labour [is] apportioned as we now see it, almost in an inverse
> ratio to the labour – the largest portions to those who have never worked at
> all, the next largest to those whose work is almost nominal, and so in a
> descending scale, the remuneration dwindling as the work grows harder and
> more disagreeable, until the most fatiguing and exhausting bodily labour
> cannot count with certainty on being able to earn even the necessaries of
> life. (1965: 207)

They also condemned the system of inheritance which perpetuates these
inequalities (1965: 201ff). Yet they did not see this situation as
inherent to capitalism, but as an anomaly which could be corrected by
appropriate reforms. The superficiality of this analysis leads to a failure
to identify the causes of capitalist economic injustice.

A parallel *démarche* is extant in Mill's political theory, which advocates perfecting rather than challenging bourgeois democracy. Similarly, patriarchal institutions are viewed as obsolete, extinct even, as
attested by the statement that 'the feudal family, *the last historical form
of patriarchal life*, has long perished' (1965: 219). Its survival was seen
as a further anomaly to be eliminated.[39] Hence Marx's remark that Mill
attempts 'to reconcile irreconcilables' (1967: 16) obtains in domains
other than political economy.

The main shortcoming in Mill's feminist analysis is his refusal to
question and to examine existing sex roles and the concomitant sexual
division of labour. This flaw has its source in Mill's subscription to a
bourgeois Victorian view of woman's 'nature' in spite of his own
statement that sexual characteristics and roles are not natural but
socially or culturally determined.

His own writings contain contradictions on the subject of women's
nature. He identifies ideology and education as the sources of women's
secondary status in society: 'All women are brought up . . . in the belief
that their ideal of character is the very opposite to that of men . . . that
it is the duty of women [. . . and] their nature, to live for others' (1970a:
141). He comments: 'I deny that anyone knows, or can know, the nature
of the two sexes, as long as they have only been seen in their present
relation to one another' (1970a: 148). Yet it is clear that, for him,
women are the gentle sex while men are the 'stronger sex'. Women have

a civilizing, 'softening influence' on the world (1970a: 223). Mill identifies a number of 'feminine' characteristics: 'a woman seldom runs wild after an abstraction', she is practical, realistic (1970a: 192–3).

A younger Mill wrote in 1832: 'the great occupation of woman should be to *beautify* life: to cultivate . . . all her faculties of mind, soul and body; all her powers of enjoyment, and powers of giving enjoyment; and to diffuse beauty, elegance, and grace, everywhere'; and further: 'her occupation should be to adorn and beautify [life . . .] that will be her natural task . . . which will be . . . accomplished rather by *being* than by *doing*' (1970b: 75, 73). It is clear from these passages that Mill saw the purpose of women's *being* as providing enjoyment *for others* (men).

His later writings do not state these beliefs as clearly, yet similar ideas are expressed in Mill's views that marriage and employment are incompatible for women (not men), and that women's nature may prevent them from being able to compete with men in some occupations, or may put limits on what they can do:

> what is contrary to women's nature to do, they never will be made to do by simply giving their nature free play. . . . What women by nature cannot do, it is quite superfluous to forbid them from doing. What they can do, but not so well as the men who are their competitors, competition suffices to exclude them from. (1970a: 154)

He also postulated that the 'majority of women' are likely to elect to engage in 'the one vocation in which there is nobody to compete with them': motherhood (1970a: 183). The purpose of these arguments might be to reassure the opponents of equality, but they are insistently present and show a profound attachment to a certain view of women and their place in society.

Mill's patriarchal views on sex roles represent the one instance of irreconcilable disagreement with Harriet Taylor.[40] Although her writings on the question are not extensive, her 1851 essay on *The Enfranchisement of Women* (1970), shows that she accepted no limits to what women could do and prioritized women's economic autonomy over their assigned 'duties' as wife and mother.

Mill's deep attachment to a Victorian conception of women's nature seems to be linked to his ideal of the relationship between the sexes within the family unit. Brought to light in Richard Krouse's analysis of the contradictions in Mill's liberal view of the family is his vision of a fusion between the sexes in marriage where both remain autonomous yet contribute to a synergistic whole. Essential to this result is the replacement of marital despotism with a form of democratic equality.

Yet, in Mill's ideal marriage, equality of the sexes is precluded by the denial of full economic autonomy and equality to married women.[41] The stumbling block in Mill's ideal is his belief that the preservation of a private sphere of personal and moral values, as a necessary antidote to the impersonal and competitive public realm, necessarily requires the full-time nurturing and 'beautifying' presence of the wife/mother (Krouse, 1983: 49).

Mill's view of an 'equal but separate' role for women opens him up to serious feminist criticism as it provides no guarantee against power imbalances and abuses. Seemingly aware of this problem, he tries to deflect it: 'There will naturally also be more potential voice on the side, whichever it is, that brings the means of support. Inequality from this source does not depend on the law of marriage, but on the general conditions of human society, as now constituted' (1970a: 170). If this inequality 'does not depend on the law of marriage', it remains unaltered by a prohibition of (or a convention against) married women's employment, which denies them access to financial autonomy and reinforces their inferior status in 'human society'. Mill refuses to acknowledge that, under his ideal system, the *material* conditions for the subjection of women are perpetuated.

Mill's liberalism blinds him to the fact that, in a capitalist market system, denying women equal access to monetary means of subsistence, not only as an alternative to marriage but within marriage, can only result in the maintenance of women's economic and social subordination. The changes he proposes are therefore superficial, providing only a formal façade of equality for women without assailing the very foundations of patriarchal power.

Although more enlightened, the values informing Mill's position on women and the family are not inherently different from those of Adam Smith and of the eighteenth- and nineteenth-century political philosophers. Whereas Mill attempts to resolve the contradictions presented by the unequal status of women in liberal capitalist society, he is unable to offer a viable solution because he is, in the last instance, unable to cast off the patriarchal privileges which arise from the traditional sexual division of labour.[42]

The main weakness of Mill's liberalism is his parallel belief in the perfectibility of the basic institutions of patriarchy (marriage and the family) and capitalism (private property) as evidenced by his declarations that none of these institutions have 'had a fair trial'.[43] He fails to see that both systems rely on power relations, between the classes and between the sexes, and are incompatible with equality.[44] He further fails to understand the interconnectedness of the two systems and their institutions when it comes to the question of the economic and social status of women.[45]

Harriet Taylor seems to have developed a better grasp of these connections. Unfortunately, there were limits to her influence on Mill and the writing in her own hand is not extensive. *The Enfranchisement of Women* is a very short, early essay, which dwells more on legal and philosophical than on economic matters. A more substantial feminist economic approach to some of the issues is provided by one of Mill and Taylor's contemporaries, Barbara Bodichon, who penned the first treatise on women's work written by a woman.

## Barbara Leigh Smith Bodichon

For the feminists of the first women's movement, pay and the position of women in the workforce were seen as essential to women's access to economic independence.[46] These issues followed closely the issues of the vote, legal rights, and women's status within the institution of marriage. This order of priorities, reflecting the class nature of the early feminists, is precisely that followed by Barbara Bodichon.

Barbara Bodichon (1827–91) was directly involved in early British feminist activism (Strachey, 1969). At the age of twenty-two she reacted critically to the first edition of John Stuart Mill's *Principles of Political Economy*, deploring that 'touching so often on unsettled questions of the greatest importance and interest, [he] has not gone away from Political Economy and . . . given us his valuable opinion on them', and also that 'philosophers and reformers have generally been afraid to say anything about the unjust laws both of society and country which crush women'.[47] These criticisms led her to publish, in 1854, *A Brief Summary, in Plain Language, of the Most Important Laws Concerning Women*, where women's lack of rights, in particular the denial to them of property rights due to marriage laws, is denounced. This was followed in 1857 by another short précis, *Women and Work*.[48]

Bodichon held that employment is not unfeminine and women should be seen as belonging in the labour market where they participate in large numbers in spite of dominant ideology. The reason why women want work is clear: it is 'often because they must eat and because they have children and others dependent on them – for all the reasons that men want work' (1859: 35).

Barbara Bodichon was one of the first to name the conditions that plague women's employment: 'they are not skilled labourers and therefore badly paid. They rarely have any training' (1859: 35). For her, this seems to be due not to women's lack of abilities, but to their treatment as women rather than as workers. She identifies the impact of 'crowding': large numbers of women being concentrated in very few jobs, resulting in low market wages. She gives the specific example of such a situation in the Philadelphia Mint:

> I saw 20 or 30 young ladies who received half, sometimes less than half, the wages given to men for the same work. They were working ten hours a day for a dollar (4s. English). This proportion shows the lamentable amount of competition among women, even in the United States, for any work which is open to them. (1859: 17)

She elaborates on how difficult it is for a woman in need to gain access to economic independence through employment, quoting *The Times*: 'the resources for gaining a livelihood left open to women are so few. At present the language practically held by modern society to destitute women may be resolved into Marry – Stitch – Die – or do worse' (Bodichon, 1987: 44). In comparison to a man losing his fortune, 'the case of most women who are left destitute is much harder, and there are fewer paths open to them, and these are choke full' (1859: 16).

She identifies the cause of women's lack of access to employment as men's monopoly over most remunerative employment and their control of the training necessary to gain such employment: 'So long as nearly every remunerative employment is engrossed by men only, so long must the wretchedness and slavery of women remain what it is' (1987: 60).

Bodichon's analytical skills are evidenced by her warning that women are losing some of the few industries that were traditionally theirs.[49] 'The work of our ancestresses is taken away from us' (1987: 26). New technologies, the cause of these alarming changes, make obsolete the few traditional skills of women: 'Women in modern life, even in the humblest, are no longer spinsters. Their spinning is all done by the steam engine; their sewing will soon all be done by that same mighty worker' (1859: 26). Women must act to stop this trend – 'We must find fresh work' (1859: 26) – otherwise, their economic and social position will go from bad to worse. Bodichon describes at length the impact on women, and on society as a whole, of their forced idleness, poverty and dependence on men. She passionately advocates women's access to employment in industries and the professions, to training and to decent wages.

Anticipating opposition, Bodichon argues that training and employment are not contrary to the established duties and roles of women in British society at the time. 'A girl will make a better wife for having had such serious training' (1859: 29). She also states that 'Work – not drudgery, but work – is the great beautifier. Activity of brain, heart, and limb, gives health and beauty, and makes women fit to be mothers of children' (1859: 21) She challenges the Victorian creed: 'To think a woman is more feminine because she is frivolous, ignorant, weak, and sickly, is absurd; the larger-natured a woman is, the more decidedly feminine she will be; the stronger she is, the more strongly feminine' (1859: 21). She denounces the social conventions that maintain women in a lifelong state of economic dependence:

> Fathers have no right to cast the burden of the support of their daughters on other men. It lowers the dignity of women; and tends to prostitution, whether legal or in the streets. As long as fathers regard the sex of a child as a reason why it should not be taught to earn its own bread, so long must women be degraded. Adult women must not be supported by men, if they are to stand as dignified, rational beings before God. (1987: 41)

Barbara Bodichon also challenges the patriarchal ideology which implies that all women marry and that, from father to husband, a man will always provide for them. She points out that 'of women at the age of twenty and upward, 43 out of the 100 in England and Wales are unmarried' (1859: 28). She admonishes the fathers of young girls to give them access to the training that will equip them for economic survival:

> Your daughter may not marry. It is your duty to provide for that possibility; and she will surely be ill, miserable, or go mad, if she has no occupation. . . . It may be years before your daughter finds a husband. It is your duty to give her worthy work, or to allow her to choose it; . . . Suppose the man she may love is poor, by her labor she can help to form their mutual home. . . . Your daughter may be left to act as both father and mother to children dependent on her for daily bread. (1859: 29)

This commonsense advice went against the dominant view that young women only needed training in domestic skills to prepare for their future. She counters:

> It is often said, it is wrong of daughters to leave their parents to follow this or that pursuit. Mothers and fathers say nothing, if their daughters leave them to be married. It is much more important to the welfare of a girl's soul that she be trained to work than that she marry. (1987: 45)

In this way she exposes the flawed logic of patriarchal ideology.

What makes Bodichon radical among the feminists of her time is her position that, for women, marriage and employment are not incompatible:

> But is it certain that a girl will give up her occupation when married? There are thousands of married women who are in want of a pursuit – a profession. It is a mistake to suppose marriage gives occupation enough to employ all

the faculties of all women. To bring a family of 12 children into the world is not in itself a noble vocation, or always a certain benefit to humanity. (1859: 29)

This was anathema to the ideologues of the day who vehemently ridiculed and denounced her proposals,[50] finding no better response than the assertion that woman's place was in the home. Critics protested that if the single life was made 'remunerative and pleasant for women its only upshot would be to make marriage a matter of "cold philosophic choice", and it would be more and more frequently declined' (Strachey, 1969: 92), a candid admission of the purpose of denying women access to employment.

Bodichon's position is based on her deep conviction that the sexual division of labour and the sex roles that were being constructed in her day were detrimental to women, as well as to men and to society as a whole. Like Harriet Taylor, she believed that women could not be equal to men in marriage without access to independent means: 'Unless a woman can earn her own livelihood or has a certain income, she has little chance of forming an equal union' (1859: 19). She also outlines a vision of a social division of labour on a wider social scale where 'some association of families' would allow some women to pursue a profession while others would manage the 'domestic concerns' of the community. Unfortunately, she does not address the changes in roles and responsibilities that would be open to men in this new social arrangement.

Bodichon challenges the common prejudices (some of which still hold today) against women's work. In her opinion, the work that women do in the home as wives and mothers should be recognized, and the women who perform it should not be seen as dependants.

Women who act as housekeepers, nurses, and instructors of their children, often do as much for the support of the household as their husbands; and it is very unfair of men to speak of supporting a wife and children when such is the case. When a woman gives up a profitable employment to be governess of her own family, she earns her right to live. (1859: 31)

This position has been emphatically expressed by some contemporary feminists,[51] yet the prejudice holds as strong as ever.

Barbara Bodichon also denounces the 'prejudice against women accepting money for their work'.[52] She clearly identifies money as representative of value and a means of access to power, 'for money is power'. Giving one's work or product for free is all right sometimes, but not all the time, as exchanging them for money gives women the confirmation that 'we are as valuable as we think'. For her, insisting on 'work for love of Christ only . . . is a profound and mischievous mistake. It tends to lessen the dignity of necessary labour' (1859: 33). She here identifies a social convention which (even today) plagues women's economic position as their availability to perform work for free is taken for granted.

A further 'fallacy' identified by Bodichon is the ideological position that women who work deprive others – who 'need' the work – of employment: 'It is often said that ladies should not take the bread out of the mouths of the poor working man or woman by selling in their market' (1859: 34).[53] Against this, she develops an argument involving a concept of full-employment welfare-maximizing general equilibrium. The more people there are in the workforce, she states, the greater the contribution to overall production and hence the easier it is to satisfy everyone's needs. This simple and self-evident view is still ignored today by those who scapegoat women and members of minority groups as the cause of unemployment.

Bodichon did not just write about and analyse the situation women faced in the labour market in her day. She put into practice her own admonition: 'we must find fresh work'. With the other women of the Langham Place group,[54] she worked to open up new areas of employment for women. In 1858 she was involved in setting up the Women's Employment Bureau, which served as a referral service and a training institute to give women access to new occupations. The group actively opposed any restriction of women's opportunities in the labour market, in particular the exclusion of women by trade unions and the Factory Acts of the 1870s. It also exerted pressure for the enactment of equal pay when women and men performed the same work (Strachey, 1969: 226–7; Lacey, 1987: *passim*).

Barbara Bodichon was seen by her feminist contemporaries as having some of the most radical views. She had a definite influence on the feminist movement of her day, both through her ideas and analyses and through her energetic activism. On the matter of women's work, there is no doubt that she contributed greatly to the challenge of Victorian ideology. She went well beyond the then common feminist concern for the economic status of single women, advocating married women's access to employment and laying the foundation for a critique of marriage as the primary vocation of women and their sole source of livelihood.

For her, women's access to equality and the development of their potential came before social conventions. Yet there are some limitations to her views. Her arguments for women's access to equality do not go as far as they could: she does not explicitly argue that women should have unlimited access to all the elements that constitute male status (political, economic, social); moreover, she does not address the nature of men's social roles and how a change in these could further lead to equality. Her analysis also focuses exclusively on individual actions (by women themselves or by their parents) as the means to change, which leaves untouched the overwhelming social and political element that composes ideology and social conventions. However, a recognition of the radicalism of her views and of the perceptiveness of her economic analysis are long overdue.

In this chapter we have identified some of the themes which announce the neoclassical approach to women's place in the economy and some of the feminist bases for a challenge to this approach.

Smith inaugurated the tradition of making women and their work (productive and reproductive) invisible, of ignoring the sexual division of labour and its articulation with the reproduction of the capitalist system, and of obscuring the part played by women in the creation of 'human capital'. He started the theoretical institutionalization of a rigid (as well as arbitrary and biased in so far as it comes from a male and capitalist point of view) separation between public and private, economic and non-economic, male and female, dichotomies of which the first half only is the object of 'science' and 'economic inquiry'.[55] The invisibility of women in Smith's economic and political theory under-scores the patriarchal values that inform his vision of a world where women must provide harmony, beauty, ethics and nurturance, for the benefit of men, and outside market mechanisms.

These tendencies are only superficially challenged by John Stuart Mill in spite of his feminist creed. His patriarchal tunnel vision kept him from rejecting the structural basis of male privilege and accepting the challenge to the traditional sexual division of labour and to its corollary, the public/private split, which was initiated by Harriet Taylor and Barbara Bodichon. Suffering no such impediment, Taylor and Bodichon took further the analysis of the connections between the political and the economic as they affect the situation of women.

With allowances made for Mill's liberal attempts to integrate women in his economic analysis and to advocate their equal integration into the market system, the classical approach prefigures the neoclassical treatment of women's economic status. The difference between the two is the blatant apologetic nature of neoclassical attempts to reaffirm the capitalist and patriarchal order at all costs.

# Notes

1. According to E. K. Hunt, 'he was the first to develop a complete and relatively consistent abstract model of the nature, structure, and workings of the capitalist system' (1979: 34).
2. See for instance Sir James Steuart: 'Oeconomy, in general, is the art of providing for all the wants of a family, with prudence and frugality. . . . What oeconomy is in a family, political oeconomy is in a state' (1967: 1, 2). This point is made by Jane Rendall (1987: 77).
3. Scott and Tilly (1978) offer a detailed and fascinating account of the impact of the industrial revolution on the nature and volume of women's market work in several European countries. They document the contribution of women to the economic survival of their families and the changes brought about by the growth of market and industry to the structure of women's involvement in market work and to the nature of their social and economic position within the family and society.
4. That Smith sees the family, as opposed to the individual, as the unit serving as a basis for calculation of subsistence needs is evidenced also in *The Theory of Moral Sentiments*: 'what is the end of avarice and ambition, of the pursuit of wealth, of power and preeminence? Is it to supply the necessities of nature? The wages of the meanest labourer can supply them. We see that they afford him food and clothing, the comfort of a house, and of a family' (*TMS*: I.iii.2.1). References to *WN* and to *TMS* are to paragraphs.
5. Some specific instances are documented by Marglin (1974 and 1975) and Lazonick (1978).
6. This omission is the rule rather than the exception among male economists. It is interesting, for instance, to see Blaug regret that in Smith's 'grand theme of the *social* division of labor', 'the territorial division of labor is ignored without any apparent reason' (1962: 39–40). Sex is even more invisible than geography.
7. The one exception is the example of women knitters and spinners in Scotland (*WN*: I.x.b.50).
8. This was written before the above passage referring to 'nunneries and boarding-schools' (*TMS*: VI.ii.1.10n.).
9. Jane Rendall shows that, for Smith, the sentiment of jealousy among husbands is legitimized by their right to their wife's fidelity and by the superiority of men's over women's rights (1987: 63–4).
10. In the conclusion of her article, Jane Rendall states: 'there were important elements in his treatment of the role of women, though largely unnoticed, which were fundamental themes in what has come to be thought of as the "Victorian" concept of womanhood: his implication that women were the moral educators of the family; the limited social and economic role of women of the middling classes; his view of the monogamous European family as representing the highest form of family life' (1987: 72).
11. Similar statements are made by Marshall and Pigou; see Chapters 8–10.
12. Marshall makes the same argument, yet more explicitly (1930: 195–6, and see Chapter 8 below).
13. For a feminist analysis of modern political and social theory see, for instance, Clark and Lange (1979); Okin (1979); Elshtain (1981, 1982); Kennedy and Mendus (1987).
14. The same questions can be asked about his treatment of the working class and the poor.
15. Quoted by Jane Rendall (1987: 64).
16. His attitude may not be as 'severe': in *The Theory of Moral Sentiments* he shows towards women the polite courteousness requisite of patriarchal condescension. But it is clear that his theory of 'sympathy' does not evenly apply to men and women. This is especially the case where the actions and feelings of men and women are contradictory, as in his discussion of husbands' jealousy, or where patriarchal values are at stake, as in his discussion of rape.

17. 'Political Economy is to the state what domestic economy is to the family' (1965: 1–2).
18. Besides the constraints to freedom presented by the patriarchal structure of capitalism, Mill was also aware that its class system stood in contradiction to a liberal ideal of society.
19. James Mill's position on women's suffrage was expressed in his *Article on Government* (1814; repr in Bell and Offen, 1983: 119, 122).
20. In his *Autobiography* (1935: IV and VI), Mill describes in detail their intellectual partnership: 'When two persons have their thoughts and speculations completely in common . . . it is of little consequence in respect to the question of originality, which of them holds the pen, the one who contributes least to the composition may contribute most to the thought; the writings which result are the joint product of both. . . . In this wide sense, not only during the years of our married life, but during many of the years of confidential friendship which preceded, all my published writings were as much her work as mine' (1935: 204–5). There is a debate on the extent and nature of Taylor's influence and of their collaboration. V. W. Bladen, one of the editors of Mill's *Collected Works*, describes his 'account of the part played by Harriet Taylor' as 'generous, perhaps over-generous' (Bladen, 1965: II.lxii). Historians of economic thought do not mention Harriet Taylor and are usually silent on Mill's feminism; such is the case with Blaug (1962) and Hunt (1979). Maurice Dobb (1973) mentions Harriet Taylor's socialist influence on Mill but is silent on her contribution to his work and on Mill's feminism. Feminism is clearly not one of the 'ideologies' he considers. Jacob Oser (1970) mentions Mill's 'passionate defense of the rights of women' and Harriet Taylor's influence. However, after quoting the above passage from the *Autobiography*, he casts doubts on its veracity. Alice Rossi comments: 'The hypothesis that a mere woman was the collaborator of so logical and intellectual a thinker as Mill, much less that she influenced the development of his thought, can be expected to meet resistance in the mind of men right up to the 1970s' (1970: 36). Rossi's thesis is that Harriet Taylor made significant contributions to the *Principles*. Gertrude Himmelfarb describes Taylor's influence as one that drastically altered the course of Mill's thought and generated the specific 'Millian' doctrine of liberty: 'It took only a shift in the weight of the argument to convert the balanced, modulated, complicated view that was distinctly his into the simple and extreme view that was distinctly hers [. . .] this] marks the transition from a whiggish mode of liberalism, in which liberty was one of several values making for a good society, to the contemporary mode, in which it is the supreme and indeed the only value' (1974: 272).
21. Zillah Eisenstein (1981: Ch. 6) attributes to Mill and Taylor jointly all writings published by either during the span of their partnership (1830 to 1858). I will differ from Eisenstein on the authorship of *The Enfranchisement of Women* (Taylor, 1970), which is clearly attributable to Taylor, and on the two 'Early Essays on Marriage and Divorce' (Rossi, 1970) authored, one by Mill, (67–84), the other by Taylor (84–7). The *Principles* were drafted fifteen years after the start of the Mill–Taylor partnership. In the dedication to the first edition, Mill declares that 'many' of the ideas in the book 'were first learned from' Taylor (1965: 1026). There is also strong evidence of continued collaboration for the revisions to the *Principles* for all editions up to Taylor's death.
22. He is matched only by the socialists Fourier and William Thompson. No other major mainstream economist has, since Mill, taken a visible position in support of feminism.
23. Mill introduced the first women's suffrage amendment in Parliament on 20 May 1867. He took this action at the suggestion of Barbara Bodichon and after the Langham Place group, at his request, gathered over 1,500 names on a petition (Strachey, 1969: 102–16; Bell and Offen, 1983: 482–8).
24. As a political philosopher, Mill distinguishes himself from the authoritarian

patriarchal leanings of Hobbes and Locke. He denies that the need for final or ultimate decision in the common affairs of the family requires the investment of sovereign authority exclusively in the hands of the husband/father. Instead, he argues that in the marriage partnership . . . there is no inherent necessity for a univocally hierarchical, much less specifically patriarchal, distribution of authority (Krouse, 1982: 145–72, 160). The neoclassical economists opted for the position of Hobbes and Locke rather than Mill in their approach to the question of consumption and utility functions for members of a family household, choosing the hierarchical model and subsuming all individual utility functions under that of the male head of household. One can only speculate about the outlook of the paradigm if it had followed instead Mill's ideal of autonomous individuals and democratic decision-making in the family.

25. Interestingly, Mill and Taylor use gender-neutral language in their passage on property: 'The institution of property . . . consists in the recognition, in each person, of a right to the exclusive disposal of what he or she have produced by their own exertions' (Mill, 1965: 215). See also pp. 218–20 where pronouns were changed to both genders or the plural from the 1952 edition on. No doubt they wanted to assert women's equal right to property. This must be a unique instance of non-sexist terminology in economics texts.

26. Mill's denunciation of chivalry is to be contrasted with Marshall and Pigou's appeals to this feudal patriarchal value system as a justification for the maintenance of this dependent status of women, and for the Factory Acts in particular. See Chapters 8–10 below.

27. Things have obviously not changed much since Mill and Taylor's times. They continue: 'That the law does not prevent these atrocities . . . is no matter of necessity, but the deep disgrace of those by whom the laws are made and administered' (Mill, 1965: 761). The theme of men's marital tyranny is a recurrent one. It is present even in the speech Mill made to Parliament when he introduced the women's suffrage amendment (Bell and Offen, 1983: 487). It is one of the main arguments he used to back his support for equality in marriage and women's suffrage. Mill's outspoken and consistent denunciation of wife battering and marital rape, in spite of the Victorian rule of silence on such topics, makes him unique among male advocates of feminism and testifies to the sincerity of his convictions.

28. Fawcett (1892: 173–6). See the next chapter for a review of her analysis.

29. This remark predates today's feminist criticism that most knowledge and science has been developed from a narrow sexist perspective, by taking only men's experience and reality into account, and by analysing the world from a male perspective. See in particular Eichler and Lapointe (1985); Canadian Research Institute on the Advancement of Women (1984); Vickers (1984), and Spender (1985).

30. Precisely the same type of comparison of the work processes of the home and the factory have been used in the early twentieth century to declare housework 'inefficient' and to advocate the need to rationalize it by imitating as much as possible the industrial work process and the principle of labour specialization. Smith's axioms had prevailed. This reinforced the characterization of housework as an archaic and inferior form of economic activity, and the questioning of its economic nature. See the positions held by the Domestic Science Movement and the Home Economics Movement as described by Ehrenreich and English (1975), and by Chafe (1972). See also Reid (1934).

31. See Mill (1970a: 161; 1970b: 77 84) and Krouse (1983: 36–76, 50–1).

32. This passage, clearly by Mill's hand, was deleted from the 1852, 1857 and 1862 editions and reintroduced in the 1865 and 1871 editions, a result of Harriet Taylor's influence which did not survive her death.

33. Similarly they exclude 'the labour employed in keeping up productive powers; in preventing them from being destroyed or weakened by accident or disease' because the main motive here is health, not productivity (1965: 41).

34. Mill included in the list in his original manuscript 'parents, so far as they concern themselves in the education of their children', but this never appeared in any of the editions of the *Principles* (1965: 47). It is not clear what Taylor's precise role in the construction of the categories of productive and unproductive labour was. Her own writings (1970) do not address the question of the nature of women's reproductive work. One not insignificant influence on Mill and Taylor's position may have been their own class, and the class bias of the dominant ideology. Women in Taylor's class supervised domestics and presumably performed little work in their home as part of their ascribed function as status symbols of the 'leisure class' (see Veblen, 1902).

35. The position that the intent of having children is not the increase in productive capacity can particularly be questioned in the case of agrarian or settlement economies. Mill and Taylor's position can be contrasted to that of Adam Smith discussing large families in North America.

36. Mill and Taylor's opposition to growth for growth's sake, their view that 'the stationary state is not in itself undesirable . . . that it would be, on the whole, a very considerable improvement of our present condition', denotes amazingly modern ecological thought. They offer an eloquent indictment of the ethics of capitalist competition as an ideal for human nature and behaviour. They propose a redistribution of wealth and limits to population as alternatives, adding that 'a stationary condition of capital and population implies no stationary state of human improvement' (1965: 343ff; IV.vi). It is clear that their ecological and feminist ideas are linked.

37. Keeping women dependent and defining their purpose as exclusively reproductive contributes to unnecessary population growth: 'It is by devoting one-half of the human species to that exclusive function, by making it fill the entire life of one sex, and interweave itself with almost all the objects of the other, that the animal instinct in question is nursed into the disproportionate preponderance which it has hitherto exercised in human life' (1965: 766). A similar argument, reinforced by evolutionary theory, was given full development by Charlotte Perkins Gilman (1962).

38. On Mill's undying attachment to a romantic ideal of womanhood and to a liberal ideal of the family, see Krouse (1982, 1983).

39. This position is typical of bourgeois malestream periodization which locates patriarchal relations exclusively within feudalism. See Krouse: 'The central inspiration of Mill's liberal feminism, both in *The Subjection of Women* and elsewhere, perhaps best can be understood as a desire to purge liberalism of its patriarchal vestiges' (1983: 39).

40. This is evidenced by Mill's inclusion of passages which were closer to Taylor's thought in editions of the *Principles* during her lifetime, and reverting to his own position after her death (see for instance 1965: 394). It is also illustrated by the lesser radicalism of the *Subjection*.

41. See Krouse (1982, 1983). He points out that Mill was the first political philosopher correctly to identify the political nature of marital and family relations (1982: 160).

42. Again, this is practically evidenced in the results of Mill's intellectual association with Harriet Taylor, the outcome of which has historically been attributed solely to him.

43. 'The principle of private property has never yet had a fair trial in any country' (1965: 207); 'his nonpatriarchal ideal of marriage, and vision of a reformed family life, have "not yet had a fair trial" ' (Krouse, 1983: 52, quoting from Mill's later letters).

44. The difference in his approach towards the two is that he wants to abolish patriarchy while remaining attached to its basic institutions whereas he only wants to reform capitalism by reforming private property, failing to see that capitalist property is inherently based on inequality and exploitation.

45. Krouse comments that he 'recognizes that liberalism must sometimes be protected from liberalism' (1983: 52). It would be more correct to explain Mill's 'violat[ion]

of his own liberal values' as his recognition that patriarchy must, in the end, be protected from liberalism

46. In the United States, a similar concern emerged. The resolutions of the Seneca Falls Convention (New York, 1848) for instance state that Man 'has monopolized nearly all the profitable employments, and from those [woman] is permitted to follow, she receives but a scanty remuneration' (Rossi, 1973: 417).

47. From unpublished notes in the Leigh Smith Papers, quoted by Matthews (1983: 92).

48. Both essays are reprinted in Lacey (1987). Quotations from the English edition of *Women and Work* will be taken from this source. As the American edition (1859) differs substantially, I will be quoting from both.

49. Similar observations were made by feminists much later, one instance being Charlotte Perkins Gilman in 1898 (1962).

50. An article in the *Saturday Review* entitled 'Bloomerania' dismissed *Women and Work* as 'pretty Fanny's talk . . . fatally deficient in the power of consecutive thought' (Matthews, 1983: 117–18). It also scoffed at the crowding hypothesis presented, attributing the low wages of governesses to the poor quality of their work (Strachey, 1969: 92).

51. See for instance Dalla Costa and James (1972) and the Wages for Housework tendency of the women's movement. More recently, this argument has been empirically and theoretically developed by Vandelac *et al.* (1985).

52. An illustration of this 'prejudice' which exposes the patriarchal power relations at its roots is provided by the instance of Sophia Jex-Blake, who was to become the first woman doctor of Great Britain. In 1859 her father forbade her to receive payment for a tutorship she was offered. He insisted she should do the work for free and that he could provide for her needs. Arguing that being paid for her work would be 'quite beneath' her, it is clear that his real motive was to keep her under his authority by maintaining her economic dependence on him. See Woolf (1982: 74–7).

53. In this argument of undeniable hypocrisy, the presumably opposite interests of two groups of low economic status are pitted against each other in a sycophantic attempt to rationalize a status quo where neither has access to adequate economic means.

54. Under the initiative of Barbara Bodichon, a group of women published *The English Woman's Journal* out of an office at Langham Place. The office also became the locale for The Society for Promoting the Employment of Women. Some of the women involved were Bessie Rayner Parkes, Jessie Boucherett and Emily Faithful. Emily Davies and other prominent feminists of these early days also participated in the group's activities (Lacey, 1987).

55. See Hartsock: 'Dualism, along with the dominance of one side of the dichotomy over the other, marks phallocentric society and social theory' (1985: 241).

# PART II

# THE EQUAL PAY DEBATES: 1890 TO 1923

# 2   Introduction

John Stuart Mill's initial, tentative discussion of the economic condition of women did not generate a lot of response among economists. Yet, in British society, these issues were being debated at the initiative of the feminists, propelled by Barbara Bodichon and the activities of the Langham Place group. Feminists were active in the 1870s and 1880s in opposing discrimination against women in the labour force, pressuring trade unions to adopt the principle of equal pay and to remove their restrictions on entry to trades and apprenticeship and agitating against the discriminatory impact of the Factory Acts.[1] The obvious economic nature of the questions raised by the feminists must have then escaped most economists.

It is not until the 1890s that some economists start approaching the question of women's wages with more than a passing and dismissive comment. This issue, central to women's economic welfare, remained marginal to economic thought. Women's employment itself was obstinately treated as a negligible phenomenon by the economists in spite of census data and a growing body of historical and empirical studies establishing that women worked, had always worked and constituted a significant proportion of the total workforce (Hill, 1896; Hutchins and Harrison, 1903; Hutchins, 1913; Clark, 1919).[2]

It is apparent that the few economic writings on the issue of women's wages and equal pay represent only the tip of an iceberg of public debate at that time. It involved the varied and conflicting views of women and feminists (who were by no means homogeneous in interests, class, analysis and political priorities), capitalist employers, trade unions, politicians, social reformers, and men in general (again, not necessarily all homogeneous groups). Besides equal pay for men and women, the concepts debated included the 'living wage' (family wage) for male workers, market wages, minimum wages for women (and sometimes for men), subsistence requirements, family allowances and other forms of transfer payment.

In historical writings on the first wave of feminism, these issues attracted less attention than did suffrage for women, which at that time was the utmost feminist priority, yet they are crucial to the economic position of women.[3] It is significant that the debate on equal pay occurred before the development of the welfare state and state

*51*

intervention in wage determination. The eventual forms of state intervention were without doubt influenced by the arguments of the debate
and the relative clout of the various social groups involved. Furthermore, as stated by Heidi Hartmann,

> Examining the literature from this period, especially the Webb–Rathbone–
> Fawcett–Edgeworth series in the *Economic Journal*, is important because it
> sets the framework for nearly all the explanations of women's position in the
> labour market that have been used since. (1976: 156)

The next three chapters further this examination by following the
issue of equal pay for equal work as it was discussed and debated among
economists and feminists. Chapter 3 scans the period between 1890 and
World War I. Chapter 4 details and contrasts the analyses and positions
of Millicent Fawcett, Eleanor Rathbone and Beatrice Webb during the
war. The fifth examines F. Y. Edgeworth's position on the question as
shown in his 1922 and 1923 articles.

**Notes**
1. For instance, in 1872, Emily Davies and Dr Louisa Garrett Anderson petitioned the
   London County Council to apply the equal pay principle to teachers (Strachey, 1969:
   ch. 12).
2. The issue of women's work was also brought to the forefront of public debate by the
   1893 Royal Commission on Labour and the Employment of Women.
3. Some exceptions are Barrett and McIntosh (1980); Folbre (1989); Hartmann (1976);
   Humphries (1975, 1977); Land (1980).

# 3 Early approaches by economists and feminists to the question of equal pay, 1890–1914

Between the 1860s and 1890, women's work and women's pay do not appear among the concerns of the economists. One exception, however, was Mary Paley and Alfred Marshall's *The Economics of Industry* (1881), where women's low wages are attributed to the 'habit' of women and of their employers 'of taking it for granted that the wages of women must be low' (Marshall and Paley, 1881: 175). For the authors, general opinion rather than any observable deficiency in women's productivity was the determinant of women's wages. It is likely that such statements were from Mary Paley's pen as in the first edition of his *Principles of Economics* (1890) Marshall opposes equal pay for women, seeing it as detrimental to a socially desirable sexual division of labour (Marshall and Paley, 1881; Marshall, 1930).[1]

In 1891, however, Sidney Webb directly addresses the question of equal pay. His empirical documentation and his proposals are followed, over the next two decades, by occasional writings on the subject, which overall tend to favour payment of wages to women according to their productivity levels. Some of the authors must be commended for taking on the ideology of the time and denouncing the sophistry of some of the rationalizations for women's starvation wages (Smart, Cadbury). These writings also see some attempts to develop theoretical explanations for the level of women's pay which prefigure more recent theorizing (Fawcett, Smart).

## Sidney Webb

Sidney Webb seems to be the first male economist to give the question of equal pay some serious thought: in his 1891 empirical article, 'Alleged Differences in Wages Paid to Women and Men for Similar Work'. In this first comprehensive empirical attempt to address the question of wage differences between the sexes, he uses data collected by the Fabian Society from working women and from its own female members, data which he acknowledges as an 'insufficient . . . heterogeneous collection' (Webb, 1891: 636). He draws from his study the following general conclusion:

Women workers appear almost invariably to earn less than men except in a few instances of exceptional ability, and in a few occupations where sexual attraction enters in. Where the inferiority of earnings exists, it is almost always coexistent with an inferiority of work. And the general inferiority of women's work seems to influence their wages in industries in which no such inferiority exists. (ibid.: 657)

This definitive statement is not in effect supported by Webb's empirical data.

His data mainly document two categories of occupation: 'manual labour' and 'routine mental work', and show that women are paid at a level often significantly below men's wages in the same industries. Webb does not document – statistically or otherwise – the 'few instances of exceptional ability',[2] and the 'few occupations where sexual attraction enters in'. These statements are nothing but hypotheses applied to two of the job classifications he defines: intellectual work where he presumes equal treatment for exceptional women, and artistic work where he asserts that women 'seem' to enjoy a monopoly rent due to 'the market value of sexual attraction' (ibid.: 656).[3]

In the first category, 'manual labour', he notes 'the impossibility of discovering more than a very few instances in which men and women do precisely similar work, in the same place, at the same epoch' (ibid.: 638). This mars his attempts at comparing the most comparable: task wages. In the very few instances of similar work he provides little data on task wages, asserting only that they are 'the same' or 'nearly as much' (ibid.: 640, 645). He does provide a substantial amount of data on average weekly earnings for men and women in these industries which seem irrelevant to his argument on task wages.

Webb nevertheless uses this data to support his finding of 'equality or near equality' of men's and women's wages. This statement is easily contradicted by the data itself showing that women get wages higher (3 cases) or within 1 shilling per week of men's wages (10 cases) in only 13 cases out of the 74 listed. Average earnings for women in these industries fall in some cases below half of men's.

Webb also notes that when women replace men, 'the women almost invariably receive less than the men did' (ibid.: 647). This can be explained in some cases by mechanization of the trade, yet 'in other cases the substitution of women for men has taken place without any change in the industrial process' (ibid.). Lower wages are also attributed to 'women's lack of industrial experience' or to their 'fail[ure] to master some incidental small part' of the industrial process (ibid.: 658, 659).[4] Whereas Webb notes these facts as 'curious', he does not question their purpose of keeping some higher-paid occupations as male preserves.[5]

These 'incidental small' differences are the only specific evidence of the alleged inferior productivity of women.

To conclude his section on manual labour, Webb finds it 'difficult to draw any general conclusion from the foregoing facts' (ibid.: 649). He nevertheless proffers that these facts 'suggest' to him that lower wages are due to women's lower productivity.

In 'routine mental work', Webb discovers more occupations where women and men do the same work. There, he finds that 'women's earnings . . . are invariably less than men's' (ibid). Women clerks get between 30 and 80 per cent of men clerks' salaries in the Post Office. In an insurance company, women perform work 'rather better and more rapidly than men' yet their salaries are 'perhaps less than half what would have to be paid to men for similar work'. Women teachers 'almost invariably receive lower salaries than men teachers' (ibid.: 652–3).

Not finding fault in women's productivity, Webb resorts to other explanations: women teachers are paid less 'partly for the reason of "gentility" '; 'it has been found as yet impossible to train the women employees to higher duties' in the Post Office and insurance companies, or in teaching; night duty cannot be required of women; they cannot be given 'any but the merest routine work'; women's work is 'a mere prelude to matrimony, and often only a source of pocket money' (ibid.: 650–5).

The 'market' rather than the type of work is seen to set women's wages below men's: 'women typewriters employed by the Government receive . . . only 14s. a week, the reason given being that this is the market rate for women typewriters, though not for men' (ibid.: 649).

Most of Webb's analysis of routine mental work is spent trying to demonstrate higher absenteeism on the part of women. But here again, his data are not conclusive. Women actually show sickness rates lower than or equivalent to those of men in 38 per cent of the Post Office departments listed by Webb (ibid.: 651–2).[6]

In his study, Webb fails to establish conclusively 'the general inferiority of women's work'. A lot of the factors cited which are seen to decrease the 'nett advantageousness' of women workers are either quite marginal or structurally determined (for example, factory legislation). They have nothing to do with productivity *per se*. Webb also fails to demonstrate that 'where the inferiority of earnings exists, it is almost always coexistent with an inferiority of work'. On the contrary, his data show inferiority of earnings where there is equivalent or superior work performed by women. In a lot of cases the comparison is not possible due to the extreme segregation of men and women in the labour market, a situation which does not warrant the blanket statement Webb makes on women's pay and their productivity.[7]

At the end of his article, Webb is probably aware of the weakness of his 'demonstration' and brings in the *Deus ex machina* of the market to explain women's low wages. They are 'set less by their efficiency in that particular industry than by comparison with what women earn elsewhere' (ibid.: 658). At this point Webb's argument becomes tautological and the exercise he has engaged in is made pointless.

The market is then used for a further assertion. Webb ventures into a comparison of pay where work is segregated by sex: 'Women's work is usually less highly paid than work of equivalent difficulty and productivity done by men'. The reason for this is that 'what they produce is usually valued in the market at a lower rate' (ibid.: 659–60). No data are provided to support this statement.

Webb must have been aware that women's wages were low regardless of their comparative productivity, something he could have logically concluded from his own empirical research. He, in fact, identifies two factors unrelated to productivity: the 'lower standard of life of women', and 'the influence of "make weights", the assistance received by so many women workers from parents, husbands, or lovers' (ibid.: 649).

In the end, for Sidney Webb, 'the problem of the inequality of wages is one of great plurality of causes and intermixture of effects' (ibid.: 659). He cannot come up with any 'definitive conclusion' on the cause of wage differences between the sexes. He can only recognize its universality:

> It exists both where the women are subject to exceptional legislative restrictions, and where these do not prevail; it exists in the United States, the Colonies and France, as well as in this country; it exists in clerical and educational as well as in manufacturing work; in mental as well as manual labour; where payment is made by the piece and where it is made by time; where custom rules and where competition. [*sic*] (ibid.: 660)

Some of the possible causes for lower wages are the lack of 'combination' of women, their relative 'redundancy' and 'inefficience [*sic*]'. To these Webb adds the following overriding statement: 'it is impossible to overlook the effect of the fact that the woman has something else to sell besides her labour . . . many women are partially maintained out of other incomes than their own' (ibid.: 660), making their case similar to that of 'male unskilled labourers receiving a rate in aid of wages' under the Poor Laws. His presumption (which no doubt is reflective of common patriarchal beliefs) is that *all* women have an alternative source of livelihood: marriage, prostitution or 'the possession of small means' (ibid.: 660n.). Women's primary commodity is sex, offered on the market either through marriage or prostitution. Labour is only a secondary commodity which they may choose to offer to gain additional income. As for the women who choose not to supply the sex commodity, it is obvious that they must have access to a further alternative source of livelihood: independent means.[8]

Webb's statement illuminates the patriarchal ideology which underlies economic analyses of women's work and women's pay. It is disconcerting, however, that Webb chose to conclude his study with such a general and definitive observation and with no attempt to elaborate or demonstrate the point. It is as if the mere statement of this 'fact' is expected to draw appreciative and knowing nods on the part of his fellow economists, who will not require further convincing. It is clear that, if Webb's presumption is right and if this element is as much a determinant of women's wages as he seems to believe, women's pay is governed more by their sex and the ideology that surrounds it in a patriarchal capitalist society than by their actual productivity, or, for that matter, their actual subsistence needs.

At the end of his article Webb classifies the causes for women's lower pay into four general categories. He sees custom and public opinion as the major one, the others being lower standards due to lower needs and 'make weights', lower productivity, and lack of trade union organization. He suggests various approaches to remedy the situation, the main one being an idealist call for a change in public opinion. Women are admonished to 'insist on a higher standard both of physical needs and mental demands' and to achieve 'greater freedom and independence'. They are called upon to exert more 'public influence' (ibid.: 660–1). Webb also puts a lot of faith into a 'gradual spread of trade unions among women workers', which he expects to have the multiple effect of educating women, improving their productivity and wages and giving them protective organization.

However well intentioned, Webb's treatment of the question of equal pay is flawed by his belief – unsubstantiated by his data – that women are generally less productive than men, and by his failure to explore the contention that women's place and conditions in the labour market are determined by their sex.

**Millicent Garrett Fawcett**
Millicent Garrett Fawcett's name has remained closely associated with the battle for women's suffrage in England. Yet she was also committed to some of the wider issues of women's emancipation such as access to education, employment and the professions. Married to the Liberal

politician and economist Henry Fawcett, she developed an interest in economics.[9] In the 1890s she contributed reviews and comments on the issues of women's wages and women's employment.[10]

In her 1892 review of Sidney Webb's article, Millicent Fawcett is generally uncritical of his approach, stating her 'almost complete agreement' (Fawcett, 1892: 173) with him at the start of her review, and proposing only to offer 'an addition' to it. She does not address his biased use of data, nor does she try to reinterpret the data. Instead she agrees with his overall conclusion that women are less productive. While attributing this lower productivity to women's lack of opportunities in the labour market, she claims it could be remedied by improved access to training.

The 'addition' she offers is the development of an analysis of women's lower wages based on her observation of the structure of the labour market. She indeed elaborates an early theory of segregated or dual labour markets.[11] What she sees is the presence of 'non-competing groups' in the labour market, 'limited both industrially and geographically', with 'the equalizing effect of competition in wages only operat[ing] within each of these groups' (ibid.: 173). What inhibits the equalization of wages between the groups is the impossibility for workers to transfer their labour from low-wage to high-wage areas of employment.

She sees the wages within each group as being determined by 'the value of the produce of labour in the most productive industry in the group' (ibid.: 174). Employers have to keep paying matching wage rates to be able to maintain their access to a skilled labour force within each group. Fawcett illustrates this with a number of examples in the case of male workers. She also applies the principle to female workers in cases where women can use the existence of alternative, better-paid employment to their advantage. Hence, the 'women servants command better wages in Lancashire than in Dorsetshire . . . because enough has to be paid them in the former county to induce them to take up domestic work, instead of going into a mill' (ibid.: 175).

Similarly, she remarks that 'the opening of more professions to women has had an important effect in preventing a sharp fall in women's wages in the professional group' (ibid.). As a result, women teachers have been able to maintain their wages in spite of an increase in the supply of women teachers because some women have entered the better-paid professions.

For Fawcett, the main reason for the inequality of wages between the sexes is the lack of direct competition between them in the labour market along with a situation where 'the most wealth-producing of men's industries, such as engineering, mining, banking . . . are more wealth-producing than the most wealth-producing of women's industries, such as cotton spinning and weaving, schoolkeeping, etc.' (ibid.: 174–5). Consequently, where the two sexes meet and perform similar work, their pay is unequal:

> A woman servant, who may be, and generally is, a much more desirable person to have about one than a man servant, and who, therefore, if mere utility governed value, would get more, is paid about half as much, because the other employments within her reach are only about half as productive of wealth as the man's. (ibid.: 175)[12]

Fawcett identifies some of the crucial characteristics of the labour market conditions women face. Yet she does not acknowledge, for instance, that women's mobility in the labour market is seriously hindered by family responsibilities and by traditions which limit women's freedom of movement. Hence the women from Dorsetshire cannot threaten to leave for Lancashire to obtain higher wages from their employers. This omission is to be contrasted with Fawcett's apparent view that men's mobility is unrestrained across occupations and geographical areas.

One can also question her view that competition within one group of workers has the unidirectional effect of pulling wages up towards those prevalent in the 'most wealth-producing industry'. The market for women's labour is, on the contrary, overwhelmingly influenced by the existence of occupations that procure either no remuneration (for example, housewife) or utterly low pay (for example, governess). This, coupled with the crowding phenomenon, can only generate a downward pull on wages. What clearly is a factor as well, in either the male or the female labour market, is the relative scarcity of skilled labour in relation to employers' demand. If taken into account, these elements would have strengthened Fawcett's analysis of relative pay among 'non-competing groups' in the labour market.

Fawcett forcefully expresses her opposition to the demand for equal pay for equal work:[13]

> I have always regarded it as an error, both in principle and in tactics to advise women under all circumstances to demand the same wages for the same work as men. . . . The cry 'the same wages for the same work' is very plausible, but it is proved impossible of achievement when the economic conditions of the two sexes are so widely different. (ibid.: 176)[14]

Crowding is the condition she refers to which in her eyes makes it impossible for employers to apply the equal pay principle. She gives the example of the London School Board: when female teachers flock towards job opportunities they get paid less than the rare male teachers who apply for the vacancies. She comments: 'Under these circumstances no one can accuse the Board of injustice to their women teachers' (ibid.). And when a school in Hertfordshire decided to pay women and men teachers equally, it was able to hire 'exceptionally well qualified' female teachers and 'mere average' male ones. For Fawcett, the 'equality therefore was only nominal; the same money bought a better article in the female labour market than it did in the male labour market' (ibid.). But, we must ask, isn't the latter situation a significant improvement for the women hired? And isn't it likely to have a positive impact on the overall market wage for female teachers? One wonders why the feminist does not applaud and encourage the Hertfordshire initiative as a means towards the improvement of female teachers' pay over time.

Fawcett suggests two remedies to the employment situation faced by women. She endorses Sidney Webb's support for the goal of women's unionization, but, more forcefully, proposes that 'what women most want is more training, to enable them to pursue more skilled handicrafts and a large number of professional occupations' (ibid.).[15] She sees this as already happening, and resulting in 'higher wages earned by women as compared with a former period, notwithstanding the . . . almost complete absence of trade unionism, and the vast increase in the number of women seeking employment'. Yet, as she pointed out earlier, the movement of women into the higher-paid professions was only able to prevent a fall in the pay of female teachers. Clearly, her faith in training is unrealistically optimistic. It exposes her faith in the free working of a presumably perfectly competitive, albeit segregated, labour market.

Whereas her analysis is far from perfect, it is clear that in 1892 Fawcett developed a more perceptive understanding of the position of women in the labour market than economists such as Sidney Webb, and subsequently A. C. Pigou or F. Y. Edgeworth, who all refer to 'market wages elsewhere' as a major cause for women's lower wages without ever elaborating an economic analysis of what precisely is at work here.

### Ada Heather-Bigg

Another feminist tackled the dominant Victorian ideology on women's work in the pages of the *Economic Journal* in the 1890s. In 1894 Ada Heather-Bigg published a short article, 'The Wife's Contribution to Family Income'. In it she takes head-on the argument that married women should not work. She documents the history of women's work and cites Adam Smith and Nassau Senior's statements on the necessity of a wife's labour and income to provide adequate support for the family. She argues that the reason for present-day opposition to women's employment is that it has been made visible by the wage earning that accompanies it.

Heather-Bigg deduces that when men oppose women's employment, 'what they object to is the *wage-earning* not the *work* of wives' (1894: 55). What they are attempting to protect is their status as breadwinners: they see women's wage-earning, no matter how minimal their wages, as a threat to that status. She exclaims: 'Such a fear is the veriest scooped-out, sheet-draped turnip that ever made a village dolt take to his heels and run' (ibid.).

She also denounces the common idea that women are 'kept' by their husbands: 'So far from keeping his wife, the true account of the matter is that he and she have together kept themselves and the younger children.' While she emphasizes women's contribution to overall family support, she is well aware that the wages women get ensure that they cannot effectively threaten the male breadwinner status. In conclusion she asserts women's right to contribute economically to their family's livelihood and to receive recognition rather than denigration for it:

> The ideal to be aimed at, I submit, is not that the man should be the sole bread-winner, but that bread-winning should go on under circumstances which secure the most comfortable life for the men, women, and children composing the family, which permit the fullest development of all powers, and which openly substitute economic co-operation on the part of the wife for economic dependence. (ibid.: 58)

She would like to see the end of the power imbalance that exists in the family.

In this short article Ada Heather-Bigg puts her finger on some important features of the patriarchal power system and the ideology that supports it. In this system, there is nothing wrong with women's work; actually the more the better, as long as this work does not give women access to economic or social power. Hence an oppressive ideology surrounds women's work: denying its existence, its value, its contribution to economic well-being and opposing its monetary compensation. Added to this is the violent reaction to any potential threat women's work presents to male power. This article marks possibly the first publication in an economic journal of a feminist analysis of the patriarchal economic power attached to the denial of economic status to women's work, the barring of women from employment, the non-recognition of their contribution (monetary and in kind) to the family and the maintenance of women in a role secondary to that of the male breadwinner.

**William Smart**

William Smart (1853–1915) occupied the Adam Smith Chair of Political
Economy at the University of Glasgow from 1896 until his death. He
gained notoriety as the translator and editor of the Austrian School
economists who influenced his own approach to marginalism. His
interest in issues of income distribution and housing led to his appointment to the Poor Law Commission in 1905 (Jones, 1916).[16]

In 1891 William Smart gave an address on women's wages to the
Philosophical Society of Glasgow. Smart uses Sidney Webb's article and
data as the basis for his argument. He remarks that women's labour 'is
not by any means unskilled, as anyone who has seen a spinning or
weaving factory knows' (Smart, 1892: 87). Yet women get on average
10s. a week while '20s. a week . . . is a low average for a man possessing
any degree of skill whatever'. He sets out to find the reason for the
'great disparity between men's and women's wages' (ibid.: 88).

The first part of Smart's address is a review and a refutation of five
common answers to the question of pay differences between men and
women. He shows that, even though 'there is truth in all these answers
. . . each of them is at best a half truth, raising as many questions as it
settles' (ibid.). Smart subsequently proceeds to develop an explanation
of his own which drew the following comment from Edgeworth: 'The
answer which Mr. Smart gives to the question thus generalised is worthy
of being read along with Mrs. Fawcett's important contribution to the
subject in the *Economic Journal*' (Edgeworth 1893: 118).

The first common answer to the question addressed by Smart is 'that
women's wages are low because of the equation of supply and demand'
in crowded industries (Smart, 1892: 88–9). For him, this explanation
resorts to a wage fund approach to wage determination, 'which is now
one of the antiquities of political economy' (ibid.: 89). Low
wages can be the result of 'overstocking' only if this is 'the sole possible
cause of low wages – which might be doubted'. Besides, Smart holds
that '[t]here is, indeed, no formula in political economy on which the
modern economist looks with more suspicion than that of Supply and
Demand'. Such law would be 'tolerable only under absolutely free
competition, which would involve perfect mobility of labour', a condition which does not apply (ibid.: 90). Smart finds that relying on supply
and demand for an explanation is tautological: 'To say, then, that wages
are low because there are enough women to take the low wage, is little
more than to say that wages are low because people are paid low wages.'
This explanation does not deal with the question: 'What are the factors,
or influences or motives, that make women take a wage below that of

men, and what are the factors that make employers offer the low wage?'
(ibid.).

The second type of explanation evaluated by Smart is that of women
as auxiliary breadwinners of the family. He finds this reason dubious
because it is based on 'an assumption which is at least questionable[:]
that the economic or wage earning unit is the *family*. This is an old time
idea which, however beautiful and desirable, is a little out of place in
the conditions to which the factory system has brought us' (ibid.). He
describes a system of a male-earned family wage sufficient to bring up
a family and train the next generation of workers, with possible
supplementary wages earned by other family members, as a system of
the past. He adds that, at the time of his writing, 'many married women
[are] not members of a family, and . . . many married women and
widows [are] the sole breadwinners of the family' (ibid.: 91). Smart also
points out the inconsistency of an explanation which seems to apply to
working-class women but not to women in professional or artistic
occupations. 'If the sex of the author, artist, musician, doctor,
intellectual or artistic worker generally, has nothing to do with her
remuneration, why should sex determine the wage of the factory girl?'
(ibid.).

Similarly, Smart dismisses an explanation based on women's lower
standard of living. He disputes that women have lower needs than men
and points out that in the upper classes they are seen as having higher
needs. What creates this belief is that women 'will live on a shilling a-
day' when forced to while men will rather 'become a tramp or go to the
workhouse first'. So, 'women's wages are less than men's because, for
some reason, women accept less' (ibid.: 91–2). The reason for this needs
to be determined.

Smart rejects the subsistence wage approach of these last two
explanations: 'it is quite against our modern ideas to represent wage
[*sic*] as regulated by wants'. His definitive comment challenges the *ad
hoc* approach of economic theorist: 'If a man-worker, then, is supposed
to get a high wage when he produces much, a low wage when he
produces little, why should a woman's wage be determined by another
principle?' (ibid.: 92). Some who have pondered the question since have
been in great need of such a reminder.

Smart then reviews two arguments which are based on a value of
marginal product approach to wages: one being that women's wages
reflect lower productivity levels, the other that they reflect a lower value
of commodities in industries employing women.

He admits that women's work may be inferior. However, some of the
reasons he reviews are not intrinsic to their sex, but rather to such

socioeconomic factors as factory legislation or low nutrition levels due to low wages, as well as the fact that women are not allowed access to some skills. Given these, wage differences are justified in Smart's eyes and only represent differences in skills or actual productivity, so the principle of 'Equal Wages for Equal Work' could be adopted without major consequences (ibid.: 93). Yet, as pointed out by Webb, there are very few occupations in which women and men work side by side.[17]

The last explanation has been used to justify the overall lower wages in women's industry.[18] Based on observations of sex segregation in the labour market and lower average industrial wages for women, it uses a 'cart before the horse' application of the value of marginal product approach to wages. Smart fails to see any necessary causality in this argument. Wages are not low because the prices of commodities produced are low, rather, 'it was the reduction in wages, among other things, that made the reduction of prices possible' (ibid.: 96). For Smart, employers, seeking access to a larger share of the market, attempt to reduce their prices. This can be achieved in a number of ways, the lowering of wages being only one of them. And, once they are low, 'it is a very difficult thing to raise wages' given the pressure of consumers to keep prices low (ibid.). Both employers and the public are therefore responsible for the low wages of women.

Although this last explanation is not satisfactory, it provides Smart with an avenue towards further elucidation of the question. He remarks that 'women are in almost exclusive possession of certain branches of trade . . . indeed . . . there is a well marked relegation of women-workers towards certain ill-paid trades', while men move to the 'better-paid trades'. Here what Smart sees at work 'is not a difference of wage between workers of various degrees of efficiency. It is very much a question of difference of wage between two non-competing groups, and of groups where the level of wage are determined by a different law' (ibid.: 97).

So the relevant question is *'Why is the wage-level of skilled female labour lower even than that of unskilled male labour?'* (ibid.; my emphasis). This is the question which has had to be addressed all along and which still needs to be addressed today. And, even though it was so clearly formulated in 1891, most economists who came after Smart chose to ignore it.

Wages are not set through the workings of the market for all workers considered together. Two elements are at work: a difference in wage determination between the sexes and a situation where the lower-paid sex drives out the other one in trades where both are at some point employed. Smart describes how women, when brought into some trade alongside men, initially receive smaller wages because of 'certain disabilities of their sex'. This keeps the overall wage level down and drives away the men, leaving the whole trade to women. 'Unscrupulous employers' can then further lower the women's wages, and competition in the trade leads all employers to follow suit.

Whether the initial move is due to technological change or to the mere hiring of women in competition with men, the wage women end up receiving is observed to be at the level of 10s. a week: 'It is quite certain that the women's remuneration will not be determined by the 20s. wage which they displace' (ibid.: 98). Women's wages are a 'customary wage', applied to their sex regardless of the line of employment, productivity levels or skills required.[19] This wage originated 'at a time when the world was poorer, and capital was more powerful' (ibid.: 99). Smart's conclusion is reinforced by the counter-example of the Lancashire weavers, where women earn the same wages for working alongside men. The reason for this anomaly is the presence of a strong trade union representing both sexes which has been able to countervail the employers' power.

But what gave rise to the custom of paying women such low wages? This question is explored by Smart to some extent. He remarks that women's wages vary very little from the average of 10s. a week: 'this is not an average made up from widely different wage-bills, and from widely varying individual wages'.[20] He also states that 'the reason why it [the wage] does not go lower is chiefly because it cannot . . . women's wages are very near the only quite definite level that political economy has ever pointed out, the level of subsistence' (ibid.: 100).

Smart contrasts two methods of wage determination: productivity wages which apply 'in a progressive society, where wealth is rapidly increasing' and subsistence wages found 'in a poor or backward society'. That women's wages are still determined under the second principle in England which 'long ago passed from the latter to the former' type of society is attributed to the lack of trade union organization by women. Male workers have used their organization to force a redistribution of the product of industry to bring their wages to the level of productivity wages while female workers, unorganized, are still in a situation where the capitalists employing them reap all the returns from their productivity.

Smart adds that women's wages are kept down – and brought below the subsistence requirements of a single woman – by competition between women; those in desperate need for an income (widows) or those whose wages only supplement (married women, young girls) 'will take any wage' (ibid.: 101). The 'make-weight' situation of some women has an influence on the overall level of women's wages, but only a secondary, after-the-fact influence, as competition within the group determines how far below the customary subsistence wage women's market wage will go.[21] To remedy the problem, Smart proposes organization 'to protect women against employers and against themselves', and the 'enlightenment of the public conscience'.

> It should not be difficult to convince educated people that women's work should be paid on the same principle as that of men . . . – according to their products, and not according to their wants; and to make them pay, or insist on the worker being paid, equal wages for equal work. (ibid.: 102)

Where Smart sees the difficulty is in eradicating the belief in the 'supposed necessity for low wages'. Towards that goal, he attacks 'the most deplorable of current fallacies . . . the idea that the cheapness of goods makes up for everything in the workers' circumstances' (ibid.: 103). Low prices are not an acceptable justification for lowering workers' wages to (or below) subsistence levels. 'The goal of economic effort is not the accumulation of wealth, but the support of wealthy human beings.' Smart shows that the benefits of lower prices do not all go to the workers who receive lower wages. Wealth is redistributed away from the workers who create it.

To conclude his address, Smart states that, given the increase in overall wealth in Britain since the industrial revolution, there is no justification for keeping women's wages at the subsistence level. 'If this was a fair wage fifty years ago, it cannot be so now' (ibid.: 105).

Smart shows economic and general common sense as well as integrity and honesty towards the subject at hand. His detailed treatment of the question of women's wages is, in the history of economic thought up to his time and for some time thereafter, the most cogent and sensible look at the question by a male economist. Although it is clear that Smart has overall a favourable opinion of capitalists, he does not try to develop an ideological tract in support of their interests. He is not an apologist for capitalists reaping maximum profit. Instead he supports a 'fair' distribution of returns between all factors, believing that the real purpose of economic growth is the increased welfare of all. Nor does he attempt to manipulate economic theory into an argument supporting the capitalist and patriarchal status quo.

Yet William Smart shows amazing naïvety in his description of the motives of capitalists and in his optimistic belief that the capitalist system is synonymous with progress for humanity. He states: 'I am sanguine enough to believe that most employers are anxious to pay their workers as high a wage as they can', and attributes exploitative behaviour to a small minority of employers, in the face of the reality of generalized underpayment of women's work.

Smart's concept of a 'customary wage' for women, regardless of trade, skill or industry, is an important innovation. It is unfortunate that he did not elaborate on what he meant exactly by 'customary', restricting his comments to the level of this wage and its relationship to subsistence requirements. It would have been useful to know exactly how Smart envisioned the determination of this wage.

The main flaw in his argument is his marginalist approach to income distribution. He confuses theory and reality when he asserts that the wages received by male workers represent their contribution to the value of the product. If the market works naturally towards the optimal income distribution predicted by the marginalist model, why is it necessary for trade unions to intervene on behalf of male workers to bring their wages up to the value of product contributed? And why is it that women's lack of organization leads to a separate, and in Smart's view antiquated, system of wage determination?

Clearly he sees that there is a double standard at work in the determination of men's and women's wages. However, his adherence to marginalism prevents him from developing a sound and comprehensive theoretical explanation for this reality. Smart's inquiry indicates that something else is at work in the determination of wages for both men and women, yet he resorts to an *ad hoc* theory of labour market equilibrium whereby wages reach the optimum level (productivity wages)[22] when trade unions represent workers and stay at a sub-optimum level (subsistence wages) when there is no labour organization. In Smart's analysis, unions are paradoxically essential to the achievement of optimal market equilibrium and income distribution. Without unions, the outcome is that rents accrue to capitalist employers and consumers at the expense of workers.

Nevertheless, Smart did contribute some important insights to the question of women's wages. He developed further the application to women of the theory of 'non-competing groups' initiated by Millicent Fawcett, he introduced the concept of a 'customary wage' applied to women workers, he identified the relationship between this customary wage and women's perceived subsistence requirements and, last but not least, he thoroughly debunked the array of trite and apologetic exertions on the subject which prevailed in his day and continue to survive to date.

After the initial interest in the question of woman's pay generated by Sidney Webb, Millicent Fawcett and William Smart, the issue receded into semi-oblivion. In England, two exceptions to this neglect are the massive survey of women workers in Birmingham, *Women's Work and Wages*, by Edward Cadbury *et al.*, in 1906,[23] and some passages of Edwin Cannan's *Wealth*, published in 1914.

## Cadbury, Matheson and Shann

Cadbury and his co-authors essentially restate W. Smart's position on women's wages. The main purpose of the study is not to formulate new theory, but to offer a comprehensive synthesis of knowledge on women workers for the 'general reader', 'the social worker amongst women' and social reformers, and to provide a substantial data base on women workers for present and future social scientists (pp. 11–12). Cadbury's team must have produced the first ever large-scale, systematic sociological study of working-class women.[24] Far from focusing only on working conditions and wages, the study breaks new ground by documenting their living conditions, including housework duties.[25]

Direct investigation of facts allows Cadbury *et al.* to throw light on some elements of the debate on women's wages. The important element they contribute is the insight that married women do not have the impact on wages denounced by most writers. Cadbury's data show higher average wages for the older age group and for married women:

> Again, the . . . answer that a women's wage is low because her wage is an auxiliary one, because she is subsidised by the other members of the family, is not borne out by facts. . . . The almost invariable reply to the question whether married women tend to bring down the wages was: 'No, they are more independent and better skilled and therefore always get more on piece-work. . . . Married women are in responsible positions, and are steadier and more skilled and so get better wages.' (p. 128)

Furthermore, rather than increasing competitive pressure, married women are observed to exercise an influence 'towards the shortening of hours' (ibid.).[26]

The study also documented that male-dominated trade unions do not feel the pressure of competition from female workers, since jobs are segregated by sex. Their general position is one of indifference towards women's wages and complete lack of interest in the organizing of women workers (pp. 130–1). As for employers, Cadbury *et al.* note: 'one of the most striking facts brought out by our investigation . . . is the thoughtless way in which they take women's work, its conditions and wages, for granted' (p. 132). The general position of the authors is that:

A woman should be paid at a rate based on the quality or quantity of her work. It is not fair that the rate should be based on the fact of her sex and not on her living requirements as a human being; that she should give the chief and best part of her life to hard toil, whether intellectual or manual and yet be partially dependent. (p. 191)

The authors assess that neither productivity nor subsistence seem to determine women's wages. They feel that 'far-reaching' remedies are necessary. Minimum wages and wage boards, discussed at length, are seen as mere palliatives. What is required is a 'social and industrial policy having for its end and aim a better and more equitable redistribution' (p. 305).

New arguments are brought into the discussion of women's wages. *Women's Work* criticizes the argument, not apparent in earlier writings, that any increase in women's wages would have to occur at the expense of men's. Such a position assumes that the labour factor is receiving its 'fair share' of the National Dividend and that the market could only suffer a redistribution of labour income among workers. Cadbury *et al.* see that position as 'sounding dangerously near the echo of the old wage fund fallacy' (p. 143), and as based on the erroneous assumption that income distribution between factors resulting from the market approximates that obtained under perfect competition. Drawing on *The Economics of Industry* (Marshall and Paley, 1881), they argue that the power imbalance between labour and capital and the lack of mobility of labour prevent an optimal factorial income distribution.

They advocate a redistribution from profits to wages (p. 143), targeting especially, but not exclusively, the profits of the 'parasitic' industries who benefit from women's cheap labour.[27] The authors also suggest redistribution from the 'considerable consumer surplus' of the cheap goods industries (ibid.).

Cadbury, Matheson and Shann situate their analysis of women's wages within an overall understanding of the economic and social situation of women. They reject a family-based approach to income distribution and the consideration that women's income is secondary to men's which informs the new 'wage fund fallacy'. They state firmly that 'a woman is not a mere appendage to a man' (ibid.) and denounce the deliberate maintenance of women in a state of economic dependence: 'it is imperative that . . . the economic status of women be raised; for, while their economic inferiority is due to their past subjection, yet in turn the inferiority tends to perpetuate the subjection' (p. 144).

Women's economic dependence is condemned as having major adverse ethical and social consequences, pushing women to 'early improvident marriages' and to prostitution (ibid.). The authors insist: 'That this [prostitution] is an economic element in the wage question is beyond all doubt.' The hypocrisy and silence surrounding 'the dread trade' allow 'the true cost of "cheap labour" ' to be kept hidden (p. 190).[28]

The Cadbury study threw much-needed light on the reality of economic and social conditions faced by women workers and earnestly questioned the ideological foundations of women's economic dependence. Unfortunately, this valuable, empirically based analysis does not seem to have been taken into consideration by subsequent writers on the subject.

### Edwin Cannan

Cannan deals briefly with women's wages in the chapter 'Incomes from Work' of his 1914 book, *Wealth*. His approach differs from the ordinary in that he recognizes that women are not uniformly inferior to men: 'there are . . . employments in which women are superior to men', for which he stereotypically gives the example of 'the care of children' (1914: 203). Men could not compete with women and would fail to be hired in these occupations, the obvious reason being that 'the men's output would be much inferior to the women's' (ibid.). Yet, in spite of this localized superiority of women, their earnings in these occupations remain low in comparison 'with the earnings of men employed in occupations of the same class'.

Cannan's approach here is original. He is probably the first male economist explicitly to address the issue of the *value* of women's work. He very clearly describes how women's wages should be compared to men's:

> It would be absurd, for example, to compare the earnings of the average children's nurse with the earnings which we might suppose her brother might make as a nurse, and consequently to declare her earnings high. What we must do is to compare her earnings with the actual earnings of her brother in his occupation of, say, carting coal, and then we find that her earnings are low – at any rate when hours, loss of freedom, and other considerations are taken into account. Now, it is clearly no use to say that the woman earns less than her brother because she cannot heave as much coal; we might just as well say that he should earn less than his sister because he cannot wash as much baby. (ibid.: 204)

He thus proposes to compare the wages of individuals of both sexes who have similar characteristics (age, education, and so on) to determine the respective value of their work regardless of the biases attached to the nature of the work and the sex of those traditionally performing it. He also interestingly reverses one of the age-old justifications for women's wages by showing its absurdity when symmetrically applied to the other sex.

The 'ultimate judge, the consumer' determines the value of one's production, and in the case of the children's nurse, the consumer finds women's 'output superior to men's' (ibid.). The reason for low wages is not, therefore, found in a low value of the product or a lack of demand for it. Rather, crowding, 'the fact of the restricted area of employment offered by these occupations in comparison with the number of girls choosing them' is, according to Cannan, the explanation. Consequently, 'it is an economic advantage to be born a boy rather than a girl' (ibid.: 202).

Cannan dismisses the argument that the limited employment opportunities of women might be due to their presumed 'inferior capacity' and points instead to the fact of restricted entry to many occupations. If there were free entry – of both women and men – in all occupations, 'men's and women's earnings would tend to be more equal' (ibid.: 206). Cannan advocates such freedom of entry and chastises the 'inertia of employers and their fear of inconvenience from the active resistance of the men employed at present', which he sees as one of the main blocks in the way of women's opportunities.

He denounces another major obstacle: 'the cry for equal wages for men and women', and claims that 'the most powerful lever for increasing the opportunities of women is taken away if they are not to do the work cheaper' (ibid.: 207).[29]

Changes in consumer demand might generate more fields of employment for women. But, for Cannan, the approach of increasing women's productivity, suggested by some (Webb, Fawcett, Smart) offers only the dismal outcome of further reductions in their pay if the existing crowding conditions are maintained. The unit price of output would decrease.

In conclusion, he states that the 'disparity of incomes between the sexes is one of the two most prominent features in the inequality of the distribution of income' (ibid.: 207–8). Yet his analysis does not offer any radical solutions. His observations are useful, and point to some of the biases that work strongly against women's equality in the labour market. But Cannan, ensconced in his *laissez-faire* dogma, resorts to the habitual indictment of interference in the free work of the market and proposes the sole solution of restoring the free working of supply and demand.

These early discussions of the question of women's wages and the principle of equal pay for women and men show the beginnings of constructive theoretical approaches. They attempt to use empirical observation to document women's work and determine whether the dominant ideology applied to it has any foundation in fact.

Sidney Webb documents the segregation existing in the labour market, while Millicent Fawcett elaborates the theory of non-competing groups and links it to the crowding theory. Cadbury *et al.* empirically challenge the views that married women effect a downward pull on wages and that women present a threat to unionized men. William Smart contributes the concept of a 'customary wage' for women based on dire subsistence and exposes the double standard applied to male and female wage determination. His analysis leads to a questioning of the marginalist theory of wages. Cannan's insights prefigure the modern feminist concept of 'comparable worth'. He provides a candid recognition, rare among male economists, that women's work has a social value and that this value is not appropriately reflected in the wages they receive. Fawcett and Heather-Bigg contribute, in the pages of an economic journal, an early feminist analysis of the effect of the patriarchal power structure and ideology on the economic situation of women.

Although not comprehensive and fully elaborated, the surveys and theories reviewed in this chapter presented genuine attempts at an explanation of women's wage level. Unfortunately, a large portion of these writings were ignored by contemporary or subsequent writers: some of the data and analysis stood in too great a contradiction to dominant ideology. We will see for instance that Edgeworth, Marshall and Pigou all but disregard the facts and theories reviewed here and revert instead, in pure theoretical regress, to the commonplace sophistry critically denounced by Smart.

**Notes**
1. See Chapter 5.
2. An early statement that women have to be exceptional to deserve equality.
3. These latter two categories are very superficially looked at. Interestingly, Webb does not analyse the occupations where women were statistically the most numerous in the 1890s: domestic and related work.
4. 'Women weavers can seldom "tune" or set their own looms. Women heraldic engravers have, curiously enough, never been able to point their own gravers' (Webb, 1891: 659).
5. In a similar way, Webb notes but does not question the use of Factory legislation to keep women in lower-paid occupations.
6. Webb does not state whether pregnancy is included in his definition of 'sickness'.
7. Interestingly, Webb makes no mention of the 'crowding' phenomenon. Rather, he sees women entering an increased range of occupations.

8. Since there is, no doubt, an overall greater proportion of men than women who have access to independent ('small means') sources of income, one must wonder why the overall effect on men's wages is not noticeable.

9. She published *Political Economy for Beginners* (Fawcett, 1870) and some of the *Essays and Lectures on Social and Political Subjects* (Fawcett and Fawcett, 1872).

10. Fawcett (1892, 1904). Millicent Fawcett's writings on women's wages do not seem to have been particularly influenced by her husband, who remained until the end of his life (1884) an adherent of the classical school and of the wages fund doctrine. Having initially expounded the doctrine in her early writings (1870), she seems to have followed Mill in his recantation by the time she wrote on women's wages.

11. This 'addition' was described as an 'important contribution' by F. Y. Edgeworth (1893). Such theories were subsequently developed in the institutionalist school of economics (Doeringer, 1967; Doeringer and Piore, 1971; Reich *et al.*, 1973; Edwards *et al.*, 1975).

12. Fawcett's use of terms here is unfortunate as it implies that women are generally less productive than men. Where similar statements have been made (see S. Webb, the Marshalls and Pigou), the terminology used refers to 'women's wages elsewhere' rather than to the productivity of women's jobs elsewhere. In a later article Fawcett looks at the demand side of the situation: 'it is more *chic*, more fashionable, to have a butler than a parlourmaid, and people are willing to pay in hard cash and even in actual discomfort for this emblem of aristocracy and wealth' (1918: 5).

13. We will see later that she switches to a position of support for the demand in her subsequent writings, partly due to the demonstration of women's abilities in the war industries (Fawcett, 1916, 1918).

14. It is not entirely clear why she sees the demand as wrong in principle and in tactics.

15. One can only wonder at the apparent contradiction between this recommendation and the preceding discussion of women teachers who get paid less for relatively greater skills and abilities.

16. Beatrice Webb was also a member of the Commission.

17. 'And here it is that Mr. Sidney Webb deserves thanks for having accented a fact which we all indeed knew, but of which few of us saw the bearing (93).'

18. It might be inferred from the organization of Smart's argument that a possible reason for sex segregation in industry is the avoidance by employers of instances of equally productive men and women working side by side, to circumvent pressures to pay women a 'man's wage'.

19. Although reminiscent of Alfred and Mary Paley Marshall's noting that the 'habit' of women and their employers is the cause for women's low wages (1881), Smart's idea of a 'customary wage' for women is a new concept in economic theory. It is to be noted that Smart feels the need to reassure his readers that this is no mere 'theorizing' on his part and substantiates his idea with a number of real-life examples.

20. Smart must only be focusing on industrial wages in this discussion. It would be interesting to see what relation he thinks exists between women's industrial wages and the wages received by domestics or by professional women.

21. Smart blames women for the low wages they receive: the intra-group competition drives wages down. In his proposed solutions he recommends that 'the average working woman' protect herself 'against the more helpless members of her own sex' (1892: 102).

22. The concept of market-determined optimum had not been fully developed at the time of Smart's writing, but he is clearly speaking of an optimal wage in the modern sense of the term.

23. All quotations are from the 1907 American edition.

24. Over 6,000 working women in the varied industrial setting of Birmingham were interviewed. Employers, trade unionists and people in various social professions and organizations offering services to women workers were surveyed as well. One earlier

      attempt to comprehensively document women's work and wages in England was the Royal Commission on Labour, The Employment of Women, 1893.

25.  The study for instance discusses the double workday of working-class women and the double standard of the sexual division of labour: 'Again, the pathetic drudgery of the ordinary working class wife is accepted as the proper thing. . . . Where the man and wife both work during the day, the woman accepts it as right that she should do all the housework at night while the husband amuses himself in any way he thinks fit. And often where a working man assists his wife in household duties he does not like his mates to know' (Cadbury *et al.*, 1906: 137).

26.  These findings are nothing but sensible and point out the rhetorical length to which the enemies of women's work will go. Why should someone whose livelihood is at least partially secured out of somebody else's income want to work at any low wage level? It makes a lot more sense to speculate that married women are able to use that partial support to bargain for higher wages, better jobs and working conditions.

27.  The concept of 'parasitic industries' was developed by the Webbs in *Industrial Democracy* (1897; see Chapter 4 below).

28.  These remarks may have been influenced by the advocacy and analysis of Josephine Butler (1828–1906) who actively opposed victimization of prostitutes and developed the argument that the economic situation of women was the main cause of prostitution. See Uglow (1983).

29.  A similar argument is made today by opponents of comparable worth policies (see Hildebrand, 1980; Block, 1982).

# 4   Feminist positions on equal pay for equal work during World War I

The war, with its massive use of female labour in industry, gave women's work and their productive ability a lot more visibility than they had ever enjoyed. This provided the basis for feminist demands for equal pay and equal working conditions for women workers. The issue of equal pay was actively debated during and after the war. Some of the feminists involved publicly in the debate on the issue of equal pay for women and men, during and after the war, were Millicent Garrett Fawcett, Eleanor Rathbone and Beatrice Potter Webb.

In 1916 Fawcett states the argument for equal pay on the basis of women's ability to be efficient industrial workers, as demonstrated during the war. In her 1917 article, Rathbone attempts to redefine the priorities of the women's movement away from the issue of equal pay for equal work. Fawcett's rebuttal appears in 1918. That same year, Beatrice Webb addresses the question from the distance and authority afforded by her membership of the War Cabinet Committee on Women in Industry. Her Minority Report situates the issue of equal pay for men and women within her overall vision of necessary reforms to industrial society. These three positions reflect three distinct feminist tendencies: liberal or equal rights feminism in the case of Fawcett, welfare or maternal feminism in the case of Rathbone, and Webb's socialist feminism.

## Millicent Garrett Fawcett: the case for equal pay

Fawcett's position on the question of Equal Pay for Women is developed in two articles she published during the war (1916, 1918). Whereas in 1892 she thought the demand for equal pay 'very plausible, but . . . impossible of achievement' (1892: 176), by 1916 she had become a strong advocate for the demand. This is most likely to be due to her assessment that women workers' war experience would make the argument for equal pay stronger.

In 1916, Fawcett notes that women's productive power was 'discovered' during the war, but she adds, 'the great mass of our countrywomen always have worked for their living; whether as wage-earners or as home-keepers, and sometimes as both' (1916: 191). Yet for their work women were paid 'less than half' of what men received, women's wages being often set below subsistence level (ibid.: 193). Quoting a Fabian Women's Group study which showed that 85 per cent of the women surveyed had dependants or were wholly supporting themselves,[1] she denounces the common rationale offered for women's low pay: 'The extraordinary low level of women's wages before the war cannot therefore be explained either on the "pocket money" theory or by the fiction that they have no one dependent upon them' (ibid.: 196). Rather, she attributes women's low pay to discriminatory practices which bar them from access to numerous industries and to skilled employment, to apprenticeship and to trades classes. Trade unions and professional organizations who practise such exclusion contribute to the crowding of women into a few unskilled occupations. She denounces this situation as 'a hideous tyranny, which has kept huge masses of industrial women in a sort of serfage' (ibid.: 199).

Fawcett reviews evidence of women's high productivity in war jobs and calls for an end to the 'gross waste of national resources' caused by the exclusion of women from industrial work and by their systematic underpayment and overwork in the crowded industries. Her case for equal pay is based on the evidence of women's equal – or higher – productivity, their ability to receive training to perform 'men's work' and the necessary improvement in women's overall health and welfare that would derive from wages providing more than bare subsistence. She calls for a change of beliefs and attitudes towards women: 'We have to root out of people's minds the notion which largely prevails that 15 shillings a week is a sort of "natural" wage for women' (ibid.: 197). She sees trade unions as necessary allies of the feminists in the fight for better pay and opportunities for women:

> We have to convince the men Trade-Unionists that their right line of policy is not to keep the women out, but to help the women in, to welcome their entry to well paid work, to give them the benefit of their own larger knowledge and wider experience, and either to enrol them in their own Trade-Unions or to help them form Trade Unions of their own. (ibid.)[2]

In this article Fawcett does not make specific proposals on how the goals of equal pay and access to employment for women can be achieved.

### Eleanor Rathbone: family allowances first
Eleanor Rathbone succeeded Millicent Garrett Fawcett as President of the NUWSS in 1919. The first woman to be elected city councillor, in Liverpool in 1909, she concentrated on the issues of housing, working-class families' budgets and financial support for widows.[3] Her expertise

led the City Council to put her in charge of separation allowances for
wives and dependants of Liverpool war conscripts. From her observations she developed her position on women's pay and her proposal for
family allowances. Family allowances became the issue she agitated for
the rest of her life, within the NUWSS at first and as a Member of
Parliament after 1929.

In 1917 Eleanor Rathbone sees the two main post-war issues of
concern to women as 'the position of women in industry' and the
conditions under which working-class mothers raise their children.[4] She
argues that these issues are 'closely related' (1917: 55) by the question
of women's pay and the way income earning is organized in industrial
society. Women receive lower wages because they are not seen as
responsible for dependants, or even for their own upkeep. This in turn
makes working-class mothers dependent on their husband's wages for
their own and their children's subsistence needs. She denounces an
income distribution system which 'leaves it to "blind economic forces"
to bring it about that the wages of men shall be sufficient for the
purposes of bringing up families' (ibid.: 61).

Rathbone urges permanent changes by seizing the opportunity
presented by the war which has, to some extent, modified the pre-
existing conditions encountered by women in industry and in the family.
In industry, war conditions broke down some of the 'barriers that kept
[women] out of the skilled trades', barriers against which 'the "women's
movement" had beaten itself for half a century in vain' (ibid.: 55). In
the home, war separation allowances gave women independence and a
more adequate income, based on the number of children as opposed to
their husband's trade.

Rathbone predicts that war separation allowances will be phased out
once the war ends. But she is hopeful that, in industry, it will be difficult
to re-erect the barriers to women's employment. Such action would
expose them as being 'based frankly upon the desire of the male to
protect himself from competition and no longer upon the alleged
incapacity of the female to compete' (ibid.: 56). She trusts that
employers will be the 'allies' of women and of the feminists, as they will
want to maintain their access to 'a great reserve of cheap, docile, and
very effective labour'. On the other hand, she predicts that the male-
dominated trade unions will insist that the jobs belong to the men.[5]
Depending on the outcome of this controversy, women's position in
industry might improve.

For Rathbone, 'Equal Pay for Equal Work' comes into this picture
as an element of feminist manoeuvres to keep women in industrial
employment. They attempt to rally support from their opponents by

arguing that legislation would halt the undercutting of male workers by women. At the same time, Rathbone exposes the scheme of 'the more astute and enlightened trade-unionists' who endorse the call for equal pay as they 'see in it an effective way of maintaining the exclusion of women while appearing as the champions of equality between the sexes' (ibid.: 58). The congruence of these opposite interests might lead to the passage of equal pay legislation. Yet this very congruence should alert feminists to the possible flaw in their proposed solution.

She describes the 'equal wages for equal work' formula as 'vague and ill-defined'. Predating Edgeworth and Pigou, she proposes to base wages on the actual measures of the 'quality and the quantity of the output' and to incorporate elements beyond simple marginal product such as women's relative consumption of the standing charges of the factory and their 'disadvantages' to employers (prohibition on night work, higher incidence of sickness, inability to lift weights, no swearing in women's presence and, above all, 'marriage mortality') (ibid.: 59).

In spite of the evidence of war work, pointed out by Fawcett (1916) among others, Rathbone here essentially makes hers the employers' claim that women are less productive, and less 'advantageous', and thus gives credence to their rationale for paying women less than men. She argues that, unless this equal pay can be pro-rated to reflect 'any permanent recognised disadvantage that adheres to women workers', it 'will prove in practice the equivalent of total exclusion' of women from employment (ibid.). She recognizes that women also offer advantages to employers, such as docility, willingness to perform routine work, a lower incidence of strikes and less alcohol-related absenteeism than men. But these 'are likely to be regarded by the employer rather as reasons why he can safely exploit women than as reasons why he should equitably pay them as much as men' (ibid.: 58). She does not, however, list this exploitation as one of the four causes for the inferiority of women's wages, which are:

1.   Lack of trades organization
2.   Pocket money or supplementary wage earning
3.   A low standard of comfort
4.   A wage requirement based on individual subsistence. (ibid.: 60)

This list stresses what seem to be characteristics of women workers rather than socially or economically determined factors.

For the purpose of her argument, Rathbone chooses to focus on the fourth cause, which she describes as 'the most important and the most habitually under-rated'. She argues that the main reason for wage

differences between men and women is the fact that 'men have families
to keep', and women don't. In modern industrial society, 'the lives of
a considerable section of the adult female community have to be entirely
given over to the work of rearing, educating, and training' children. The
'male parent' receives the responsibility of paying for family subsistence
out of his wages and is trusted 'somehow to see things through' (ibid.:
61). Rathbone finds this arrangement 'extraordinarily clumsy' and
unsatisfactory, and incisively questions its economic basis:

> In other words, the wages of the worker represent not only the value of his
> services to the employer, and through him to the community, but also the
> value of his wife's services to him and their children, and through them to
> the community, and, in addition, the value to the State of the children
> themselves. His wages, in short, are the channel by which the community
> . . . pays for the continuance of his own existence and the rearing of fresh
> generations. The amount so paid becomes part of the cost of production of
> the commodities produced . . . and comes eventually out of the pocket of
> the community as consumers. (ibid.: 62)

For Rathbone, the main reason for women's lower wages is that
women need to support only themselves. She acknowledges that when
women have dependants it creates an upward pull on their wages (and
she refers to the Fabian Women's Group study quoted by Fawcett), but
this is offset by the downward pull exerted by those who work only for
'pocket money'. She asserts that the major stumbling block in the
struggle for equal pay is the present, deep-rooted system of family
support by the father:

> The argument that it is an indisputable principle of justice that if men and
> women do the same work they shall receive the same pay can be countered
> by the proposition, apparently equally undisputable, that if men have to pay
> for the upbringing of the rising generation they must be given some money
> to do it with. (ibid.: 63)

Rathbone characterizes a wage system based on the differing subsistence requirement of men and women as an 'impasse' which bars
indefinitely women's access to wage equality and to employment
opportunity. It makes them 'the eternal blacklegs' who, by undercutting
men in industry, threaten the social basis of economic support to the
family 'which should be most sacred to them'. The socioeconomic status
quo is maintained only by turning women into 'industrial lepers'
restricted to the few trades where they won't undercut men (ibid.).
Because this is unlikely to be acceptable to women and the majority
of public opinion after the war, Rathbone predicts the 'illogical compromise' of giving women 'free entry to occupations . . . subject to the

condition that their labour is paid for at the same rate as male labour' (ibid.: 64). Her opposition to this compromise is not well developed. She uses three arguments: this 'compromise' will not resolve the problem of women and children's dependence on male wages in most working-class families where wages do not reflect family size; the cost of implementing equal pay for equal work will be high, requiring a 'gigantic extension of the system of trade boards'; and equal pay for equal work might lead to increased sex segregation in employment. She adds that further state intervention might be required to ensure wage equality across trades, for, she asks, 'Can one justify levelling up women's wages to men's in trades where they both work, while keeping them on an altogether lower scale in wholly feminine trades of equivalent difficulty?' (ibid.: 65).

The latter argument shows her understanding that labour market segregation coupled with the undervaluation of women's work are much stronger causes for the inferiority of women's labour income than actual pay discrimination within a few mixed occupations. This observation makes Rathbone a forerunner of contemporary feminist analysis of women's conditions in the labour market.[6] However, rather than using it to expand the 'Equal Pay for Equal Work' demand beyond its limited scope, Rathbone instead adds it to her charge against that very demand.

Rathbone ends her article with an advocacy of a new system of income distribution which, including 'motherhood allowance', would directly provide for the needs of mothers and children.[7] She concludes that, with such a system,

> the main reason for the differentiation of wages between the two sexes having disappeared, competition between them that was at once free and fair would be for the first time possible, and the services of women – not only in industry, but in the house – would be remunerated on their merits. (ibid.: 68)

It is clear from the above two articles that the positions of Millicent G. Fawcett and Eleanor Rathbone on the question of equal pay were widely divergent. Rathbone, a feminist herself, criticizes the demand for 'Equal Pay for Equal Work', and attempts to influence feminists to take an indirect approach to the goal of equal pay, one which will generate a structural change in income distribution and which will provide, she argues, a more solid basis for its achievement.

**Fawcett's response to Rathbone**

In 1918 Millicent Fawcett responded to Rathbone's article. The response is not very long or debated. It is disappointing, failing to deal with Rathbone's main proposal of focusing reformist action on the source and composition of family income as a way to remove pay differences between male and female workers. Instead Fawcett reiterates some of her earlier points and rebuffs Rathbone's criticisms of the equal pay for equal work demand.

Fawcett objects to Rathbone's characterization of the feminists' demands for equal pay as 'vague and ill-defined'. For Fawcett, this demand has never meant that women should be paid the same as men when they are less efficient. She states that Rathbone's own declaration that equal pay for equal work should mean 'securing for women a fair field of competition with men, their work being accepted or rejected on its merits, recognising that any permanent disadvantage that adheres to women workers as such should be allowed for by a pro rata reduction in their standard rates' is as close a definition of the feminist equal pay principle as there could be (Fawcett, 1918: 3–4).

Fawcett takes issue with Rathbone's presumption that women are less productive than men. She questions this position given the evidence of women's war work, employers' statements on their efficiency and the evidence that much of male workers' productivity is controlled by trade union rules which do not apply to the unorganized women. Rathbone emphasized the disadvantages to employers of using women workers. 'War experience, however, has stiffened the conviction of many feminists that a large proportion of supposed feminine disadvantages exist more in imagination than in reality', replies Fawcett (ibid.: 4). To counter Rathbone's list of all the commonplace arguments against equal pay, Fawcett displays a more positive faith in women's abilities: '[N]o one knows what women . . . can do until they have had an opportunity of learning how and trying' (ibid.: 5).

For Fawcett, the causes of women's inferior pay are clear: women's crowding in very few trades and the sweated conditions they face in the trades where employers' exploitation leads to 'wages below subsistence levels'. She disagrees with Rathbone's focus on factors affecting the supply of female labour as causes of women's low pay, and with her misrepresentation of the extent of women's dependence on their own earnings. Instead of stressing the 'pocket-money' argument, Rathbone should look at the 85 per cent of women workers who support themselves and dependants and explain why this 'upward pull' (Rathbone, 1917: 62) on women's wages does not raise the average wage above subsistence level. In Fawcett's view, the demand factor of employer hiring practices which create a 'downward pull' on women's wages provides a better explanation.

Why should employers' market power be ignored for the sake of developing an argument against women's dependency on male wages in the family? Can it be assumed to disappear once income distribution elsewhere is tampered with? And what of the immediate crippling effect on women's well-being?

> The evil effects of such a state of things can hardly be exaggerated. It means physical degeneracy, not for one sex only, premature old age for women, impossibility of organising women's labour, the stamping out of any intelligent effort to acquire industrial training and a high degree of industrial efficiency. (Fawcett, 1918: 2)

Certainly, there is as much urgency in the present conditions faced by women in industry as in those faced by women within the family.

Fawcett states that 'such differences as exist between Mrs. Rathbone and myself . . . are very much a question of words and not of facts', but these differences are fundamental in the priorities they set for feminist action. The differences did affect the internal politics of the British feminist movement. After succeeding Fawcett as President of the NUWSS, Rathbone attempted to redirect the agenda of the national organization (renamed the National Union of Societies for Equal Citizenship in 1919). But it took six years of internal debate before NUSEC endorsed the demand for family allowances and economic recognition of motherhood in 1925 (Stocks, 1950: chs 8, 9).

The leading feminists were thus divided on the issue of equal pay. Fawcett's position was strong and uncompromising, but insufficiently developed. It also lacked a critical analysis of the capitalist system and how it sets women up and uses them as 'blacklegs'. Her arguments use a marginal productivity approach to wages, on the basis of which she believes that the logic and reasonableness of the equal pay proposition should be sufficient to generate trade union and public support.

In contrast, Eleanor Rathbone's position is more calculated and analytical. But it is very ambiguous in its implications for the economic position of women in patriarchal capitalist society. Her analysis leads her to a radical rejection of marginal productivity as an explanation for existing wage determination. She exposes the contradictions inherent in the capitalist wage system where, in theory, a productivity wage is supposed (through the workings of what invisible hand?) to provide sufficient subsistence for working-class families of varied sizes. Meanwhile, in practice, wage determination is based on perceived average subsistence and dependant support requirements. For her, the demand of equal pay for equal work will only satisfy a claim to equality for men and women based on their market productivity, leaving the question of dependant support unresolved and forever divisive, and leaving the mass of non-employed women dependent on male support.

Equally radical is her analysis of the income distribution system, the sex roles, the social institution of the family and the division of labour between the sexes, and her insight that equal pay would have to be achieved across industries and occupations. Her observations make her a precursor of modern socialist feminist approaches to domestic labour, the family wage and social reproduction under capitalism. Her proposal for family allowances anticipates to some extent the modern feminist demand of wages for housework and her solution to the equal pay question has some theoretical and logistic merit.

However, there are definite elements of conservatism in her position. She never challenges the capitalist and patriarchal structures of society, and also displays a very limited view of women. Her argument relies exclusively on a single function for women: that of motherhood. Her proposal for family allowances could even be seen as a way to make the capitalist labour market work more smoothly, removing the subsistence requirement element in wage determination. She could also be seen as interfering with elements of working-class autonomy – her bourgeois background shows in her patronizing attitude toward working-class women. The institution of the family is never questioned. She only challenges the income distribution system that is applied to it, carefully refraining from supporting working-class women's access to economic autonomy. Her main concern is not the economic independence of women, but the support of children.

Rathbone believes in the benevolence of the state. But how could she entrust it to serve women's interests better than men or capitalists do? She has faith in the rationality of the state and its willingness to do what is best for its subjects. In her argument for family allowances, mothers are seen to serve the state when they raise their children: the next generation is produced for the state, the state 'owns' children.

In retrospect, Fawcett and Rathbone's positions share some of the same limitations but are complementary in their approaches and proposals. Both are reformist, but with different focuses, Fawcett's being on the labour market position and income of women, Rathbone's on their family situation. These differences in focus and philosophy reflect shifts in the priorities of the women's movement of the time. This switch has been characterized as a split in the movement and subsequently as a change of emphasis from 'equal rights' to 'welfare' feminism.[8]

After the vote was 'won', numerous feminists chose to focus on issues which they deemed 'winnable' and which would, in their view, improve immediately the situation of the 'large mass of dependent women' (Holton, 1986: 152). Such is the case with Rathbone, who seems to have

abandoned as an immediate goal the fight for equality, and in particular
equal pay, on the grounds that 'it would be difficult to achieve' and
'unpopular' (Jeffreys, 1985: 153). Her demand for the 'endowment for
motherhood' could gain more popular appeal because it was based on
a widely accepted feminine role, and as such presented a much lesser
challenge to patriarchal and capitalist ideology.[9]

In retrospect, it is unfortunate that a fusion of the two tendencies in
the women's movement could not have been achieved. It could have
led to more comprehensive reform proposals, with greater chances of
success and the backing of a more united movement.

### Beatrice Potter Webb

Beatrice Webb comes to the question of equal pay from the Fabian/
Labour Party tradition and from outside the ranks (and the leadership)
of the women's movement. Her analysis, interestingly, does effect
somewhat of a synthesis of the divergent focuses of Fawcett and
Rathbone.

Government and industry use of female labour power during World
War I was met by the organized resistance of male-dominated trade
unions. The threat women presented to male employment preserves led
unions to cry out that women would bring the wages down, the hours
up and be used by employers to roll back the gains made in collective
bargaining. To allay those fears, the British government made an
agreement with the trade unions to maintain the same rate of pay and
the same piece rates as those paid to men (Strachey, 1969: 341–3). This
promise presented the advantage of paying lip-service to the feminist
demand for equal pay.

Allegations that this agreement had not been implemented and that
labour unrest had been generated by the discriminatory treatment of
women war workers led to the appointment of a special War Cabinet
Committee to investigate women in industry, and in particular the
relationship between the wages of men and women.[10] Beatrice Webb,
a member of the Committee, wrote a Minority Report. Her major
objection was that the Committee had not set out to fulfil its mandate,
which was to investigate 'the relation which should be maintained
between the wages of women and men, having regard to the interests
of both, as well as to the value of their work'. She criticizes the majority
for focusing exclusively on the employment of women, thereby
'assum[ing], perhaps inadvertently, that industry is normally a function
of the male, and that women . . . are only permitted to work for wages
at special hours, for special rates of wages, under special supervision
and subject to special restrictions by the Legislature' (Webb, 1919: 257).

As she 'cannot accept this assumption', she devotes her Minority Report to an examination of principles affecting wage determination, 'whether such principles affect differently men and women; whether such difference is justifiable . . . and whether any new principle is called for on which the relation between them can be based' (ibid.).

Beatrice Webb long remained opposed to feminism (and to women's suffrage). She finally changed her position in 1906, but maintained her stance on some of the feminist demands. Equal pay for equal work is one feminist demand which she did not fully endorse. An article she published in 1914 details her reasons and her preferred approach to the question of women's wages (Webb, 1914).

Webb thought that equal pay for equal work was irrelevant to most working women because they were segregated in separate jobs. Furthermore, she felt that the implementation of such a demand would lead to increased segregation, and keep women in the lowest-paying jobs.

> There is no getting over the fact that when an employer concludes that his work is such as to command a salary of £500 a year, he thinks it much more advantageous to employ a man; when the work seems to demand only a salary of £100 a year, he often finds it positively more advantageous to employ a woman. (1914: 526)

Instead, she favoured the immediate increase of working women's earnings and an improvement in their working conditions through a system of wage boards and factory inspections which would enforce a 'statutory minimum' (ibid.: 525).

Like Rathbone, Webb points out the irony of both feminists and male trade unionists supporting the demand for equal pay for diametrically opposite reasons, the male trade unionist's intent in imposing 'his own Standard Rate' being to obtain the exclusion of women from the trade altogether. She insists that 'each class must be left . . . to define for itself the particular conditions of employment which seem to its own members to promote their professional efficiency' (ibid.: 526). Rather than having their conditions dictated by the interests or concerns of other groups, women should define them on the basis of their own organizing in the trades and professions.

The statutory minimum advocated by Webb is seen as 'only the beginning of the story', a base on which organized working women can build: 'In their own interests, and in the interests of a progressive community, the women workers, like all other producers, must be perpetually pushing upwards towards a fuller personal life and greater collective control over the conditions of their employment' (ibid.: 525). In this process, they must be free to enter any trade or profession and to define what is best for them, in terms of wage levels and hours and conditions of work, rather than be restricted by a formula such as 'equal pay for equal work', the formula implying that women would be required to perform at the same level as men as a condition of employment.

Beatrice Webb's Minority Report essentially restates the position developed in *Industrial Democracy* (Webb and Webb, 1897): democratic collective bargaining to establish negotiated standard rates of pay and standard skill requirements and a national minimum of pay and working conditions applying in the non-organized trades.

In the Minority Report, the 'National Minimum' 'should include, at least, the fundamental requirements of leisure, sanitation, education and subsistence' and should be 'identical . . . for persons of either sex' as it 'cannot, in practice, secure more than the needs that are common to human beings as such' (Webb, 1919: 274). Beatrice Webb disagrees with any rationale to base separate minimum wages on the different average physical characteristics of the two sexes.[11] Food forms only part of the overall basic requirements of men or women. Their other needs (shelter, fuel, light, clothing, travelling, insurance and savings for lost time and sickness, holidays) can hardly be differentiated on the basis of sex.[12]

Equally she sees 'no reason why anything less should be paid to youths of either sex than the equivalent of the national minimum' (ibid.: 299). They have practically the same costs of subsistence as adult men or women. Enforcing the same minimum wage for them would also remove one of the factors that has kept women's wages low as 'it is, to a large extent, with such young persons that adult women come directly into competition' (ibid.).

In her Minority Report Beatrice Webb rejects some of the principles applied to wage determination which she finds contrary to the achievement of the highest standard of life for all and to maximum efficiency in production. She opposes leaving wage determination to the 'higgling of the market', which she identifies as 'the most potent factor prior to the war in making the statistical average of the net earnings of adult women in British industry . . . often as low . . . as "a shilling a day" ' (ibid.: 258). She also counters the argument that women's wages have to remain low due to the pressure of foreign competition. She states emphatically that 'any industry that can be maintained in this country only at the cost of "sweating" is an industry that we are better without' (ibid.: 293). She holds the same view of the 'parasitic' industries where workers are expected 'to pay in lower wages for the relative inefficiency of the employers and managers' (ibid.: 291).

Rather than an ambiguous 'equal pay for equal work formula', she recommends, beyond the national minimum which would apply to non-organized workers, a system of collectively bargained 'occupational rates' that would be attached to specific occupations and applied indiscriminately to all men and women employed in them.[13] She also favours the establishment of 'definite qualifications for employment' setting required levels of skills and training for each occupation. This system would reduce the amount of discrimination exercised by employers against women, provided that women have full access to training and that they can enter any occupation.

In connection with these recommendations, Webb opposes what she calls 'the Vested Interest of the Male': 'The long-continued exclusion of women from nearly all the better-paid occupations has largely been the result of the assumption that these occupations were the sacred preserve of men' (ibid.: 265). She lists a number of practices, such as segregation of tasks, Factory Acts' ban on women's night work, or restriction on apprenticeship, which are used to maintain male monopoly. The result is

> the exclusion of the whole class of women, as such, from the professions or occupations in which the occupational rate is relatively high, and from the training qualifying for the work, so that not even those individuals among them who might have proved their competence have been permitted to enter these favoured occupations. (ibid.: 267)

Both employers and trade unions act to maintain this male privilege. When employers introduce women into the male preserves, their only purpose is to bring down the occupational rates.[14]

Beatrice Webb also denounces the 'tacit convention that there is throughout industry a male rate and a female rate', maintained through collective bargaining and wage setting by employers (ibid.: 261). Trade unions, complicit in this arrangement, set up their members to be undercut by women workers. At the same time, overall economic efficiency is defeated as the employer is 'bribed' by the differential rates 'to get his work done by workers industrially less efficient' (ibid.: 282). A single occupational rate would, by contrast, lead the employer to hire the most efficient worker (male or female) for the job.

She points out that, 'women, like men are, for the purposes of industry, not a homogeneous class' (ibid.: 295), and that 'classifying together all the workers of one sex, and subjecting them all to a differential rate' is not justified (ibid.: 279). She concludes that 'there is no justice in, and no economic basis for, the conception of a man's rate and a woman's rate', and that 'we have no ground for making sex a reason for differentiation in the conditions of employment any more than race and creed' (ibid.: 295).

Webb denounces the hypocrisy of employers who pay women less, alleging inferior productivity, unreliability in case of emergency, or the presumed higher overhead costs involved in employing women, while paying the standard male rate to less efficient male employees. She insists that the factor of sex is irrelevant to actual productivity, that all employees should be treated across the board on the basis of their own merit.[15] She also denounces the hypocrisy of justifying differential rates with the argument of the unequal family obligations of male and female workers.

> Though the principle of determining wages by the extent of the family obligations of the wage earner has not been adopted . . . it has been frequently used as an argument for keeping down the wages or salaries of women relatively to those of men, even as their work is admitted to be of the same value to the employer. (ibid.: 264)

The trade unions, who actively promote this 'complete justification' for lower women's wages, would be the first to cry out that wages paid to male workers on the basis of number of dependants counters 'the principle of the standard rate of remuneration for effort' (ibid.: 286).

The ideology of the breadwinner needing a family wage was used during the war to deny bonuses and cost-of-living adjustments to women workers. Denouncing this added form of discrimination, Webb advocates a general cost-of-living adjustment. Such adjustments should be applied to the national minimum and to the collectively bargained occupational rates and should be paid to all workers, regardless of sex and family obligations. Webb argues that denying women a cost-of-living increase or giving them a lower increase (as in the case of proportional or even flat-rate increases), penalizes them twice and ensures that their pay will never catch up with that of men (ibid.: 262–3).

Beatrice Webb recommends that earnings correspond more closely 'to the efforts and needs' of workers (ibid.: 295). The effort element would be recognized through her proposals of uniform occupational rates and definite qualification requirements for each level of employment. The need part would be covered by her proposals of a national minimum and of cost-of-living adjustments. It is clear that her proposals include the concept of equal pay for equal work, which she leaves to be defined and enforced through collective bargaining. Yet she goes beyond this with proposals applicable where there are no trade unions, and no male work to which the female work could be compared.

Minimum wage and minimum standards are seen by her as crucial complements of equal pay.

Equally complementary are a set of social welfare proposals Webb sketches out in the concluding pages of her Report. She sees the maintenance of full employment as a responsibility of the state and proposes the establishment of a state-financed unemployment insurance system. She furthermore proposes that unemployment benefits be 'given at equal rates for men and women' (ibid.: 302). She also advocates the implementation of a 'national endowment' system, a continuation of the war separation allowances payable to mothers, as a more suitable approach to the economic support of dependent children.

[T]he community must face the necessity of seeing that adequate provision is made for children, not by statistical averages, but case by case. . . . This cannot be done under any system of wages; nor can the adoption of any conceivable principle as to the relation between men's and women's wages achieve this end. (ibid.: 306)

Her ideas on this issue are essentially the same as Eleanor Rathbone's.[16]

Beatrice Webb's recommendations form a logical, coherent and comprehensive whole and include numerous innovative ideas some of which still have to be implemented today. These include uniform occupational wage rates, uniform minimum standards of income and working conditions, uniform unemployment insurance payments, freedom of entry into all occupations, and cost-of-living adjustments which would allow women's wages to catch up with men's. These propositions demonstrate the perceptive analytical skills and visionary faculties of their author.

The main weakness of Beatrice Webb's writings on women's wages is her lack of analysis of the causes of the treatment women receive in the workforce. This leads to a relatively naïve position that discrimination will disappear once appropriate measures, such as uniform occupational rates, are implemented. Webb does identify the existence of discriminatory attitudes and actions on the part of employers and trade unions but does not attempt to explain them, and therefore does not develop specific proposals to eliminate them.

On what basis can she recommend collectively bargained single occupational rates when she clearly identified the two partners in collective bargaining – employers and trade unions – as the source of the system of separate rates for the two sexes? What makes her believe that employers will start hiring women in the 'male preserve' occupations upon the implementation of a system of specific occupational qualifications? What makes her trust in the trade unions to represent

fairly the interests of their female members, and to organize women
workers in the first place? Does she believe that employers and trade
unions will easily forget their rhetoric about women's lesser efficiency
or about their lesser subsistence needs and lack of dependants?

Webb essentially lacks an analysis of the patriarchal forces at work
within the capitalist economy. She does identify some of their manifestations, such as what she calls the 'Vested Interest of the Male', but
does not offer any analysis of their origin and their strength. This leads
her to rely on the benevolence of men and male-controlled institutions
(trade unions, the state) for the implementation of her proposals.

She herself makes a statement which would lend support to differential treatment for women in the post-war labour market. Although she
denounced the 'Vested Interest of the Male', which reserves the best-
paying jobs for the men, she seems to believe in a vested right of men
to jobs at the expense of women. She maintains that it is less costly to
the state and less detrimental to 'national well being' to see women
rather than men unemployed, not because they would be entitled to less
unemployment benefits (she proposed that these should be the same for
both sexes), but because 'the children of the unemployed have also to
be maintained at the public expense in one form or other; and male
wage earners have undoubtedly on an average more dependent children
than female wage-earners' (ibid.: 303). One wonders what happened to
Webb's proposal for dependant allowances and why she uses the
argument of average numbers of dependants when it comes to
unemployment, having rejected it in her discussion of wages.

The other reason advanced for giving women priority in unemployment is that

> temporary unemployment involves, to a woman, usually less suffering and
> less danger of demoralisation than to a man. She has nearly always domestic
> work with which to occupy herself usefully. She can be much more easily
> provided for by enabling her to improve her qualifications in domestic
> economy, than an unemployed man can be found any other occupation than
> the demoralising and costly relief works. (ibid.: 302)

Webb does not tell us why paid relief work should be more demoralizing
than unpaid domestic work. It is clear in this whole discussion that the
interests of men and the state come first in her mind.

The contradictions presented by Webb's position on women's
unemployment show how far her feminist views go. Her treatment of
this issue contradicts her earlier statements to the effect that one should
not be treated in the labour market on the basis of one's sex. The
ultimate message she gives to her readers is that women's equality and

their access to economic independence can be sacrificed to other (presumably superior) needs: those of men, those of the state, or those of the national economy.

The three feminists reviewed here show the diversity of analysis and approach which may coexist at any time within the women's movement. These three women had similar life histories in that they came from the same class, had access to education, and got involved in political activism, but their political orientations and their activist priorities differed. Fawcett was part of the initial wave of feminists, which has been described as 'equal rights' feminism, whereas Rathbone witnessed the winning of the vote in mid-life and became part of the switch to 'welfare feminism'.[17] Fawcett's politics were those of the nineteenth-century Liberals, while Rathbone was politically unaligned. Beatrice Webb came to feminism later in life than Fawcett or Rathbone and placed herself within the Fabian/socialist/Labour Party tradition.

On the issue of equal pay, both Fawcett and Webb showed flexibility, having shifted from opposition to the principle (mostly on practical grounds) to endorsement after the experience of the war. Rathbone shows inflexibility in her opposition to it (arguing practical grounds for her position), entrenching herself in a calculated single-issue strategy.

Both Fawcett and Webb see the trade unions as potential allies in the cause of working women but lack realism in their analysis of the extent of the trade unions' role in the establishment and maintenance of patriarchal privileges. Rathbone sees the unions as outright opponents to family allowances, which they perceive as a threat to the 'family wage'. She, realistically, does not trust trade unions' support for equal pay.

Fawcett and Webb show integrity towards the cause of working women while Rathbone displays opportunism when she denigrates women's productivity levels to support her argument. Her vision is hampered by her narrowing of the feminist agenda, her 'defeatism' (Jeffreys, 1985: 153) and lack of faith in the strength of the feminist movement. Given her leadership position, this had major implications for post-war feminism.

Retrospectively, we can deplore the failure of feminists and their supporters to come to a common position and capitalize on the sympathetic public opinion in post-World War I Britain. Divisions on feminist priorities left the stage open for a reassertion of capitalist and patriarchal interests. Nevertheless, all three women contributed important theoretical elements towards a feminist economic analysis of women's position within a capitalist patriarchal society. They were able to initiate a challenge to male economic power and to question the differential impact the capitalist labour market has on women.

**Notes**

1. Ellen Smith (1915). The Fabian Women's Group conducted its own survey of 2,830 working women. Of these, 1,405 or slightly less than 50 per cent were found to partially or wholly support others besides themselves, a further 1,005 (35 per cent) were 'exactly self-supporting'.

2. This position can be related to the Labour–Suffrage alliance developed in the pre-war years. See Holton (1986).

3. Mary Stocks mentions two studies by Rathbone: 'How the Casual Worker Lives' (1909) and 'The Conditions of Widows under the Poor Laws in Liverpool' (1913). (See Stocks, 1950: ch. 6.)

4. Rathbone (1917). Her position was later developed in *The Disinherited Family* (1924) and *The Case for Family Allowances* (1940).

5. Rathbone notes that the feminist organizations meanwhile argue that women themselves should decide about their position in post-war industry and not 'be treated as a football between capital and labour with the government acting as an umpire' (quoting the National Union of Women Suffrage Societies, 57).

6. An analysis which has led to the demand for 'equal pay for work of equal value'.

7. The case for family allowances is fully developed in her books (1924, 1940).

8. See Banks (1981), Jeffreys (1985: 147–55). Holton (1986) disagrees that there was such a split and traces back to the pre-war Suffrage–Labour alliance some of the 'New Feminism'.

9. Jeffreys comments: 'She [Rathbone] explained that although equal pay might be a good idea, there were too many obstacles in the way, such as the idea that men receive a "family" wage. . . . Thus she betrayed the cause of spinsterhood and the independent woman. She deserted a feminist option because it was too difficult and embraced the simpler alternative of emphasising woman's mission of motherhood. It is particularly surprising that Rathbone should opt to support the married woman and mother at the expense of the spinster considering that she was herself a lifelong spinster' (1985: 152). Rathbone lived with a woman (Elizabeth MacAdam) most of her life, she did not have children and was never much affected by the patriarchal family system, yet she chose to spend her life battling in favour of the economic recognition of motherhood and took care not to challenge the institution of the family and the dominant sex roles in a patriarchal society.

10. War Cabinet Committee on Women in Industry (1919: 1–2). Workers downed tools in July 1918 in protest against the awarding of war advances and bonuses to male and not to female workers.

11. 'But this result of statistical averages affords, as it seems to me, much less ground for differentiating between the rations of men and women as such, than between human beings over and under five-feet-five in height, or above and below nine stone in weight' (Webb, 1919: 274).

12. Webb issues here a fundamental challenge to a widely accepted tenet of patriarchal ideology: lower subsistence needs of women. This principle is fully accepted by Marxists when they apply Marx's approach to the determination of the value of labour power to women. That women's labour power has a lower value than men's due to its presumed lower reproduction cost is as pervasive a sign of patriarchal bias among Marxists as the presumption of women's inferior productivity is among neoclassical economists. Even feminists may be found to accept this pronouncement blindly. An example is Heidi Hartmann's treatment of this question (1976: 158, n. 60).

13. She does state that this proposal corresponds to one of the possible approaches to 'equal pay for equal work', where wages are defined on the basis of 'the

physiological and mental results to the operative . . . according to the efforts and sacrifices that the work involves'. The best approximation, given the difficulty of comparing effort, is a time-wage, as time can be used to measure the cost of work to the worker (Webb, 1919: 268).

14. The concept of 'Vested Interest of the Male' makes Beatrice Webb a precursor of the contemporary feminist economists who have developed a model of male monopoly to integrate an analysis of patriarchy into their theoretical approaches. See in particular Madden (1975), Hartmann (1976), Leghorn and Parker (1981).

15. 'Either it is essential . . . in view of the likelihood or the seriousness of possible emergencies, that all the operatives employed should possess the qualifications needed to deal with such emergencies, or it is not. If it is, then the workers concerned, whether men or women, should be chosen from among those so qualified and paid accordingly. If it is not – the fact being proven by the engagement of workers without such qualifications – then the lack of them cannot be pleaded as a ground for paying a lower rate because any particular workers, whether men or women, do not possess what is demonstrably not necessary for their work' (Webb, 1919: 281).

16. Rathbone applauds Beatrice Webb's position: 'the minority report, drawn up by Mrs. Sidney Webb, is notable as containing the first full statement, so far as I am aware, by a leading member of the Labour Party of the disadvantages of providing for families through wages based on the fiction of the uniform standard family . . .' (1924: 165).

17. On these categories, see Jeffreys (1985), Spender (1983), Banks (1981), Holton (1986), Lewis (1975). It is difficult to characterize individual feminists on the basis of categories that may generalize or simplify too much. Political tendencies, alliances, goals and strategies often result from subtler balances, and change over time. Categories are also often developed unidimensionally, by, for instance, focusing on a single issue, strategy or traditional approach to politics.

# 5   The impending 'débâcle': Edgeworth on equal pay

Francis Ysidro Edgeworth's life was seemingly quiet and removed from the limelight of political activism (Keynes, 1926; Bonar, 1926). One of his biographers said that he had 'realised Aristotle's notion of the βιος θεωρητικός: the life devoted to study' (Bonar, 1926: 653). Edgeworth was a supporter of women's suffrage (ibid.: 650). His biographers stated that 'no one has described more fully and faithfully than he the economic position of women and he favoured all their claims' (ibid.: 652) and that 'the problem of the inequality of men's and women's wages interested him all his life' (Keynes, 1926: 146). Yet both biographers quote some of the sexist quips and aphorisms which he proffered. The following analysis of his writings on women's pay will show the extent of his support of women's demand for equality.

The economics profession has wrongly attributed to Edgeworth the development of the overcrowding theory of women's pay (Arrow, 1976; Chiplin and Sloane, 1980). As we have already seen, this theory was actually developed by John Stuart Mill (1965), Barbara Bodichon (1857) and Millicent Garrett Fawcett (1892, 1918). Edgeworth's treatment of the equal pay question is found in his two *Economic Journal* articles (1922, 1923). He had previously contributed a number of reviews of writings on women's pay (1893, 1917).

In his 1922 and 1923 pieces he attempts to review all aspects of the question and to determine whether 'equal pay for equal work' could be endorsed as an economically sound proposition. His articles are very detailed and display great knowledge of the literature on the topic. However, they also display his definite bias against the equal pay proposition, which is only thinly veiled by his economic and mathematical treatment.[1]

Edgeworth separates the issue into two aspects. In his 1922 article he focuses on the implications of equal pay for 'external wealth' – that is, purely economic concerns. In the 1923 article he focuses on 'the attendant internal feeling of welfare', which allows him to look into the more subjective elements. However, we will see that subjectivity and 'welfare' (social and moral issues) are not absent from the earlier article.

In the 1922 article Edgeworth first undertakes to define 'equal pay for equal work' according to the principles set by the marginal calculus of welfare economics. Equal pay thus means 'pay in proportion to efficient output', or to 'equal utility to the employer' (quoting Bowley), or to 'productivity' or 'productive value' (1922: 432). What is meant by utility and whether it encompasses more than the actual value of the marginal product of the work done is not specified. At any rate, he heavily stresses the employer's interests: pay is determined solely by what the employer gets out of the worker.

Edgeworth adds, 'there must be understood a certain equality on the side of the employee as well as on the side of the employer or community' (ibid.: 432). And there, workers are seen to have access to equality of work and pay only if they enjoy 'equal freedom in the choice of work' (ibid.: 433). Given that pay is related to the market value of the final product, equally efficient workers should be able to move from low-value to high-value commodity production: a basic principle of free market adjustment applied to the labour market.

Having made this observation, Edgeworth proceeds to restate the question, 'should there be equal pay for equal work?' as 'should there be perfect competition between the sexes?' (ibid.: 433). From the workers' point of view access to equality in remuneration for work is reduced to the question of 'equal freedom in the choice of work [which] should include equal freedom to prepare for work by acquiring skill' (ibid.: 433). In summary:

> There are thus presented two attributes [of the equal pay for equal work proposition]: equality of utility to the employer as tested by the pecuniary value of the result, and equality of disutility to the employee as tested by his freedom to choose his employment. These two attributes will concur in a regime of perfect competition. (ibid.: 433)

Edgeworth restricts his inquiry to a perfect competition framework to which the usual neoclassical assumptions are applied. He does not even allude to the question of whether perfect competition exists in the commodities market. He also tacitly assumes that wages are solely determined by productivity. This leads to the conclusion that women's wages are low, not because they might receive less than the value of the marginal product, but for the sole reason that they are not allowed the same labour market opportunities as men. The self-evident solution is to give them free access to all occupations.

We have thus a one-track analytical framework: (1) equal pay for equal work would prevail under free competition; (2) free competition is lacking in the labour market; so (3) equal pay can only exist if free competition is restored. Where does this proposition stand if (1) is wrong or if free competition fails elsewhere than in the labour market?

Edgeworth does not propose the straightforward solution of opening
the 'labour market freely to women'. Instead, he asks cautiously 'should
there be perfect competition between the sexes?' and engages in a
lengthy discussion of the pros and cons of this question. Any *laissez-
faire* economist should without hesitation answer 'yes' to this question,
but Edgeworth's answer is mitigated by other factors. Even brushing
aside the social or ethical considerations – relegated to the 1923 article
– he details a number of rationales against free competition between
the sexes in the labour market.

One of these is the apocalyptic vision he paints of what would happen
if women were unleashed on the labour market. Perfect competition
might yield a maximum in total output which would not be an optimum
('greatest possible value'). Edgeworth brings in Francis Walker,
Marshall and Mill to help him support the unorthodox argument that
perfect competition, in this case, may not be optimal for the reason that
the large quantities of cheap female labour thus made available to
industry would bring underinvestment leading to a 'depression or
débâcle of industry' (ibid.: 436). Edgeworth sees no limit to how low
female wages might go in a competitive situation due to women's lower
standard of living, their subsidization by male family members and the
fact that 'the woman worker has not acquired by custom and tradition
the same unwillingness to work for less than will support a family'
(ibid.). Given this situation, Edgeworth hastens to conclude that if
'some action must be taken to avert the evils which have been glanced
at . . . our question cannot receive a categorical answer in the affirmative' (ibid.).

Edgeworth hints that a possible way to avoid a market with no bottom
price would be to institute 'minimum wages for men as well as women
. . . enabling the men to marry and support a family and the single
women to live in decent comfort' (ibid.: 437). He sees this prescription
as problematic, expecting productivity levels to stay below the minimum
wages. He does not seem to realize that minimum wages, set at
different levels for men and women, would be unlikely to lead to equal
pay or to equal access to all skills and occupations for women.
Differentiated minimum wages would entrench in society the idea that
women's work is worth less than men's work. They would also, in all
likelihood, reinforce sex segregation in the labour market.[2]

The question of equal pay is rephrased once more, from 'should there
be perfect competition between the sexes?' to the question, 'What sort
or amount of perfect competition between the sexes is advisable?'
(ibid.: 433).[3]

To address this question, Edgeworth first establishes two simplifying assumptions. First, 'desperate competition has been somehow ruled out' (ibid.: 437) possibly by a minimum wage scheme or any other mechanisms that would avert the industrial 'débâcle' predicted above. With his mind at rest, the economist can now focus solely on 'the relative market value of the services rendered' by male and female workers. Secondly, abstraction is made of 'the circumstances of family life, considering the labour world as if it was composed of bachelors and spinsters' (ibid.: 438). At this point one must wonder about the relevance of 'the circumstances of family life' to a discussion of the relative market value of services rendered by men and women.[4]

In his analysis, Edgeworth examines the nature of the labour market. He rejects the proposition that 'but for the inferiority of female labour "it is not clear why the employer should not further (than he does) substitute female labour for the dearer male labour" ' (ibid.). Here Edgeworth states clearly that women's low wages in the existing labour market could not be used to infer their lower productivity because conditions of perfect competition do not prevail. The actual productivity levels of women have to be established in other ways. Yet he never answers the very question of how this can be done.

He identifies three reasons why perfect competition does not obtain. First, 'an employer of many workmen is in himself virtually a combination' and can exert market power (ibid.). Secondly, hiring decisions may not be based on the actual value of marginal product of the workers, as employers may keep hiring men over women to their own disadvantage if this disadvantage is perceived as small.[5] Thirdly, and for Edgeworth more importantly, trade unions severely restrict women's involvement in the labour market. Their practices are 'largely responsible for that crowding of women into a comparatively few occupations, which is universally recognised as a main factor in the depression of their wages' (ibid.: 439).

It is clear here that Edgeworth does not claim authorship for the crowding theory. He does not, however, identify its authors – something remarkable given his scholarship and extant quoting of various authorities in his writings. Would this have something to do with the feminism of those who developed the theory?[6]

Edgeworth's discussion of crowding is one-sided: he does not recognize that employers may have been complicit in restricting women's employment. Is it a fact that women have been barred only from unionized occupations?

His position on crowding is ambiguous: while restrictive of the free working of the market these practices have a necessary purpose, that of avoiding a capitalist débâcle: 'It should be remembered, however, that many of the prohibitions and prejudices here mentioned as contravening free competition were adopted to avert that catastrophic competition' (ibid.: 440). This is an all too candid recognition that patriarchal and capitalist institutions work hand in hand to their best interests.

If women were to organize to counter male trade union restrictions and employers' market power, a situation might result, according to Edgeworth, where conditions close to those of perfect competition and to equal pay for equal work as earlier defined, would prevail. Yet, his biases transpire as he states his belief, informed by employers' opinions, that women's time wages would still have to be lower than men's:

> Probably an arrangement that the weekly earnings of women should be the same as those of men, in cases where the actual value of a woman as a worker was about 30 per cent below that of an average man employed in the same capacity (as testified by a majority of employers before a Committee of the British Association . . .), could not be maintained *without tyranny on a Russian scale.* (ibid.: emphasis added)

Any 'arrangement' to enact equal pay should be circumscribed 'within the limits outside which it would be futile . . . as it would be swept away by the forces of competition' and should be guided by the presumed outcome 'which would be determined by ideal competition'.

Edgeworth also warns his readers to avoid 'two opposite misconceptions: the one exaggerating the comparative efficiency of men, the other that of women'. Interestingly, he has to go back in history to Plato to illustrate the first one as if that misconception had long disappeared from the face of the earth. As for the second, his 'feminist' contemporaries provide him with the example: 'The opposite exaggeration is committed by feminists when they maintain, in the words of a generally impartial expert [Pr. Cannan] that "there is no reason save custom and lack of organization why a nursery maid should be paid less than a coal miner" ' (ibid.: 442).

He hastens to add, 'I submit it as an *inference based on general impressions and ordinary experience* that, even if all restrictions of the competition between male and female workers were removed we should still find the average weekly earnings of the former to be considerably higher' (ibid.: emphasis added). Note that this statement is not inspired by scientific – or even logical – proof of any sort. It is nothing but a statement of belief. One must wonder at this point how rigorous Edgeworth's discussion is when we compare this statement to his earlier dismissal of J. S. Mill's opinion that 'the remuneration of the peculiar employments of women is always, I believe, greatly below that of employments of equal skill and equal disagreeableness arrived at by men' (ibid.: 433–4) as involving 'more than what is given by physical observation'. What is more aggravating is Edgeworth's refusal to respond factually or analytically to the feminist statement he quotes and to give us his expert opinion on why a nursery maid's work should be less valuable to society than a coal miner's.

Edgeworth proposes to prove his 'inference' by developing a model of the labour market under perfect competition conditions (equal access to all occupations by women). Employment would 'naturally divide itself into women's jobs, men's jobs and jobs held by both sexes.[7] Edgeworth 'submits' that the average wages in the women's jobs will be lower than those in the men's jobs. In the jobs held by both sexes, piece wages will be equal but time wages will be lower for women. He does not offer any other proof for this perfectly competitive 'ideal' state of things than an Australian court ruling to pay a minimum wage higher in a male occupation than in a female one.

Edgeworth's description of this 'ideal' state seems influenced by his own perception of women's productive abilities. He speculates on the 'material changes in physique, arts and customs' that might bring about a different distribution of women and men across occupations and a different gendered pay structure. These include 'the female sex [becoming] as strong as the male sex', a decrease in employers' demand for physical strength, or else a change in 'desiderata' whereby 'type-writing, telephoning and the like become more in demand than coal mining and ironworks'. He also adds: 'if the vast amount of household work that is now unpaid could only be obtained by paying for it, the demand for women's labour and its price might be considerably raised' (ibid.: 444). He is relieved to conclude that 'these changes, however, do not appear very imminent'.

Ironically, some of these changes have happened since 1922 (though unfortunately housework is still unpaid labour). 'Typewriting' is definitely more in demand nowadays than coal mining, yet secretaries are still paid less than coal miners; women overall, although the demand for their labour has tremendously increased, still receive 50–60 per cent of what men make. Is the labour market not responding to the laws of supply and demand the way economists think it should?

Edgeworth clearly held the beliefs that physical strength is a main determinant of productivity, that women are generally incapable of it and that some trades are more 'feminine' than others. Proofs are not offered and the rationale for the last proposition is not provided.

His remark on household work misses some aspects of the question. It is true that women's overall earnings would increase if housework became a lucrative proposition, but this would be due to the fact that it would be paid, and not because of an increase in the demand for labour. The demand for that type of labour has always been there, it just does not come with a pay cheque. On the other hand, it is quite conceivable that keeping women occupied doing housework significantly reduces the supply of female labour on the labour market. This, according to the laws of supply and demand (presuming they apply to female labour), should have had the effect of keeping women's employment wages at a higher level than they would otherwise be (*ceteris paribus*).

Given that employers are able to distinguish between male and female job applicants and that 'it will often be within [their] knowledge . . . that it is more profitable to employ a man than a woman, although the work performed by each is identical' (ibid.: 444), pay differences between the sexes seem inevitable to Edgeworth. Where productivities are equal, he sees two reasons for their persistence. First, the 'secondary differences' such as 'marriage mortality' or 'inability to "tune" the machines', are introduced by quoting (or misquoting) Rathbone or Fawcett, using feminist writers to emphasize what he describes as women's shortcomings in industry. He fails to present their analysis or prescriptions (for instance, equal access to training) for eliminating these 'secondary differences'. Instead he focuses on the mechanisms of prorating women's pay downward as a means of achieving equal pay according to his definition (ensuring 'equality of utility for the employers'), worries about the 'risks' incurred by employers of women and their necessary compensation, and prescribes that the outcome should approximate that which perfect competition would achieve.

The 'tertiary differences' are those arising where, for instance, male employees are sought for jobs predominantly held by women (school teaching of boys is the example provided), and can be attracted only by paying them at a rate that reflects the 'market rate' in male jobs elsewhere. Edgeworth acknowledges that female teachers 'might, indeed, be more diligent and . . . better teachers than men' (ibid.: 447). Yet they would receive a lower salary, owing to the overall inferiority of female wages compared to male wages in the market. Edgeworth asserts that this does not violate his definition of equal pay for equal work since the freedom of male teachers to choose this line of employment would be enhanced.

It is useful at this point to remark that in his discussion Edgeworth has taken great care to ensure that the employers' side as well as the male workers' side of his definition of equal pay are enforced. He never indicates how women get their utility or freedom to choose heightened.

In the remainder of the article, Edgeworth drops his earlier 'abstraction' from the 'circumstances of family life'. As he does this, his analytical framework switches abruptly from one based on marginal productivity wages to one based on subsistence wages. He quotes a number of male writers (Rowntree, Taussig, Mill) to establish, from their 'authoritative expression of belief' the normality of the male breadwinner role. To paraphrase, it is 'normal for men to marry' and have families, so their wages must 'normally' be sufficient to support a family. His statements would be stronger if backed by specific statistics on the actual nature and extent of family support by men, but he provides none.

The 'wiser and more moderate advocates of equal pay for women' are also quoted to document this normality. However, a more radical feminist (whom he does not name) who advocates female economic independence from husband support is dismissed (ibid.: 449).[8] Equally dismissed are the data provided by the Fabian survey of women workers' responsibility for dependants (quoted by both Fawcett and Rathbone). A 'more elaborate' study by Rowntree (whose purpose seemed to be the countering of the Fabian Study)[9] is given more weight as it concludes that 'only 12.06% of women have either partially or wholly to support others besides themselves' (ibid.). Women's responsibility for dependants should not, at any rate, be taken too seriously:

> The figure would not be serious even if it proved on further inquiry to be somewhat greater. For the figure has not the same significance as that which relates to the dependents of the male wage-earners. The sustenation of the old and infirm cannot be compared, as regards at least economic importance, with the support of the young, the cost of which normally falls on the male breadwinner. The world got on tolerably before the institution of Old Age Pensions; but it could not have got on at all without the support of young children by their fathers. (ibid.)

We can see that, for Edgeworth, not only are men more productive than women, but their dependants are more valuable to society than those of women. It is not surprising then to see him argue in favour of higher pay on the second ground. 'If the bulk of working men support families, and the bulk of working women do not, it seems not unreasonable that the men should have some advantage in the labour market.' Given these circumstances, 'Equal pay for equal work . . . no longer appears quite equitable'.

By this stage it becomes apparent that Edgeworth has forgotten the marginalist principles and switched entirely to an approach to wage determination based on each sex's assumed living requirement needs, and on their perceived familial responsibilities. His statement can be interpreted to mean that it would not be equitable to pay women according to the value of their contribution to production. Similarly, given Edgeworth's initial redefinition of 'equal pay for equal work', it would not be equitable for employers to pay equal wages for equal utility received from male and female workers.

Having completely rejected the feminist demand for equal pay he sees fit to chastise its proponents for not representing men's interests: 'It can hardly be expected that the representatives of female interests should look at the question from the masculine point of view' (ibid.). As if he himself had fairly represented women's point of view! Rathbone is, however, one of the two feminists (the other one being Elizabeth Hutchins) who exceptionally meet his approval, due to her position that family support should take precedence over equal pay among feminist priorities. Yet he does not at this point endorse her proposal of an 'endowment for motherhood', although it 'has the merit of being logical'. He reviews the pros and cons of the scheme and finds the 'evils' in excess of the 'good' on a purely economic basis. Two advantages are presented: it would provide more adequate support of children and remove the 'excuse for the under-payment of women' (ibid.: 450). Whereas he sees this as a move toward the conditions of perfect competition he advocates, he is not satisfied that the threat to male employment and male wages caused by 'the transitory and episodical character of female labour' would be sufficiently removed to avoid the threat of industrial débâcle mentioned earlier.

The disadvantages he lists are numerous: the logistics of the scheme (bureaucracy, tax system), its impact on the national dividend, the 'seriously deleterious' effect that 'relieving the average house-father from the necessity of providing necessaries for his family . . . would remove a great part of his incentive to work' (ibid.: 453),[10] and implications for the size and nature of population growth sufficient to send a Malthusian eugenist into a panic.

Edgeworth ends his 1922 article with a series of alternative proposals. He advocates greater contributions by all family members to the family's income needs: children can earn their upkeep, wives can contribute, possibly by part-time work or by taking in homework, spinsters should accumulate a dowry to help set up their future families. As a result, Edgeworth expects increased access to employment by women, increased female efficiency and increased competition – conditions of his equal pay definition. He does not address the question of whether his proposal might generate a degree of competition among all these new entrants in the labour market such that it could lead to the much-feared industrial 'débâcle'.

It is at any rate not clear how women's increased entry into the labour market on a part-time or homework basis will lead to equal pay (as generally defined by the feminists). Edgeworth's proposals in general favour capitalists, who would gain access to a larger labour supply with overall lower wages: neither women, children nor spinsters could claim wages covering their own subsistence, while men's wages could be depressed by the presumption that they no longer solely support families. As long as workers have freedom to move in the labour market and employers receive good utility for the wages they pay, Edgeworth's equal pay conditions would be satisfied.

In his 1923 article, Edgeworth goes beyond the question of 'what relation between the wages of men and women is most conducive to production of wealth in the narrower sense of the term' to consider the issues of economic welfare involved (1923: 487).[11] In the article, assumptions about the existing state of welfare are not always set out clearly; neither are the author's own (patriarchal and capitalist) biases, as he addresses the welfare implications of increasing women's pay, opening occupations to them, and instituting a system of family allowances.

An existing state of perfect competition, and its corollary of maximum economic welfare are presumed: 'the economic equilibrium which is determined by competition may be considered as realising the *maximum* of advantage (attainable in the existing state of things)'. Furthermore,

> by the theory of maxima, a slight modification of the arrangements which secure maximum advantage will be attended with only a *very slight* diminution of the total advantage. There would not be an appreciable loss *in globo*, but a transference conducive to economic welfare. (ibid.: 490)[12]

This should lead to a straightforward argument in favour of the increase in women's wages, if at present they result from a perfectly competitive market, or to the restoration of a competitive situation if it were ascertained that they result from a non-competitive situation. This argument should be reinforced by Edgeworth's observation that 'the gain to the women workers would not always involve an equal loss to the men . . . and so would result in an increase of the wealth to be distributed' (ibid.).[13]

As the community's economic welfare does not just depend on 'the amount of wealth added or subtracted', but also on its distribution among individuals (ibid.: 487), the outcome of an increase in women's labour income could lead to a higher welfare maximum, especially if women's marginal utility from increased income exceeds any resulting decrease in men's utility.[14] A clear discussion of this question by Edgeworth would have been helpful, but although he engages in a discussion of the merits of marginal tax changes given the relative utility of money to members of different classes, he nowhere elaborates a hypothesis on the relative utility of money to the two sexes. We can only speculate on his thoughts on the matter.

In a footnote, Edgeworth sets out a mathematical argument to demonstrate that if women, being weaker, suffer more disutility from work, the condition for the minimization of total disutility (of men and women) is that women perform less work than men. This argument could be used to support greater compensation for women in the form of equal pay for equal work at the margin. Instead, Edgeworth insists that 'it does not follow that $\Xi$ (the man's portion of goods) should be greater than (the woman's) $\xi$' (ibid.: 489n).[15]

His argument, like his conclusion, is incomplete. He clearly assumes that women suffer greater marginal disutility from work than men do, but no assumption is made on the relative utility they derive from consumption. Similarly, the actual distribution of income and goods between the two sexes is not considered as having an impact on the conditions of welfare maximization.

Edgeworth provides us here with another clear instance of a male economist making pronouncements about national economic welfare maximization and the optimal distribution of work and income between the sexes, while missing some crucial elements and obvious conclusions. Nothing in the whole article indicates whether he believes women derive any utility from earning an income. Furthermore, the assumption that women do not need an income while men do permeates Edgeworth's thought. This goes along with his further assumption that men's income goes to the support of dependants while women's does not.[16] Edgeworth totally disregards women's contribution to family subsistence needs. This leads him to imply that any relative redistribution of income from men to women would be detrimental to family support and to the economy as a whole. He restates the case made in his 1922 article that equal pay for men and women would be unjust as 'one of the parties is subject to unequal deductions from his pay' (ibid.: 493); support of dependants is seen as a tax on men's income. This 'injustice' is rightfully corrected by giving men an 'advantage in the labour market'.

In a manner much more explicit than in the previous article, Edgeworth disagrees with feminists, including Olive Schreiner, whom he quotes. Paying women less for equal work, she says, 'is the nearest approach to a willful and unqualified "wrong" in the whole relations of women to Society to-day'.[17] The only 'wrong' he acknowledges in the matter is the 'infraction of *laissez-faire*' inherent in the situation. 'But,' he adds, 'it is not "unqualified" in so far as it is *calculated* to correct another sort of wrong', the 'unequal deductions' from men's pay (ibid.; emphasis added).[18] Edgeworth compares the impact on welfare of the 'infraction of *laissez-faire*' and the unequal 'taxation' of men's income and decides that the latter injustice deserves more to be corrected, at the expense of the former. He never explains why simultaneous correction of both 'injustices' is impossible.

Edgeworth thereby supports the maintenance of men's privileged treatment in the labour force. He is oblivious to the implications that men are compensated twice in his reasoning: with higher pay and with 'their advantage in the labour market', that is, greater opportunities for employment. As in the 1922 article, Edgeworth does not allow women improved access to occupations, as the predicted débâcle would be detrimental to economic welfare:

> Moreover, those barriers against the entrance of women workers into certain occupations . . . appear to subserve the purpose of preventing the *débâcle*, ultimately ruinous alike to wealth and family life, which the hasty substitution of low-paid female operatives for well-paid men threatens to bring about. (ibid.)

Thus, once again, a 'welfare-maximizing' infraction to *laissez-faire* has been 'calculated': the economy and the family must be protected against women. This is a more pressing imperative than the correction of the identified major cause of pay inequality.

Yet elsewhere in the article Edgeworth feels protective towards women. He deplores the fact that 'chivalry' is no longer part of social values and has been replaced by competition between the sexes. Following Walker's recommendations,[19] he agrees that women could be allowed to enter more occupations and receive training for them. Yet he is not convinced that they could do this on the basis of their own merit:

> On the ground of economic welfare it is now further demanded that women workers should at least have *the benefit of any doubt* that may arise with regard to *the apportionment of industries between the sexes*. If in effect . . . there comes in an element of chance in determinations about work and wages . . . *let us weight the chances somewhat in favour of the weaker sex*. (ibid.: 490; emphasis added)

He clearly does not propose that women have free access to *all* occupations and training, in competition with men. Instead he suggests an expanded share for women in a segregated labour market, one that would not be decided by the women themselves, but by a patronizing invisible hand 'drawing lots'. Patriarchal sentiments are appealed to:

> The man who is hesitating between the older policy of exclusion and greater freedom of competition (safeguarded by subsidies to families) is exhorted *to give the benefit of the doubt* to the course which makes for the higher remuneration and larger independence of the woman worker. To thwart her wishes and degrade her status would not be consistent with *economic chivalry*. (ibid.: 493–4; emphasis added)[20]

Chivalry is eminently consistent with the patriarchal outlook, where women are not judged on their own capacities or merit but allowed some privileges under strict control, lest they take advantage of them, where they are considered weak, unable to compete, and hence in need of protection, and where these very privileges and protection are misrepresented as proof of women's higher social status.

While Edgeworth is posturing as a supporter of expanded opportunities for women in the labour market, he questions their abilities. He enjoins his male readers to give them 'the benefit of the doubt', but what is to be doubted? Haven't women proven themselves in industry during the war? And haven't the feminists stated that women do not want more protection, but equal treatment and equal opportunities?

Edgeworth equally displays condescension, chivalry and bad faith on the question of family allowances. He has to concede that the case for family allowances is strengthened in his economic welfare approach, yet again he uses 'the benefit of the doubt'. While he – surprisingly – states that family allowances 'should be paid in the hands of the mother' (ibid.: 494), he warns that 'the objections to its injudicious use are nowise weakened'. He suggests that state control may be needed to avoid 'the evil effects on the future of population' and suggests that allowances may be given out only in cases 'of births sanctioned by the authorities'. Eugenic and Malthusian concerns, as well as the fear of lost productivity,[21] motivate the suggestion. Hence, while mothers would receive the payment, women would not be allowed free choice in their reproductive decisions.

In the conclusion of the 1923 article, Edgeworth exhorts social reformers to gradualism and reasserts his belief in the optimality of existing economic structures.

> But the economist, remembering how often the appearance of easy remedies to human ills, in his sphere at least, have proven deceptive, will not expect much from a stroke, gentle or violent, intended to revolutionise established

institutions which have worked well for the production of wealth and economic welfare. The only reform of such institutions which the economist can approve are tentative and gradual. (ibid.: 495)

Edgeworth presumes to speak for the economic profession as a whole, and negates the presence in its midst of more daring reformers, or revolutionaries.

Edgeworth was prompted to write his two articles on the question of 'equal pay for equal work' by the demands of his feminist contemporaries, demands which he appeared to support liberally by giving some of the feminists space in the pages of the *Economic Journal*, of which he was editor. Reviewing his position, however, one must question his biographer's assertion that 'no one has described more fully and faithfully than he the economic position of women and he favoured all their causes' (Bonar, 1926: 652). It is clear that he was more concerned with the defence of the privileges of men (as breadwinners) and of capitalists (hiding behind the perfect competition concept) than with the interests of women. Indeed at no time does he represent their position or take up their point of view, while he busily detracts or misrepresents feminists. He curiously ignores the feminists' definition of equal pay for equal work, one that takes the point of view of women and that would eminently make sense to an economist taking the perspective of maximizing women's utility and incorporating it in overall welfare maximization. Edgeworth's look at women's utility functions is narrowly restricted to their presumed disutility from work and is predetermined by the assumption that it is greater than men's disutility from work.

Furthermore, given that the *laissez-faire* approach hinders his objectives, Edgeworth sees the necessity of shifting his argument to a 'higher plane' of economic welfare where the infraction to the economic optimum of *laissez-faire* is secondary to a perceived need for justice for male workers whose incomes are 'taxed' by dependant support.

All this is compounded by the unstated assumption that the status quo itself is an economic welfare optimum. This status quo includes the existing division of labour between the sexes, women's responsibility for family care, reproductive and domestic labour, the existing distribution of income between the sexes, the system of labour income determination, the patriarchal family as the basic socioeconomic institution for the purposes of consumption, reproduction of labour and income earning, the breadwinner role for men and the definition of men's wages as a 'family wage', along with the presumption that men are solely responsible for dependants.

These assumptions inscribe themselves in a familialist ideology whereby the heterosexual patriarchal and nuclear family is the social norm, *all* men are defined as supporters of dependants, bachelors do not exist,[22] all women are mothers, and spinsters have no rights.[23] Whereas the actual optimality of this status quo is never established, Edgeworth clearly sees any interference with it as threatening a welfare optimum.

Some elements of women's utility functions are invisible to Edgeworth, and some women, those who are not mothers, are themselves invisible to him. Edgeworth consistently ignores studies that show that a significant proportion of women are self-supporting and have partial or full responsibility for dependants. He chooses to neglect the part played by women in contributing to family incomes. Assuming that their income does not further family welfare, he proclaims any redistribution of income from men to women a severe threat to family well-being.

This warning parallels his hysterical fear of a débâcle. His initial concern that women should have greater mobility in the labour market is subsequently dropped and replaced by a very tentative recommendation to provide limited entry of women into some occupations. Free entry of women into occupations is, for the otherwise *laissez-faire* economist, too great a threat to the stability of the market, and to 'family life'. Edgeworth sees women as a threat to society if they are allowed to stray from their patriarchally assigned role and place.

Overall, Edgeworth's treatment of the question of equal pay is based on and reinforces what Beatrice Webb has called 'the Vested Interest of the Male'. His rationale that men have to be compensated for their support of dependants makes him reassert men's rights to employment free from female competition and their right to a family wage. Consequently, in a baffling ideological twist, he implies that the feminist demand for equal pay is inequitable. This implication is facilitated by his misrepresentation of the feminist position. Edgeworth's bias leads to an unscholarly and dishonest presentation of feminist views. Some of the proponents of equal pay are never mentioned in the two articles. Neither William Smart's nor Edward Cadbury's position is referred to,[24] yet they provided sensible economic arguments and factual data in support of equal pay which could hardly be ignored. Edgeworth's amnesia is an expedient way to avoid confronting their ideas. After all, male social scientists could not be misrepresented or derided as easily as feminist women.

In his 1922 article Edgeworth uses Beatrice Webb's socialism against her proposals: 'The Socialist who aims at a closer approximation of pay to efforts and needs does not acquiesce in the present arrangements. . . . But these considerations lie outside pure economics, and must be postponed to our sequel' (1922: 447–8). Yet her *Minority Report* is not discussed in the 1923 article.

In addition, Edgeworth elects to focus only on some elements of the feminist analysis of women's economic position. In particular, he completely ignores the demand for economic recognition of women's unpaid work in the home which forms part of the argument for family allowances. He sees family endowment schemes solely as a form of support for children. Yet the feminist analysis of women's unpaid economic contribution (which is developed, among the feminists he quotes, by Eleanor Rathbone, Olive Schreiner and Ellen Key) should have alerted the welfare economist to contributions to economic welfare by women which should be taken into account in any discussion of overall welfare optima.

The only reference made to this particular feminist analysis is dismissive. At the end of the 1923 article he quotes Ellen Key, whom he describes as 'the Swedish *sentimentalist*', who advocated 'economic appreciation of [women's] domestic work', 'subsidy from the community for the bringing up of children', and society's maintenance of women similar to maintenance of 'its army and navy'. He comments: 'Naturally conditions of wealth and economic welfare are not considered by reformers intent upon some object of a higher or at least a different order' (1923: 495). But these conditions definitely enter into consideration in the feminist writings. Edgeworth, afflicted with sexist myopia, just does not see it as such and typically dismisses the feminist proposal as one that is outside the realm of economics.

Edgeworth constructs an argument against equal pay entirely based on the need to compensate men for the deductions to their income resulting from their support of dependants. This one-sided approach to national economic welfare is exposed when one takes into account women's support of dependants (and men), not only out of their meagre earnings, but also through the performance of unpaid domestic and reproductive work.

In conclusion, it is imperative to question Edgeworth's reputation both as a welfare economist and as a supporter of 'all [women's] causes'. His approach to economic welfare in these two articles is nothing but a pure apology for the patriarchal status quo.

## Notes

1. Edgeworth's articles also often lack clarity, in the argument and in the position he takes. This seems to reflect his style and personality. Bonar says that 'he loved to hold the balances and elude a positive answer' and that it was 'out of character' for him to have a definite opinion on issues of political economy (1926: 650). According to Bowley, 'Readers of Edgeworth's writings are often deterred by what appears to be deliberate obscurantism in the arguments' (1934: 123). And Keynes, in his 'Obituary', mentions the 'obscurity and allusiveness and half-apologetic air in which he served up his intellectual dishes' (1926: 146) and elaborates: 'Edgeworth seldom looked the reader or interlocutor straight in the face; he is allusive, obscure and devious as one who would slip by unnoticed, hurrying on if stopped by another traveller' (ibid.: 150).

2. Here Edgeworth ignores Beatrice Webb's argument that, if minimum wages are implemented to ensure that minimum subsistence requirements are met for workers of both sexes, there is no reason to hold that these requirements should be inferior in the case of women (and children) compared to men (see Chapter 4).

3. As if there could be such thing as 'partial' perfect competition.

4. This assumption will later be dropped when Edgeworth switches from productivity to subsistence needs in his approach to wage determination.

5. This statement seems quite speculative; however, Edgeworth attempts to back it up with a seemingly inapplicable discussion on the shape of maxima.

6. While Fawcett is not acknowledged as one of the feminists who developed the crowding theory, she is quoted twice in support of Edgeworth's charge against the exclusionary practices of trade unions. Edgeworth is also oblivious of her general support of trade unionism and of her attempts to rally trade unions to the equal pay demand.

7. Pigou developed a similar argument in his treatment of the equal pay question (see Chapter 9).

8. It is curious to see here that Edgeworth, renowned for his fastidiousness and encyclopaedic quoting of sources manages, in two pages (448–9), to give two different titles for the same book by B. L. Hutchins (*Conflicting Ideals* or *Conflict of Ideals*), to neglect naming the 'radical' feminist he quotes, and to give an erroneous title for her book: '*A Sane* [sic] *Feminism*' while using irony to discredit her. Presumably he is there quoting Wilma Meikle's *Towards a Sane Feminism*.

9. (Rowntree and Stuart, 1921.) The methodology and definitions used by Rowntree vary significantly from those of the Fabian survey. Rowntree does not investigate the degree of self-sufficiency of working women, yet his sample shows that 87 per cent were single. He limited his sample to women over the age of 18 while the Fabian study went down to 16. More importantly, whereas in the Fabian survey women themselves declared whether they were self-supporting or supporting others, in Rowntree's survey the answer was determined by the investigators, who had 'to decide to what extent the woman worker was really responsible for dependants' (1921: 14). The judgement was based on a preconceived idea of the amount of wage necessary to support an adult or a child (a subsistence requirement), no matter what the reality of the situation. Hence, by this logic, a woman supporting a child on a wage insufficient for herself alone would not be deemed to have a dependant. Rowntree also did not consider as dependants individuals performing housekeeping tasks in exchange for financial support. By this definition wives should never be considered dependants.

   Edgeworth forgets to mention Hogg's survey (1921), which shows, on a sample basis, for five cities, that 28 per cent of the working women have partial responsibility and a further 5 per cent full responsibility for dependants. These proportions are much higher than those resulting from Rowntree's survey. One wonders if this is because it contradicts both Rowntree's findings (which are criticized by Hogg) and Edgeworth's argument and because Hogg's methodology cannot be easily dismissed.

   We must note too that the focus of discussion on dependants is one-sided. None of the studies quoted try to determine the exact extent of male support of dependants. The first author to approach this question is Rathbone (1924) who documents the numbers of 'phantom children' that bachelor men are presumed to maintain out of their 'family wage'.

10. Here Edgeworth identifies one of the purposes served in a capitalist labour market by the norm of family economic dependence on the father's income: without it, male workers would lose a major 'incentive to work', capitalists would lose a relatively stable and docile supply of labour. He elaborates this in his 1923 article: 'It is a fearfully rash assumption that, because each man now generally works hard for the sake of his own wife and children, all men will work equally hard for all wives and children' (1923: 494).

11. Surprisingly, since the point is a contentious one, Edgeworth asserts 'the postulate that the satisfactions felt by different persons admit of comparison'. This allows him to envision 'the aggregate economic welfare of a community as the sum of satisfactions enjoyed by the individual members' (1923: 487) and to speculate on the comparative gains or losses in welfare to separate individuals (men vs. women) brought about by specific policy measures.

12. This statement assumes a flat configuration of the maximum. Edgeworth had speculated in the 1922 article that economic welfare maxima may have a 'dumpling-shape' (1922: 438–9).

13. Edgeworth does not specifically address here whether the increase in women's wages would lead to a decrease in men's wages. His discussion focuses more on non-pecuniary changes resulting from the entry of women into industry. He ignores the arguments of the feminists (B. Webb, Smart) that equal pay *per se* would increase total economic welfare.

14. That there might be a reduction in men's wages and utility as a consequence of increasing women's pay is asserted, not demonstrated.

15. He hastens to add that the assumption of no family support applies to this argument.

16. It is actually not clear what, in Edgeworth's mind, women use their income for since they are presumed not to derive utility from it and not to support dependants out of it.

17. Quoted from Schreiner (1978: 24). Edgeworth does not mention the title of her book or give a whole reference for it. He further quotes: 'That males of enlightenment and equity can for an hour tolerate the existence of this inequality has seemed to me always incomprehensible', but does not respond to Olive Schreiner's statement, which he should have taken personally.

Interestingly, he ignores other observations by Schreiner which might have given him a more balanced view of the relative burdens falling on men's and women's shoulders when it comes to family support. In the same passage, she denounces 'the gigantic evils which arise from the fact that her labour, especially domestic labour, often the most wearisome and unending known to any section of the human race, is not adequately recognised and recompensed'.

18. Apparently some invisible hand has computed the extent to which *laissez-faire* should be restricted to compensate the men while maintaining an overall welfare optimum.

19. Francis Walker states that women's wages are 'to a degree inadequate to the service rendered' (1906: 375). He did not endorse the demand for equal pay, believing that women's labour is worth less than men's. He proffered, talking about industries where women and children were employed together, 'that which is only a child's labour can be remunerated only by a child's wage' (ibid.: 373).

20. Credit is given to Marshall (1907) for the concept of 'economic chivalry', along with an admonition to retain plain old chivalry: 'And certainly if chivalry in the general sense of knightly virtue has been shown by another great economist to be compatible with modern industry, why would not this be true also of chivalry in that special sense which was the crown and glory of the knightly character?' (1923: 491).

21. 'It is a fearfully rash assumption that, because each man now generally works hard

for the sake of his own wife and children, all men will work equally hard for all wives and children collectively' (1923: 494).

22. Ironically, Edgeworth was a bachelor, yet the economic situation of bachelors and their existence, which presents a problem for his argument, are not addressed in his two articles.

23. In the 1923 article Edgeworth expresses the concern that changes in labour income determination should not 'alter the balance between the wages of spinsters and that of married men to the detriment of families' (p. 493). On familialism, see Barrett and McIntosh (1982).

24. The Cadbury study is mentioned only as a way to criticize the lack of good saving habits of 'working girls' (1922: 456). It is also apparent that male economists who support equal pay are quoted by Edgeworth, when they are, not directly but through the writings of feminist writers, as if with the implication that the feminists are misusing them (see quoting of Cannan, 1922: 442).

# 6 Conclusion

Chapters 3–5 trace the discussion of equal pay for equal work in economic writings by economists and by feminists over the period 1890 to 1923. This era saw the development and maturing of modern capitalist organizations and, in particular, initial attempts to structure sex roles in society in a fashion that would serve the requirements of capital for labour power and for its effective reproduction.

The writings reviewed here reflect the tensions in society created by this evolution of capitalism: fledgling attempts by economists to participate in the rationalization of women's place in capitalist society, feminist activism to challenge inherited Victorian values and generate reforms towards the equality and recognition of women's participation in the economy, socialist and trade union efforts to alter the course of capitalist development.

The positions reviewed represent various approaches and tendencies: from plain neoclassical, *laissez-faire* economists (Cannan, Edgeworth) to the reform-minded or less dogmatically entrenched William Smart, from the mildly feminist Fabian socialist Sidney Webb to the more resolute supporters of women's rights: Cadbury, Matheson and Shann, and with Beatrice Webb, Millicent Fawcett, Ada Heather-Bigg and Eleanor Rathbone representing diverse tendencies of feminism. The socialist approach is most strongly presented by Beatrice Webb, and to some extent by Cadbury, Matheson and Shann.

In the literature reviewed, the focus on the question of equal pay brought out the wider issues of women's economic role in capitalist society: women's access to employment and the conditions they face in the labour market; the family as the commonly accepted locus of women's existence; women's contribution – monetary and non-monetary – to its livelihood; the global reliance of the capitalist system on women's labour, paid and unpaid; and the connection between the hierarchical systems of class and sex in a patriarchal capitalist society.

The discussion shows both the beginnings of feminist theorizing on the economic position of women in the labour force, and the characteristic tendency of a mainstream/malestream economist like Edgeworth to use his expert authority towards apologetic goals, which, in this particular case, serve a patriarchal order to a greater extent than a capitalist order. This tendency was not shared by all the economists who wrote on the subject; Smart and Cadbury in particular seem more committed to unbiased theorizing than the rest of their male colleagues. The consequence of their earnest questioning of the dominant ideology was their erasure from the history of economic thought, their obliteration from patriarchal memory.[1]

The major issue at stake in the debate was the remuneration of women's contribution to the economy, and more particularly of their contribution in the form of paid employment. The core of the question is whether their wages represent an appropriate remuneration: whether the wage level represents women's contribution to production for some writers, and whether it constitutes a sufficient subsistence income for others. The two concepts of subsistence and productivity wages are present in the approaches of all writers.

Although strongly suggested in the early stages of the debate (Sidney Webb), the proposition that women's low wages reflect their low productivity does not appear to stand on its own in the opinions of the writers reviewed. That proposition is usually qualified by observations on the labour market conditions faced by working women: crowding, limited entry, limited access to skills, education and training. Consequently, none of the writers concludes that women's pay should remain what it is because it reflects their actual productivity. The focus of discussion is instead shifted to the merit of measures to alter labour market conditions to allow working women access to a full expression of their productive potential and to allow wages to freely reflect actual productivity.

Of all the writers, Edgeworth is the only one who does not clearly advocate either the equating of women's wages with the value of their marginal product, or the alteration of market conditions to allow approximation of this perfectly competitive outcome (he endorses such alterations only if they are gradual). By asserting that women should be paid less than men because they don't have families to support, he is equivocal on the exact relationship that should exist between women's (and men's) wages and marginal productivity. At any rate, the whole debate (including Beatrice Webb's contribution) inscribes itself within an approach centred on the assumption that a free market (or, failing that, a set of conditions which approximate the free market) yields optimum levels of production and remuneration of factors.

Very characteristic of this approach is the overall lack of questioning, except by Eleanor Rathbone, of the basis of men's wages. They are assumed to reflect male productivity levels and to be the outcome of the free interaction of demand and supply for men's labour. This assumption reaches the height of sophistry with the rationale that the higher trade union bargained rates for male workers reflect their actual productivity levels (Smart). Men's wages, whether 'family wages' or trade union 'standard rates', are taken as the norm in the labour market and are, consequently and without second thoughts, equated with the orthodox theoretical concept of marginal productivity wages, which neoclassical theory declares as the normal and optimal labour market outcome. Whereas some of the debaters may be plainly naive or unsophisticated in making such assumptions, this cannot be the case for Edgeworth, who clearly muddles the issues to avoid confronting the basic inconsistency and 'ad hocery' of this curious mixture of patriarchal and capitalist apologetics.

In contrast, Rathbone squarely questions the neoclassical dogma by stating that men's wages have more to do with the belief that they have families to support than with their actual productivity level. She subscribes to a subsistence needs approach to wage determination. Smart goes half-way by theorizing that women's wages are subsistence based, which he denounces as an antiquated survival of early capitalist times,[2] while men's are productivity based.

Sidney Webb and Edgeworth rationalize women's wage levels on the basis of their presumed low subsistence needs and lack of family responsibilities. The latter issue is itself the object of heated discussion and contradictory empirical measures. Meanwhile Fawcett, Heather-Bigg, Cadbury and Beatrice Webb denounce the perception of women's low subsistence needs as one of the causes for their low pay, and argue that this perception should be erased from public opinion. Beatrice Webb and William Smart go further: they challenge the ideology that women's subsistence needs are lower than men's. Overall the debate reveals the centrality of the question of women's subsistence needs and of their relation to women's wage level. This issue presents a strong challenge to the validity and universality of the neoclassical theory of wage (and price) determination.

Besides the fundamental issues of productivity levels and subsistence requirements as determinants of women's wages, a number of other elements are identified by the various authors as intervening in the determination of women's wages. Subsequent to Sidney Webb's initial observation and Millicent Fawcett's ensuing elaboration of a theory of non-competing groups, all writers agree that a major obstacle for women is their lack of employment options, their restricted access to trades and to training, and the resulting crowding conditions they face.

The 'make-weight' argument (women's subsistence being ensured by male family members) is referred to by Sidney Webb and Edgeworth, while its exploitation by 'parasitic industries' is denounced by Beatrice

Webb. The explanation of 'market wages elsewhere' setting women's wages regardless of their actual productivity in the job is employed by Sidney Webb and Millicent Fawcett, with the additional observation that the set rate is close to if not below what a single woman would require for subsistence. Smart denounces this situation while using the concept of 'customary wage', which may be another description of these 'market wages elsewhere' but seems to comprise an element of tradition. Beatrice Webb locates customary practice in the setting of separate men's and women's rates. At the same time she observes that the free 'higgling of the market' in women's jobs is a main reason for below-subsistence wage rates. She joins Fawcett, Rathbone and Sidney Webb in assigning further causality to women's weak bargaining power, their restricted mobility and lack of trade union organization.

Some newer and more challenging – although at times embryonic – observations were contributed by the feminist writers. Millicent Fawcett and Beatrice Webb observe a situation of male monopoly over remunerative employment, enforced through collective bargaining, and involving the obvious collusion of employers. The issue of economic power, held by men and enforced through labour market conditions which discriminate against women, is identified by Ada Heather-Bigg. The question of the comparative social value of women's work is raised, albeit tangentially, by Rathbone, and in a much clearer fashion by Cannan.

The solutions proposed differ widely due to the varied political beliefs and theoretical approaches of the debaters. Both Cannan and Edgeworth warn their readers against any intervention in the labour market. Cannan sees equal pay as detrimental to women's future in the labour market and Edgeworth paints the increased access of women to occupations as a threat to the stability of capitalism and to the fabric of society. The other writers, however, agree that the door preventing women's access to trades, professions and training should be burst open. With the identification of crowding as one of the main reasons for women's low wages, entry into new occupations is seen as the necessary complement of approaches giving women equal remuneration or wages reflecting their actual productivity levels.

The support for an equal pay for equal work policy seems to come from the least interventionist of the advocates of women's equality (Fawcett and Smart). They propose the application of the same rule of marginal productivity wage determination to women and men without being clear on the enforcement mechanisms required. By contrast, Cadbury *et al.*, Rathbone and Beatrice Webb suggest major revisions to the existing income distribution structure (based on the more or less free market). The proposals made by Rathbone and Beatrice Webb required definite state intervention and involve an alternative form of dependant support (family allowances). To this Webb adds unemployment insurance, minimum wages and minimum standards, and cost-of-living adjustments. Her proposals go the farthest in challenging the income distribution 'chaos' engendered by the free market.

Ultimately, the debate revealed the double standard existing in the capitalist labour market with respect to the determination of men's and women's wages. Rathbone put her finger on the reason for this: wages are based on the perceived average subsistence requirements of male and female workers. This position is not fundamentally denied by Edgeworth, who rationalizes the pay difference with an appeal to a 'higher concept of justice'. The double standard is founded on the underlying patriarchal structure of capitalist society. In it men are 'breadwinners' in charge of a family and women are wives and mothers with no claim to access to their own means of subsistence through employment.

Edgeworth's position illustrates how the dogmatism of neoclassical economists and their profound and blind acceptance of the patriarchal structure of society lead to a completely incoherent theoretical position. Typically, their stubborn clinging to the marginal productivity theory of factor payments as unchallengeable dogma forces them to engage in acrobatic sophistry to 'explain' women's wage rates. When the acrobatics become too painful (or the position too untenable) all pretence of theoretical consistency is abandoned to be replaced by outright normative edicts.[3] When all else fails, patriarchal power raises its ugly head to simply assert: 'men ought to be paid more'. Hence the need to reassert male rights under the onslaught of feminist attacks reveals the internal weakness and ideological nature of the cornerstone of neoclassical theory. Surprisingly, the theoretical and ideological inadequacies of marginalism are admitted by the theorists themselves. Yet if the neoclassical economists end up with no clothes they can still maintain their views as dominant, speaking from the side of the powerful in a capitalist and patriarchal society.

The feminists were able to initiate a challenge to male economic power and to question the differential impact the capitalist system has on women. The central questions are: why, in modern society, should men control women's access to market production and income? And why should women's economic contributions be undervalued or altogether denied and made invisible? The main/malestream economists who participated in the debate do not directly address these fundamental questions, taking refuge in vague pronouncements on the need to protect the economy and society against the disorders that economically free women would generate. These positions are more clearly asserted by two leading neoclassical economists: Alfred Marshall and A. C. Pigou.

**Notes**
1.  Including the immediate memories of Edgeworth and Pigou.
2.  Amazingly, capitalist history is supposed to evolve as paradigms change.
3.  Another illustration of this is also provided by Pigou; see Chapter 9.

# PART III

# WOMEN IN THE
# ECONOMICS OF
# MARSHALL AND PIGOU

# 7   Introduction

Marshall and Pigou, like Edgeworth, did not involve themselves in political activism.[1] They kept a lofty distance from the controversies initiated by the feminists, bridging this distance only occasionally to issue their learned opinion. Yet their work contains pronouncements on the issues raised in the debate just reviewed. Furthermore, although at no point the place of women in society and their economic activities are given the specific focus of, say a full chapter or section in their work, one can find, in filigree, a consistent construct of opinions and prescriptions on these subjects. It is thus possible to analyse these economists' approaches to the place of women in a capitalist economy.

Marshall was one of the founders of neoclassical economics as well as an initiator of welfare economics, which was subsequently developed by Pigou. A study of both economists' work is crucial to an understanding of the treatment of women in the hegemonic theoretical framework of contemporary neoclassical economics. The following chapters will review Marshall and Pigou's approaches to the sexual division of labour, and to women's economic contribution and remuneration. Their application to women of the principles of economic efficiency and welfare maximization will be scrutinized. The configuration of their ideological approaches to an incipient human capital theory and to a state welfare system will be assessed.

**Note**
1.   One exception is Marshall's activism in the Cambridge 'battle of the degree', on the 'anti' side.

# 8 Gender and class in Marshall's *Principles of Economics*[1]

Marshall held that economics was a positive and not a normative science[2] and emphasized the scientificity imported to the discipline's approach and object by the measurability of the phenomena observed,[3] this measurability being permitted (and limited) by the use of money in economic transactions and decision-making (1930: 15).

Marshall's marginalist model rests on the assumption of individualistic rational economic behaviour, behaviour directed at 'the attainment and . . . the use of the material requisites of well being' (ibid.: 1) involving marginal calculations by the individual to reach a welfare optimum. In this model, income shares – and wages – are determined by the marginal product of the individual factors of production. Market mechanisms yield the maximization of economic returns and an optimal state of economic welfare.

Yet Marshall departs from that model in at least two instances. In particular, the unit to be considered for consumption, welfare decisions or income levels is often not the individual, but the family. Interestingly, individualistic (selfish) economic motivations break down within the family unit, especially in the case of inter-generational transfers (ibid.: 24).[4] Elsewhere, Marshall breaks with the market-oriented *laissez-faire* tradition when he approves of state intervention (Factory Acts) and advocates further state involvement in the economy (education, family wage). As we shall see, these divergences from the model find a unity in the economist's treatment of the role of women in a capitalist economy.

Marshall's argument about women rests on his development of a 'human capital' theory in Book IV of his *Principles*. His intent there is to provide advice on how to improve the productivity of the working class. Education is a major element in his proposal. But, to enhance the environment in which male workers and their children live and to generate greater health, 'character and ability', working-class women are required to build a 'true home'. Marshall therefore opposes employment for married women and advocates a 'family wage' paid to male workers. He consistently applies bourgeois Victorian values to the working class in a system where women are assigned to contributing their time to investment in the human capital of male workers without receiving a direct return for it.

## Marshall's human capital theory

Marshall states that, of the factors of production, labour has superior properties: it creates capital.[5] As such it deserves special study:

> The growth of mankind in number, in health and strength, in knowledge, ability, and in richness of character is the end of all our studies. . . . We cannot avoid taking account of the direct agency of man in production, and of the conditions which govern his efficiency as a producer. (ibid.: 139)

The labour force of a country is clearly seen as its most important asset and as such requires proper investment to maintain and augment it: 'The most valuable capital is that invested in human beings' (ibid.: 564). At the same time, this asset has to be shaped in a specific way, to meet the production requirements of an industrial society:

> To be able to bear in mind many things at a time, to have everything ready when wanted, to act promptly and show resource when anything goes wrong, to accommodate oneself quickly to changes in detail of the work done, to be steady and trustworthy, to have always a reserve of force which will come out in emergency, these are the qualities which make a great industrial people. They are not peculiar to any occupations, but are wanted in all. (ibid.: 206–7)[6]

Marshall's approach to the study of labour, its characteristics and the determining factors of labour supply is more prescriptive than analytical. The role of the economist, in his view, is to enlighten society as to how this asset must be maintained and improved through 'human capital investment'. Marshall's proposals include the following elements.

First of all, poverty must be eradicated to allow a better use of the labour potential of the poor. 'Prompt action is needed in regard to the large . . . "Residuum" of persons who are physically, mentally or morally incapable of doing a good day's work with which to earn a good day's wage' (ibid.: 714). Eradication of poverty requires the increase in incomes and wages of the poorer classes which will lower the death rate and provide the poor with the subsistence levels required to improve their working ability: 'there is a certain consumption which is strictly necessary for each grade of work in this sense, that if any of it is curtailed the work cannot be done efficiently' (ibid.: 529). Marshall writes at length on the food requirements of various types of labourer (ibid.: 529–30), and on the other 'necessaries': clothing, shorter hours and healthier surroundings.

> Rest is essential for the growth of vigorous population. . . . Overwork of
> every form lowers vitality; while anxiety, worrying, and excessive mental
> strain have a fatal influence in undermining the constitution, impairing
> fecundity and diminishing the vigour of the race. (ibid.: 197)

Marshall argues that improved conditions will have cumulative effects
on the workforce: 'an increase in wages unless earned under unwhole-
some conditions, almost always increases the strength, physical, mental,
and even moral, of the coming generations' (ibid.: 532).

He prescribes direct government intervention to achieve the above-
stated goals. This includes the upholding of the Factory Acts (ibid.:
198), the establishment of a 'minimum wages . . . fixed by authority of
government below which no man may work, and another below which
no woman may work' (715), and control by the state of child-rearing
in the Residuum class:

> The case of those, who are responsible for young children would call for
> greater expenditure of public funds, and a more strict subordination of
> *personal freedom to public necessity*. The most urgent among the first steps
> towards causing the Residuum to cease from the land, is to insist on regular
> school attendance in decent clothing, and with bodies clean and well fed. In
> case of failure the parents should be warned and advised: as a last resource
> the homes might be closed or regulated with some *limitation of the freedom
> of the parents*. The expense would be great: but there is no other so urgent
> need for bold expenditure. It would remove the great canker that infects
> the whole body of the nation. (ibid.: 714–15n.; emphasis added)

The second set of measures proposed by Marshall to improve the
country's supply of labour concerns the education of the working
classes. Education is necessary to improve the supply of skilled labour:
'the children of unskilled workers need similar means to be made
capable of earning the wages of skilled work: and the children of skilled
workers need similar means to be made capable of doing still more
responsible work' (ibid.: 718). The main goal of education is clearly
identified by Marshall as serving the needs of industry for a skilled
labour force, to make the future workers 'efficient producers'. To that
effect,

> Education must be made more thorough. The schoolmaster must learn that
> his main duty is not to impart knowledge, for a few shillings will buy more
> printed knowledge than a man's brain can hold. It is to educate character,
> faculties and activities. (ibid.: 717–18)

Providing education is 'a national investment' (ibid.: 216). 'To this
end, public money must flow freely', as it is 'the most imperative duty

of this generation . . . to provide for the young' (ibid.: 718–20) and as 'the wisdom of expanding public and private funds on education is not to be measured by its direct fruits alone' (ibid.: 216). In effect, the benefits of working-class education will be cumulative over time as it will generate among more educated parents a greater willingness to educate their children and more resources to devote to that goal (ibid.: 516–63, 718).

Although benefits from education go in a great part to society at large and to private industry, the decision whether children should receive education, and what particular education, rests with the parents.

> [T]he investment of capital in the rearing and early training of the workers of England is limited by the resources of parents on the various grades of society, by their power of forecasting the future, and by their willingness to sacrifice themselves for the sake of their children. (ibid.: 561)

While Marshall recognizes that this 'willingness to sacrifice' oneself for the sake of one's children does exist 'now even among the poorer classes', he perceives that the propensity to provide education for their offspring is stronger in 'the higher grades' who have more information on employment opportunities, who 'are generally willing and able to incur a considerable expense for the purpose',[7] and who are more able to 'distinctly realise the future', and 'discount it at a low rate of interest' (561–3).[8]

Human capital investment by parents in their children is obviously complicated by the generational transfers involved. Unlike the case of physical capital where 'he who bears the expenses of production' receives all the returns,

> Those who bear the expenses of rearing and educating [the worker] receive but very little of the price that is paid for his services in later years. . . . Consequently, the investment of capital in him is limited by the means, the forethought, and the unselfishness of his parents. (ibid.: 560–1)

So the proper habits and attitudes of parents must be generated within society. In a capitalist society, human capital investment depends entirely on the unselfishness of parents *vis-à-vis* their children, on their willingness to sacrifice themselves for their future, behaviour quite contrary to the individual greed and selfishness that is assumed, in the marginalist model, to motivate rational economic decisions, yet crucial to the requirements of reproduction and growth of a capitalist society.

While Marshall takes for granted that the 'willingness' to insure the 'wellbeing of their children' is present among parents, 'even among the poorest classes', he makes it clear that this propensity should be increased through education (ibid.: 561–3). What is to be thus obtained is a sense of social duty, of responsibility for the next generation's welfare: 'Education is a *duty* of parents' (ibid.: 216; emphasis added).

## Women's duty to their family

This sense of duty is particularly required of women; mothers, more than fathers, are called upon to sacrifice themselves for the sake of their children. One thing women have to give up is employment: Marshall consistently maintains that women's employment is detrimental because 'it tempts them to neglect their duty of building a true home, and investing their efforts in the personal capital of their children's character and abilities' (ibid.: 685). In Marshall's opinion, a mother's care of her children is one of the most essential elements in the production of the human capital that is required by modern industry:

> [T]he degradation of the working classes varies almost uniformly with the amount of rough work done by women. The most valuable of all capital is that invested in human beings; and of that capital, the most precious part is the results of the care and influence of the mother, so long as she retains her tender and unselfish instincts, and has not been hardened by the strain and stress of unfeminine work. (ibid.: 564)

While Marshall exposes his sympathies for the 'cult of the Home' and the 'cult of true womanhood', he does not attempt to back up his assertions on the relation between 'the degradation of the working classes' and the employment of women with any specific data. Neither does he try to correlate other variables (wage levels, length of the working day, diet) to that 'degradation' to test whether it could be attributed to women's employment alone.

The same criticism applies to Marshall's argument that infant mortality is directly linked to women's employment: infant mortality is higher in towns 'especially where there are many mothers who neglect their parental duties in order to earn money wages' (ibid.: 198); 'an increase in wages is almost certain to diminish the death rate, unless it has been obtained at the price of the neglect by mothers of their duties to their children' (ibid.: 529). Here again, Marshall is found to depart significantly from his positivist posture.[9]

Furthermore, work interferes with an efficient use of women's reproductive capacity: overwork impairs fecundity, and 'the birth of children who die early from the want of care and adequate means is a useless strain to the mother' (ibid.: 202). Work, especially if 'unfeminine' (no example provided), is seen by Marshall as destructive of these qualities (tenderness and unselfishness) required for the building of a 'true home' and the nurturing of children.[10] These feminine qualities are an essential ingredient of the human capital investment in children: 'general ability', the faculties, general knowledge and intelligence that must be developed among workers, 'depends largely on the surroundings of childhood and youth. In this the first and far the most powerful influence is that of the mother' (ibid.: 207).[11]

One further requirement is the mother's full-time presence in the home. 'Able workers and good citizens are not likely to come from homes from which the mother is absent during a great part of the day' (ibid.: 721). In this respect, the son of the artisan enjoys an advantage over the son of the unskilled worker: 'He generally lives in a better and cleaner house. . . . His parents are likely to be better educated . . . and, last but not least, his mother is likely to be able to give more of her time to the care of her family' (ibid.: 563–4).

While Marshall holds that women have a 'tender and unselfish instinct' to give priority to the care of their children, he does not seem to trust it to be sufficient to generate in them the qualities and behaviour that will benefit industrial society the most. This can be helped by some form of state intervention.

In the first place, women require education, not for the purpose of improving their skills as workers, but for the purpose of contributing to the human capital investment in their children.[12] Marshall insists that the need to educate men cannot be separated from the need to educate women, as a part of the social design of improving the workforce as a whole:

> in estimating the cost of production of efficient labour, we must take as our unit the family. At all events, we cannot treat the cost of production of efficient men as an isolated problem; it must be taken as part of the broader problem of the cost of production of efficient men together with the women who are fitted to make their home happy, and to bring up their children vigorous in body and mind, truthful and cleanly, gentle and brave. (ibid.: 564)

The education of women must be directed towards developing specific skills and knowledge. The mother and housewife must know how best to take care of her family. To this end she requires, besides a knowledge of, among other things, health care and nutrition, some notion of household economy to make the best of the tight working-class household budget:

> a skilled housewife with ten shillings a week to spend on food will often do more for the health and strength of her family than an unskilled one with

twenty. The great mortality of infants among the poor is largely due to the want of care and judgement in preparing their food; and those who do not entirely succumb to this want of motherly care often grow up with enfeebled constitutions. (ibid.: 195–6)

The value of housewives' skills to society seems therefore to be great. On the one hand they produce a stronger, healthier and better-prepared workforce; they prevent the social waste of infant and child mortality. On the other hand they provide industry with a quality workforce at reduced expense: subsistence wages paid to male workers can be lowered without negative consequences for their productivity.

In spite of this, Marshall does not prescribe any system to socially recognize the value of the housewife's contribution to industrial society, or to induce the development of such skills by women. While, for instance, male workers benefit from the human capital invested in them as they earn better wages, women get no return from their education (and *a fortiori* from their contribution to the 'investment' of human capital in their children). The 'virtue of those who have aided [the worker in acquiring better skills] must remain for the greater part its *own* reward' (ibid.: 564).[13] For Marshall, 'virtue', or the accomplishment of motherly or housewifely 'duties', is a sufficient reward for women's contribution to society. He holds that women's 'neglect of their duties' is reprehensible but refuses to devise an economic explanation for this 'neglect' or an economic solution (monetary incentive) to it.

### Women's employment

The only kind of monetary incentive prescribed by Marshall to generate the appropriate social behaviour among women is negative and punitive. Women can be induced to stay home, discouraged from seeking the employment opportunities that will lead them to 'neglect their duties', if the wages offered to women workers on the job market are kept low.[14]

Marshall implicitly advocates low wages for women when he calls for women's minimum wage to be set below men's (ibid.: 715) and when he describes as 'injurious' a rise in women's wages relative to men's. Such a rise is detrimental, not only to men's employment and relative earning capacity but also to the performance of household duties by women (ibid.: 685).[15]

Another way to discourage and restrict women's access to the job market is through the Factory Acts. The Acts fit with Marshall's overall proposal on the improvement of the working class. The restriction of women's and children's employment gives the latter a better chance to be educated and enjoy improved physical health while it prevents the disastrous effect of overwork on women's fecundity and increases the amount of time women can consecrate to their 'family duties'.

To appease the opponents of the Acts Marshall reassures them that 'the temporary material loss' they might generate 'should be submitted to for the sake of a higher and ultimate greater gain'. No doubt he is talking about production (the National Dividend) rather than the incomes of women and children.[16] Yet his official justification for the Acts is chivalrous: 'the coming generation is interested in the *rescue* of men, and still more in that of women, from excessive work' (ibid.: 694; emphasis added). The Factory Acts 'are imposed not as a means of class domination; but with the purpose of *defending the weak*, and especially the children and the *mothers* of children, in matters in which they are not able to use the forces of competition in their own defence' (ibid.: 751; emphasis added).

Marshall does not say what renders women so 'weak' once they become mothers; nor whether he feels that women are better protected in the home (for instance against abusive husbands); nor whether they are better able 'to use the forces of competition in their own defence' in that environment; nor whether they will certainly work shorter hours and perform less strenuous tasks when engaging in homework or household drudgery.

The level and determination of women's wages are not specially investigated in the *Principles*. By contrast, in *The Economics of Industry* (jointly written with Mary Paley Marshall), a couple of pages are devoted to this question. The authors observe:

> In England, many women get low wages, not because the value of the work they do is low, but because both they and their employers have been in the habit of taking it for granted that the wages of women must be low. Sometimes even when men and women do the same work in the same factory, not only the Time-wages, but also the Task-wages of the women are lower than those of the men. (1881: 175–6)

The Marshalls do not comment on this departure from a marginal productivity determination of wages. They only speculate on some of the possible reasons for the differential treatment of women. In particular, they note that the employer's demand price for women's labour is influenced by his perception that 'the woman is of less service in the long run' owing to her responsibility for her family, and this influences the 'general opinion' on the value of women's work.[17]

With respect to the question of the minimum wage, Marshall actually proposed 'to adjust the minimum wage to the family instead of to the individual' (1930: 715). He thought a nationally set minimum wage for each sex too rigid. Regional variations in the demand for the labour of each sex create variations in the sexes' wage levels, which 'naturally' compensate one another within the family unit.

> The family is, in the main, a single unit as regards geographical migration: and therefore the wages of men are relatively high, and those of women and children low where heavy iron and other industries preponderate, while in some other districts less than half the money income of the family is earned by the father, and men's wages are relatively low. This natural adjustment is socially beneficial; and rigid national rules as to minimum wages for men and for women, which ignore or oppose it, are to be deprecated. (ibid.: 715n.)

This approach asserts that all women should be in families and that their earnings – if any – have the sole purpose of complementing men's earnings towards a family subsistence income. One can further deduce from Marshall's statement that women's wages need not be related to their own subsistence requirements or to their own productivity, but are only to be related to the prevailing male wage rate in the area considered.[18]

### Marshall's theory of wages
Marshall's theory of wages deserves notice here:

> demand and supply exert co-ordinate influences on wages; neither has a claim to predominance . . . wages tend to equal the net product of labour; its marginal productivity rules the demand price for it; and, on the other side, wages tend to retain a close though indirect and intricate relation with the cost of rearing, training, and sustaining the energy of efficient labour. (ibid.: 532)

The 'intricate relation' referred to is in fact a very close relation of the supply price of labour to subsistence wage levels: 'the earnings that are got by efficient labour are *not much above the lowest earnings that are needed* to cover the expenses of rearing and training efficient workers, and of sustaining and bringing into activity their full energies' (ibid.: 531; emphasis added).

Wages cannot go below that subsistence level, except at a cost to society: 'there is a certain consumption which is strictly necessary for each grade of work in the sense, that if any of it is curtailed, the work cannot be done efficiently' (ibid.: 529).[19] Yet if wages go beyond subsistence, industrial society suffers. Labour is used efficiently and economically if its cost does not exceed the exact wage required to maintain its optimum productivity. In this context, consumption by workers beyond subsistence levels is considered wasteful. Talking about non-subsistence 'conventional necessaries and customary comforts', Marshall states: 'the greater they are, the less economical is man as an agent of production' (ibid.: 530). Another argument in favour of subsistence level wages is the resulting greater elasticity of labour supply: 'the question of how closely the supply of labour responds to the demand for it, is . . . resolved into the question how great a part of the present consumption of the people at large consists of necessaries, strictly so called' (ibid.).

Overall, even though Marshall states his full acceptance of the marginal productivity theory of wages,[20] he cannot depart from a subsistence theory. He goes on at length parsimoniously listing the food and the non-food requirements of a representative working-class family in different categories of employment:

> the necessaries for the efficiency of an ordinary agricultural or of an unskilled town labourer and his family, in England, in this generation . . . consist of a well-drained dwelling with several rooms, warm clothing, with some changes of underclothing, pure water, a plentiful supply of cereal food, with a moderate allowance of meat and milk, and a little tea, etc., some education and some recreation, and lastly, *sufficient freedom for his wife from other work to enable her to perform properly her maternal and her household duties.* (ibid.: 69; emphasis added)[21]

Here Marshall is advocating a family wage, and subscribes entirely to the view that the nuclear family household with a specific sexual division of labour is the most efficient basic economic and reproduction unit in capitalist society.

The concept of 'necessaries' in Marshall's argument requires clarification. Why should it be a 'necessary' for the male worker that his wife be housebound?[22] And is it necessary for her? Does Marshall subscribe to Veblen's theory and suggest that workers should accede to leisure-class status by being able to afford and enjoy the luxury of the conspicuous leisure of the female household members? Far from it. This 'necessary' conveys a benefit to industrial society by ensuring full-time supervision of, and contribution to the human capital investment in working-class children, as well as a more efficient and economical use of the family income to reproduce the family members.

The 'necessaries' are socially determined. They comprise what is required – from the 'efficient' point of view of the capitalist's interests – to reproduce the labour power of the worker and the working class as a whole. They benefit the worker and his wife and children only in so far as he remains capable of earning a wage and in so far as the household is kept alive, and – for children – in so far as they will be able to work in the future.

One may wonder why Marshall takes such trouble determining exactly what the working-class family's consumption basket should hold. His concern raises the question of whether he believes that workers can act rationally and maximize their own welfare. Although he does not explicitly address that question, he seems to hold that workers would pursue their own enjoyment by, for instance, engaging in drinking and smoking, and will even 'sacrifice some things which are necessary for efficiency' to indulge in the 'consumption of alcohol and tobacco' (ibid.: 70). Such indulgence in wasteful commodities and frivolous expenses when access to luxury goods is permitted by the worker's wage level contradicts the interests of industrial society by rendering labour an uneconomical factor of production.

Consequently, workers have to be 'guided' towards the appropriate (non-wasteful) level of consumption and mix of consumption goods. To achieve this objective, wages have to be kept at the subsistence level required for efficiency – a level carefully calculated to cover the necessaries listed. This will ensure 'rational' spending by workers from the perspective of industrial society.

Working-class women are given even less opportunity to make their own utility-maximizing decisions. They are not even allowed to choose the type of economic activity they want to engage in and, should they – just in case – decide to become independent and seek employment, they would soon find that their wages could not assure their own subsistence. In short, women have access to the utility-maximizing marginal calculus only in so far as they have to allocate the meagre family budget among the various 'necessaries'.[23]

### Housework and the national dividend

While Marshall recognizes and commends the great skill deployed by the housewife in getting the greatest number of necessaries out of a thin budget, and while he maintains that women are more useful to a capitalist society as mothers and housewives than as wage workers, he evades both the issue of whether their household activities ought to be considered productive, and the question of the valuation of women's economic contribution to society.

'If we had to make a fresh start', states Marshall, 'it would be best to regard all labour as productive except that which failed to promote the aim towards which it was directed and so produced no utility' (ibid.:

65). However, he quickly abandons this concept and defines productive labour as labour which produces 'means of production and durable sources of enjoyment', or labour 'productive of necessaries', the latter being defined as 'all things required to meet wants which *must* be satisfied for existence and efficiency' (ibid.: 67–8).

Marshall also defines labour as any activity which contributes to 'income', and he notes that income can be defined in two ways. On the one hand, it can be understood in the wide sense, as real income, that includes 'all the benefits which mankind derive at any time from their efforts in the present, and in the past' (ibid.: 76). Under this definition, it is possible to recognize the social contribution of housework activities – a point Marshall acknowledges when he observes that, should a housewife work, 'the loss resulting from any consequent neglect by the wife from her household duties' must be deducted from the family income (ibid.: 556). On the other hand, income can be defined in the narrow sense, including only 'those incomings which are in the form of money' (ibid.: 71). By this definition, which Marshall (in deference to 'common practice') adopts, the contribution of housework cannot be recognized.

With respect to services performed for self (and presumably for one's household), Marshall observes that:

> no services that [a person] performs for himself are commonly reckoned as adding to his nominal income. But, though it is best generally to neglect them when they are trivial, account should for consistency be taken of them, when they are of a kind which people commonly pay for having done for them. (ibid.: 72)[24]

He does not address the question of whether all housework should be considered trivial (his example of a trivial service is the brushing of one's hat: 79n.), or whether it should be considered as a service commonly paid for. In fact, such service is 'commonly paid for' in the upper classes (where it is performed by domestics) but not in the lower classes. Perhaps this distinction is enough – for Marshall – to keep household services unacknowledged in the lower classes.

Be that as it may, the question of household activities' 'productiveness' does seem to trouble him. On the one hand, he does not hesitate to declare, in opposition to Adam Smith, that domestic workers are productive.[25] 'The work of domestic servants is always classed as "labour" in the technical sense . . . and can be assessed *en bloc* at the value of their remuneration in money and in kind', so it can be included in national income. At the same time, however, he notes that there is 'some inconsistency in omitting the heavy domestic work which is done

by women and other members of the household, where no servants are
kept' (ibid.: 79–80). He makes no attempt to resolve this inconsistency.
Rather than seeking to establish consistency between work performed
and goods and services produced, Marshall seeks to establish it by using
the mode of measurement of economic activity: by accounting for only
that which has a monetary counterpart.[26]

> It is best here to follow the *common practice*, and not count as part of the
> national income or dividend anything that is not *commonly* counted as part
> of the income of the individual. Thus . . . the services which a person renders
> to himself, and those which he renders gratuitously to members of his family
> or friends, the benefits which he derives from using his own personal goods,
> or public property . . . are not reckoned as parts of the national dividend,
> but are left to be accounted for separately. (ibid.: 524; emphasis added)

Unfortunately, Marshall does not indicate how all these services and
benefits can 'be accounted for separately' and his followers quickly
ignored this recommendation.

Notice that, in the end, Marshall abandons all pretence of 'scientific
method' in arriving at his national income accounting scheme. Instead
he is guided by the views of 'the world at large' and by 'popular
convention' as enshrined, in particular, in 'the practice of the [British]
income tax commissioners' (ibid.: 77–8) when determining what should
be included in the national income.[27] In this way Marshall helps to
institutionalize in marginalist literature, as well as in national and
international standards of income accounting, the exclusion from
consideration, in theory and practice, of an important share of total
production,[28] carried out for no monetary compensation by women in
the home.

Marshall's decision to follow the tax collectors and include in the
national dividend at least part of the value of household production in
the middle and upper classes – with the inclusion of domestics' income
in money and kind – and to exclude the value of that production when
it is carried out in households that cannot afford paid servants also
reveals a definite class bias. Services to bourgeois households are
recognized as being valuable to society while the services of working-
class women to the members of their households (and through them, to
capital) are not.

### Bourgeois Victorian values and the working class
The class bias is also present in Marshall's suggestion that what is
appropriate for middle-class and upper-class women (gentility, protection and, above all, being housebound) is also appropriate for

working-class women. It is present as well in his belief that working-class children should be cared for in the same manner as middle-class and upper-class children (with a great deal of individual attention), and that the standards of home care that apply in middle-class and upper-class households should apply in the working-class home.

In advocating the working-class woman's 'return' to the household, Marshall does not seem to worry about whether it is economically feasible for the working-class family to live on the single salary of the male member of the household. Indeed, at no point does he address the question of whether the wage levels extant at the time of his writing would 'permit' such a return. He never compares the 'going' level of men's wages to his notion of the appropriate family wage. He rather seems to assume that the housewife's skills will palliate the (inevitable, at least in the immediate term) decrease in family money income.[29]

When he argues that women and children should stay at home for the purpose of the future improvement in workers' welfare (and, of course, the future welfare of industry) he ignores the fact that this involves a cost in terms of the present welfare of the working-class family. The only costs he acknowledges are those incurred by industry losing a cheap supply of labour.

At the beginning of his *Principles*, Marshall argues that economists should not 'defend class privileges' (1930: 47); he declares that 'economic studies call for and develop the faculty of *sympathy*, and especially that rare sympathy which enables people to *put themselves in the place*, not only of their comrades, but also of other classes' (ibid.: 46; emphasis added). But can sympathy replace, in serious scientific inquiry, the *real practice* of attempting to feed a whole family on ten shillings a week?

The intent of Marshall's sympathy is specific: it is needed to study 'the ways in which the efficiency of a nation is strengthened by and strengthens the confidences and affections which hold together the members of each economic group – the family, employers and employees in the same business, citizens of the same country' (ibid.). One wonders if the expression of Marshall's sympathy – his defence of a subsistence wage and his prescription that working-class women should be made into unpaid servants to their class – will reassure the poor and the working class that he does not defend the interests of the capitalist class.

It is perhaps this 'sympathy' for members of the lower classes which guides Marshall in applying to them bourgeois standards. Such is Marshall's wish that the working class acquire 'the habit of distinctly realising the future' ('discounting the future at a low interest rate') as well as an eagerness to invest capital 'in' their children.

It seems that Marshall's use of such terminology as 'human' or 'personal' capital investment *in* human beings arises out of an attempt to apply a similar, 'symmetrical', theoretical approach to the two basic factors of production in the capitalist economy. Indeed, he contends that the two factors obey the same rules – rules which originate in the predominant social relations of the capitalist market.[30] The motivations of the owners of the two factors of production and their behaviour can, in Marshall's view, be treated in the same way since they arise from such market phenomena as demand, supply and prices. It is this 'symmetry' which provides the basis for the development of Marshall's 'human capital theory'.[31]

The similarity between the two factors, according to Marshall, is revealed by the 'general correspondence between the causes that govern the supply prices of material and personal capital':[32]

> Wages and other earnings of effort have much in common with interest on capital . . . the motives which induce a man to accumulate personal capital *in* his son's education are similar to those which control his accumulation of material capital *for* his son. (1930: 660–1)[33]

In his attempt to render the two factors of production identical, Marshall implies that *all* acts of investment are governed by a single motive: providing returns to the next generation (or, more precisely, to the male element of that generation). While the motive has to be such in the case of human capital, since the return of a wage reflecting the amount of education received accrues only to the 'son' of the investor, this is not the case for physical capital. Here, the investor can – and expects to – receive all the returns during his lifetime. The bequeathing of physical capital to one's son is an action separate, and which responds to a motivation different, from the action of investment proper. Indeed, there is sufficient motivation for capital investment in the prospect of immediate personal returns. The capitalist will invest regardless of whether he has a son to provide for.

Marshall is aware of this difference, and at one point he contradicts himself by saying that 'parents are governed by motives different from those which induce a capitalist undertaker to erect a new machine' (ibid.: 571). He also acknowledges that the inter-generational transfer necessarily involved in the case of human capital investment will generate a less than optimal level of human capital stock (ibid.: 560–1). This suboptimality also arises from the length of time required between the initial investment decision and the availability of the new skill developed (ibid.: 474). From all this, one can infer that the supplies of human and physical capital do not follow the same rules.

Moreover, Marshall is aware of another basic difference between the two factors, one which he sees as inherent in the human character of labour. '[H]uman agents of production are not bought and sold as machinery and other material agents of production are . . . the worker remains his own property' (ibid.: 560). From this perspective, it becomes doubtful whether the concept of investment is applicable at all to human beings.

**What returns for women?**
A final and, for the present purpose, most significant difference between human and physical capital – one which Marshall does not take into explicit account – is that all the transactions involved in physical capital investment are done through the capitalist market framework, whereas practically none of the elements of human capital investment, except the payment of a wage in exchange for work and skill once the investment has reached 'maturity', take place in the market. Along with this goes the complete absence of women as agents in physical capital investment while their role is of supreme importance in human capital formation.

Marshall is, characteristically, ambiguous on the exact role played by women in human capital investment. Whereas he clearly states that women have the duty of 'investing their efforts in the personal capital of their children' (ibid.: 685), and that 'the most precious part of the capital invested in human beings is the result of the care and influence of the mother' (ibid.: 564), he forgets all this when he compares human and physical capital. Here, the father 'works and waits' and invests *in* and *for* his son. Women, it seems, have no part in this process of working and waiting. The emphasis on the monetary element involved in 'investment' is decisive: since the mother does not 'work' to earn the family income, she is not seen to partake in the sacrifice involved in redirecting income from consumption to the children's education.

There is, of course, a definite 'cost' involved for the woman: she has to sacrifice, not only her consumption of goods bought out of the family budget, but also her whole being. She has to spend her whole life activity 'investing her efforts' in the human capital of her children. Her life and self-purpose is taken from her in the process. And, for that reason, it can be said that she bears the bulk of the costs involved in this 'investment'.

In terms of returns, it is clear that only male children (and capitalist employers) receive benefits from human capital investment, since only male children are called to become wage earners in Marshall's scheme. Female children must instead devote their adult life to the human capital investment of the next generation of males. Moreover, in

Marshall's writings, the form of human capital investment women receive does not yield them any 'real' return in the 'form of money'. Indeed, the only 'payment' associated with their efforts is self-denial.

If male workers get a return in the form of higher wages, industry also benefits from human capital investment by getting an improved, healthier, more skilled and adaptable supply of labour. In fact, in some cases, it seems that industry benefits more than workers do. As Marshall notes, an aggregate increase in human capital investment

> has resulted [in a] largely increased supply of trained abilities . . . but it has taken away from these trained abilities much of that scarcity value which they used to possess, and has lowered their earnings not indeed absolutely, but relatively to the general advance; and it has caused many occupations, which not long ago were accounted skilled and which are still spoken of as skilled, *to rank with unskilled labour as regards wages.* (ibid.: 681–2; emphasis added)

While capital was supplied in the process with increased quantities of skilled labour at a lower relative wage, it is not clear that the workers benefited, since their wages failed to increase proportionately with the increase in their human capital. As for the parents of these workers, it seems that they 'worked and waited' to see capital subsidized by their own earnings.

To recapitulate, in Marshall's scheme of human capital investment, fathers are seen to be the main investors but mothers happen to bear a large share of the investment cost; male children are seen to receive the returns but capital potentially receives a large proportion of these returns; women get no return from the human capital invested in them, and *a fortiori* from that they invest in their children; their sole reward for a life of toil is virtue and abnegation; men do bear some of the costs of investment and they do receive some of the benefits on an inter-generational basis; capital bears none of the costs, or only in so far as some of the training may happen on the shop floor; its labour costs are subsidized by the workers, but it gets benefits from a more productive workforce – this, however, is not seen by Marshall, as his marginalist myopia leads him to recognize only the factor returns going to the individual factor owners.[34]

In this chapter we have seen how Alfred Marshall, the leading British economist of his time and a founder of the marginalist school, approaches the questions of women's role in the economy and of the production of the factor labour. It is clear that he not only subscribes to Victorian ideology but also contributes directly to its propagation by

offering economic justifications for seemingly purely social propositions.

He proposes and justifies the extension of the Victorian bourgeois
sexual division of labour to the working class and to the poor. Working-
class women are assigned to the home to nurture male human capital
while men have to earn a 'family wage' in the labour market. In
addition, a national human capital investment policy and a minimum
wage policy are advocated. But the economic justification advanced by
Marshall for these proposals does not focus on the maximization of
individual utility and on the returns to individual factors of production.
What is stressed is the economic benefit arising from such policies for
capitalist society as a whole.

In a striking departure from the *laissez-faire* dogma that permeated
the economic doctrines of his time, Marshall supports existing state
intervention in the economy and advances and constructs new proposals
to expand such intervention into the autonomy of the labour market,
into the autonomy of the family and of individuals, and into the
mechanisms of determination and distribution of incomes. His
proposals contribute to the development and reinforcement of socioeconomic structures based on the institution of the nuclear family and
on the economic dependence of women within that family – structures
wherein appeals to 'duty' rather than 'economic motivation' serve as a
basis for the allocation of women's labour to assigned activities.

In Marshall's *Principles*, beneath the image of weakness and gentility
projected on to working-class women – following the model set in higher
classes – appears a heavy taxing of their life activity. This activity
appears to contribute nothing to the national dividend,[35] whereas his
entire human capital investment mechanism is fundamentally dependent upon its performance. Under the guise of protection, women are
assigned to the home and given a major responsibility of care for the
family and human capital investment in children while constrained by
a budget set at the minimum level for capitalist efficiency. And even
though this requires a skilled exercise of economic rationality, women
are not considered by Marshall to be economic beings.

It might be that the question of whether women are economic beings
is irrelevant to Marshall because he carefully removes them from the
economic sphere (as defined by economists) and turns them, in this
theory, from economic *actors* into mere *parameters* in the decisions
taken by other economic agents. It is more likely, however, that
Marshall's position results from his careful calculation of the most
economical (from whose point of view?) place for women in capitalist
society.

**Notes**

1.  A slightly modified version of this chapter appeared in the *Cambridge Journal of Economics* (Pujol, 1984).
2.  'Scientific inquiries are to be arranged with reference not to the practical aim which they subserve, but to the nature of the subjects with which they are concerned' (Marshall, 1930: 39).
3.  'The *raison d'être* of economics as a separate science is that it deals chiefly with that part of man's action which is most under the control of measurable motives; and which therefore lends itself better than any other to systematic reasoning and analysis' (1930: 38–9).
4.  This contradiction to the cornerstone of marginalist economics will be rationalized by Becker (1976, 1981a).
5.  'In a sense there are only two agents of production, nature and man. Capital and organisation are the results of the work of man aided by nature' (1930: 139).
6.  It is interesting to note here that Marshall's argument about the education of workers leads him to speculate on a transformation of the class structure of society and the feasibility of 'worker self-management': 'Ought we to rest content with the existing form of division of labour? Is it necessary that large numbers of people should be exclusively occupied with work that has no elevating character? Is it possible to educate gradually among the great mass of workers a new capacity for the higher kinds of work; and in particular for undertaking cooperatively the management of the business in which they are themselves employed? (1930: 4). He does not answer these questions.
7.  'The professional classes especially, while generally eager to save some capital *for* their children, are even more on the alert for opportunities of investing *in* them' (1930: 562).
8.  'Most parents are willing enough to do for their children what their own parents did for them; and perhaps even to go a little beyond it. But to do more than this requires, in addition to the moral qualities of unselfishness and a warmth of affection that are perhaps not rare, a certain habit of mind which is as yet not very common. It requires the habit of distinctly realising the future, of regarding a distant event as of nearly the same importance as if it were close at hand' (1930: 216–17).
9.  Contrast the above statement with the following methodological remark: 'It must . . . always be remembered that though observation or history may tell us that one event happened at the same time as another, or after it, they cannot tell us whether the first was the cause of the second . . . wider experience, more careful inquiry, may show that the causes to which the event is attributed could not have produced it unaided; perhaps even that they hindered the event, which was brought about in spite of them by other causes that have escaped notice' (1930: 774).
10. Marshall himself benefited from the nurturing and the building of a 'true home' by his wife Mary Paley Marshall. According to Keynes, '[d]uring forty-seven years of married life his dependence upon her devotion was complete. Her life was given to him and to his work' (in Pigou, 1956: 15). And elsewhere: 'Neither in Alfred's lifetime or afterwards did she ever ask, or expect, anything for herself' (Keynes, 1944: 276).
11. Marshall notes here that great men had great mothers: 'an earnest mother leads her child to feel deeply about great things; and a thoughtful mother does not repress, but encourages that childish curiosity which is the raw material of scientific habits of thought' (1930: 207n.).
12. This applies to both male and female children. The educational investment in the male child is to prepare him for industrial work, the investment in the female child to prepare her for the future duties of housewife and mother. Marshall did not agree that women should have the same educational opportunities as men. Edgeworth points out in his 'Reminiscences' of Alfred Marshall that 'concern for the practice of family duties was the ground of Marshall's opposition to the granting of degrees

to women' in a submission Marshall made to the Cambridge Senate in 1896 (in Pigou, 1956: 72).

The paradox in this is that Mary Paley Marshall was one of the first women to receive an education at Cambridge (Marshall taught her economics) and taught economics to women at Oxford and Cambridge (Newnham College) after marrying Marshall. She also co-authored with him the book *Economics of Industry*, which she had actually been commissioned to write. Marshall opposed the reprinting of the book. Keynes comments: 'It was, in fact, an extremely good book; nothing more serviceable for its purpose was produced for many years, if ever. I know that my father always felt that there was something ungenerous in Marshall's distaste for this book, which was originally hers, but was allowed to go out of print without a murmur of complaint from her when there was still a strong demand for it' (Keynes, 1944: 274–5).

By 1896, Marshall had come 'increasingly to the conclusion that there was nothing useful to be made of women's intellect' (Keynes, 1944: 276). Yet all his life he benefited from the partnership, advice and help (particularly for the proof-reading and indexing of his writings) of his educated and intelligent companion, 'without whose understanding and devotion his work would not have fulfilled its fruitfulness' (Keynes, 1944: 268).

13.  This quotation actually refers to the 'virtue' of employers who undertake to train their workers to new skills while knowing that they will not keep all the returns from their investment (other employers will benefit). Marshall does not even acknowledge the similar (and greater) 'virtue' of women who are called upon to sacrifice their self-interest for the future of their children and to expect no return whatsoever from their 'investment'.

14.  But, according to the hypothesis of a backward-bending supply curve for labour, low wages could in fact induce women to spend even more time in the job market.

15.  Marshall, in the same argument, and for similar reasons, opposes high relative wages for children: they would deter school attendance and human capital investment. However, unlike women, children are eventually to benefit from abstention from work, through higher future earnings.

16.  Women's income is precisely what Harriet Martineau (and other feminists) had in mind when opposing the Acts. Although Marshall never conducts specific calculations to verify the gain in production that is supposed to result from keeping women and children away from employment, he tries to discredit the opponents of the Factory Acts, and in particular Harriet Martineau. Marshall proclaims that her position is prompted by her ignorance of economics: 'Miss Martineau was not an economist in the *proper* sense of the word: she confessed that she never read more than one chapter of an economic book at a time before writing a story to illustrate economic principles, *for fear that pressure on her mind should be too great*; and before her death she expressed a just doubt whether the principles of economics (as understood by her) had any validity' (1930: 763n.; emphasis added). Curiously, Marshall's treatment of Martineau grew harsher with time. In the earlier editions of the *Principles*, he quotes Martineau's own words: 'In order to save my nerves from being overwhelmed by the thought of what I had undertaken, I resolved not to look beyond the department on which I was engaged' (1961, II: 759). His paraphrasing and interpretation of that quote from the fifth edition is an attempt to discredit her completely. Curiously, he never formulated similarly scathing commentaries on J. S. Mill's or N. Senior's opposition to the Factory Acts.

17.  *The Economics of Industry* was first published in 1879 whereas the first edition of the *Principles* appeared in 1890. In contrast with the later developed opinions of Marshall on women's education, this early work identifies the education of women as one element that will fit 'women to do more difficult work . . . making them more ready to demand, and employers more ready to grant them higher wages for it' (1881: 176).

18. Pigou states this more explicitly than Marshall: 'women are the less likely to work at industry the more money their husbands are earning'. He thus makes men's wages one of the arguments in his mathematical formulation of women's labour supply (1960: 565–6; see below, Ch.10).
19. See also 'the income of any class in the ranks of industry is below its *necessary* level, when any increase in their income would in the course of time produce a more than proportionate increase in their efficiency. . . . any stinting of necessaries is wasteful' (1930: 69).
20. For instance 'every worker will in general be able with the earnings of a hundred days' labour to buy the net product of a hundred days' labour of other workers in the same grade with himself' (1930: 539).
21. In a footnote, Marshall further evaluates the necessaries for different classes of households: 'the strict necessaries for an average agricultural family are covered by fifteen or eighteen shillings a week. . . . For the unskilled labourer in the town, a few shillings must be added. . . . For the family of the skilled workman living in town, we may take twenty-five or thirty shillings for strict necessaries. . . . For a man whose brain has to undergo great and continuous strain, the strict necessaries are perhaps two hundred or two hundred and fifty pounds per year if he is a bachelor' (1930: 70n.).
22. Presumably, the 'sufficient freedom for his wife from other work' enters into the worker's consumption and utility function, and is hence the object of a utility-maximizing decision on his part, but Marshall does not explore this point.
23. It is thus ironic that Marshall uses the particular example of a 'primitive housewife' allocating yarn between different uses to illustrate the principle of utility maximization at the margin. He clarifies that this 'illustration belongs indeed properly to domestic production rather than to domestic consumption' (1930: 117).
24. Elsewhere, Marshall considers the situation where 'a landowner with an annual income of £10,000, hires a secretary at a salary of £500, who hires a servant at wages of £50'. All of these incomes are to be included in the net national income without encountering the problem of double counting because they represent real services performed. 'But if the landlord makes an allowance of £500 to his son, that must not be counted as an independent income; because no services are rendered for it' (1930: 80). Unfortunately, Marshall does not consider the situation of services rendered without monetary compensation in the home (housework, child-rearing, etc.) nor does he even consider the case where the landlord gives an allowance to his wife. Here, would Marshall argue that the wife, like the son, renders or performs no 'real services' for the landlord and, hence, her allowance should not be counted as income?
25. Is it because they receive a wage?
26. Other non-monetary incomes he includes in national income are, besides payments in kind to domestics, the services rendered by a house to its owner, and the production for use by farm households.
27. In so doing, Marshall forgets that the purpose of the income tax commissioners, meeting the revenue needs of the British state, in no way guarantees the appropriateness of that practice to the theoretical needs of economic analysis. Indeed, had economic theorists consistently deferred to such 'common conventions' in their analytical constructions, the discipline would – by its own standards of scientificity – be nothing but mere collection of superstitious beliefs.
28. Recent surveys estimate that housework (often narrowly defined) yields a total product equivalent to 30–40 per cent of total GNP depending on estimate methods. It is likely that, in Marshall's time, housework probably yielded an even greater total product in relation to the GNP. See Vandelac (1985) for an excellent analysis of the issue of domestic production in capitalist society, in national income accounts and in economic theory.
29. Marshall could have argued that the decrease in the supply of labour caused by the

withdrawal of women and children from the labour market should induce a rise in men's wages; but he does not.

30. It is obvious that the treatment is actually not symmetrical but biased, since a capital-oriented terminology is applied to labour. Could the bias have been inverse? Probably not. Marshall here is merely being a 'reflector' of the tendency of capital to objectify labour, to appropriate it, to dominate and control it, to transform it into part of itself, to subsume labour. Hence, the 'essential' intent of Marshall's human capital theory is not only to fit labour into a capital framework, but also to transform it ultimately into capital.

31. Although Marshall is a precursor of the modern human capital theorists, his approach is slightly different to that of Becker. For Becker, human capital is an asset for a sole individual, its owner, while Marshall has the more classical view that human capital (population, labour force) is an asset to a particular country, a social asset. Becker denies the existence of externalities in the cost of production of and the returns from human capital. For him, all costs are borne by the individual (forgone earnings) and all benefits (income streams) accrue to him/her. By contrast, Marshall acknowledges the existence of externalities arising from the social and human character of the 'asset', regardless of how these externalities might be confusing for his treatment and might lead to inconsistencies in his paradigm. Thus he jettisons the assumption of selfishness to explain the inter-generational transfers of welfare, and abandons the notion that individuals – as opposed to families – are the basic economic units. Becker retains the assumptions of individualism and selfishness, and attempts to generate consistency within his model by introducing psychic, non-consumption-induced benefits to parents as a motivation for the sacrifices of consumption-oriented welfare by the present generation (Becker, 1964, 1976, 1981a and b).

32. Does Marshall mean that the supply price of capital is also governed by the 'cost of rearing, training and sustaining [its] energy' (1930: 532), that is, its subsistence level of consumption?

33. This point is further developed by Marshall when he applies to this matter his own view of economic gradualism: 'There is a continuous transition from the father who works and waits in order that he may bequeath to his son a rich and firmly established manufacturing or trading business, to the one who works and waits in order to support his son while he is slowly acquiring a thorough medical education, and ultimately to buy for him a lucrative practice . . . to one who works and waits in order that his son may stay long at school' (1930: 661). These 'continuous transitions' permit Marshall a wide generalization of investment behaviour across social classes. At all levels of society, fathers 'work and wait' – even if there is more 'waiting' at the top and more 'working' at the bottom. This generalization gives the appearance that the sacrifices of all fathers are of the same 'essential nature' and magnitude.

34. The question raised by this complicated system of welfare transfer is: how can the appropriate level of human capital investment be ensured? Given that the recipients of benefits and returns differ from those who bear the costs, and that most of the 'investment activity' does not happen through a market, marginal calculations and market mechanisms cannot be relied upon to yield this appropriate level. This leads to some considerations of state intervention through the education system and its state financing, factory legislation, minimum wages laws and through these, the setting and maintenance of an adequate family structure. State involvement indicates that the social benefits from such a scheme are greater than individual benefits.

35. But then, how does one compute the value of virtue?

# 9 The 'violent paradoxes' of A. C. Pigou: Pigouvian exploitation and women's wages

A student of Alfred Marshall, Arthur Cecil Pigou succeeded him in the Chair of Economics at Cambridge University. Pigou further developed his teacher's approach to the study of national wealth and welfare and elaborated, in his *Economics of Welfare*,[1] the first systematic approach to what has now become the field of welfare economics.

Pigou defines 'economic welfare' as 'the subject matter of economic science' (11). His goal in *The Economics of Welfare* is 'to study certain important groups of causes that affect economic welfare in actual modern societies'. Some 'elements' of welfare, however, are quite subjective, 'states of consciousness', and, for the purpose of 'scientific inquiry', Pigou finds it 'necessary to limit our subject matter' to ensure quantitative measurement is possible. Therefore economic welfare becomes only 'that part of social welfare that can be brought directly or indirectly into relation with the measuring rod of money' (ibid.).

For Pigou, the quantitative analytical unit which represents the total economic welfare of a nation is the national dividend, 'that part of the objective income of the community which can be measured in money' (ibid.: 31). Having asserted that total welfare is directly correlated with economic welfare,[2] he enjoins policy-makers to be concerned with a single goal: the maximization of the national dividend. Under the guidance of this sole concern, his treatise

> seeks to bring into clearer light some of the ways in which it now is, or eventually may become, feasible for governments to control the play of economic forces in such wise as to promote the economic welfare, and through that, the total welfare, of their citizens as a whole. (ibid.: 129–30)

In the opening discussion, Pigou speculates on the *probability* that economic and social welfare would be affected in similar ways by particular events. Yet, in the above quote, he forgets that such parallelism was speculation on his part and asserts that actions by governments to 'promote economic welfare' will also improve 'the total welfare of their citizens as a whole'. In this he does not consider the possibility that increased welfare for 'citizens as a whole' might be obtained at the cost of reduced welfare for minority groups among them. Nor does he explore the implications of such a situation given that individual states of welfare cannot be compared or ranked. It is in Pigou's treatment of women's economic and social activity in particular that certain problems inherent in this generalization become apparent.

To correct the imperfections of the market system and to give direction to state policy-makers, Pigou devises a blueprint for a state-administered welfare system and constructs an economic rationale for each specific component of this system. His proposals include attempts to counter the harmful effects of market power and to modify the distribution of income in favour of the lowest income classes in society. Here, state intervention is oriented towards assuring 'fair' payments for the resources supplied on the market by these classes. Where payment is already fair, or where it is absent, the state is to set up programmes designed to bring living standards up to a 'living' level and to enhance the market productivity of these classes. This social 'human capital' policy is necessary, Pigou contends, in order to redress the inadequate level of 'investment' in the productivity of the poor caused by discrepancies in social and private costs and benefits in the production of human resources.

Women have a distinct role in Pigou's blueprint. They are presumed to contribute more to the achievement of an optimal state of economic welfare by restricting themselves to the roles of housewife and mother, in charge of the welfare, health and education of their families, rather than by being employed in the labour market, contributing directly to the national dividend.[3] It is this overall theme which informs Pigou's treatment of women's economic activity.

The following analysis of Pigou's welfare system continues into Chapter 10. In this chapter the focus is on his treatment of women's employment in the labour market and, in particular, on the questions of the wages paid to women and their access to employment opportunities. In Chapter 10 women's place in Pigou's welfare system as a whole is assessed.

Pigou devotes a good deal of space in *The Economics of Welfare* to the analysis of unequal wages for men and women – indeed a lot more space than allocated by earlier economists in their main theoretical works. In addition, he wrote an essay, 'Men's and Women's Wages' (Pigou, 1952).

The study of Pigou's concept of 'fair wages' and its application to women allows us to test the internal consistency of his marginalist approach. His treatment of the case of women's wages will be found opportunistic rather than rigorous, informed by a sexist bias which leads him to predetermined theoretical positions and contradictory policy recommendations.

### Fair and unfair wages

In *The Economics of Welfare*, Pigou begins his discussion of women's wages with the statement:

> The common idea is that women are normally paid less than men because men's wages have, in general to support a family while women's wages have only to support themselves. This is very superficial. (p. 565)

Wages, he maintains, are based on marginal productivity, not on subsistence requirements:

> Whatever methods [of remuneration] are adopted in any industry, the general tendency of economic forces will be to cause the wages offered for each class of workpeople to approximate . . . to the value of marginal social net product of that class. (p. 473)

However, real life may stray from this general tendency and wages might differ from the value of the marginal product of the worker. For policy purposes, Pigou differentiates between fair and unfair wages in such cases.

'Fair wages' result from (1) the payment of wages 'to workpeople in all places and occupations . . . equal to the value of the marginal net product of their work', and (2) 'the distribution of all grades of workpeople among different occupations . . . such as to maximise the national dividend' (p. 549). Wages are fair when they 'are proportioned to "efficiency"; the efficiency of a worker being measured by his net product conceived as marginal, multiplied by the price of that product' (p. 550).[4]

Pigou identifies two types of 'unfair wages'. The first is when, even 'though they are equal to the value of the marginal net product of the labour' in a particular 'place or occupation', they are not 'equal to the value of the marginal net product, and, therefore, to the wage rate, of similar labour assembled elsewhere' (p. 551). Note here that Pigou's definition of 'unfair wages' implies comparison with marginal productivity wages as they are determined 'elsewhere' in the overall labour market for the particular type of labour considered (pp. 813–14). This concept is illustrated in Fig. 9.1.

For 'similar labour', $S_N$ and $S_L$ are, respectively the national and local supply curves of labour, $D_N$ and $D_L$ the national and local demand curves. $W_L$, the local, marginal productivity wage is 'unfair' because lower than $W_N$, which is the nationally determined 'fair' wage. Among

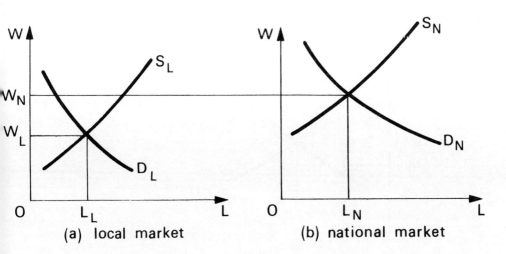

*Figure 9.1 Unfair wages*

specific groups he identifies as receiving unfair wages, Pigou lists women workers who, because they are tied to their family, display little geographic mobility; and also 'married women or widows' who engage in homework because they 'are tied by the non-economic compulsion of family cares' (p. 553).

As Pigou's main concern is for the impact on the national dividend of any interference with market forces, he advocates no intervention in this case, as wages result from localized market conditions.

The second case of unfair wages involves 'exploitation': where 'workpeople are exploited in the sense that they are paid less than the value which their marginal product has to the firms employing them' (p. 551). The concept of 'Pigouvian exploitation' involves a comparison between the workers' wages and the value of their marginal net product. It is not a relative concept like the preceding case of 'unfair wages'. Pigou illustrates exploitation as shown in Figure 9.2.

S and D being respectively the supply and demand for labour, the market equilibrium wage $W_M$ is a marginal productivity wage. OM is the quantity of labour hired at this wage. According to Pigou, 'there is necessarily exploitation if the employers succeed in paying a wage less than PM'. If 'they succeed in paying a wage RM' [and] obtain an amount of labour represented by OM', then the measure of *unfairness* in the wage is the excess of PM over RM', but the measure of *exploitation* is the excess of KM' over RM'' (p. 814).[5]

Pigou argued that, once established in an industry, exploitative

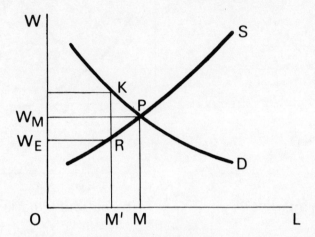

*Figure 9.2   Pigouvian exploitation*

situations, which result in higher than normal profit levels, tend to perpetuate themselves due to the character of the labour supply found in such industries. In this regard, he sees women and children as particularly vulnerable to 'exploitation': their relatively new or temporary attachment to the workforce or to a particular workplace makes them less likely to 'combine' to obtain wages 'corresponding' to the value of their marginal product (p. 559).[6]

In the case of 'exploitation', Pigou approves of intervention to raise wages to the level of the value of marginal product. This is 'desirable' because exploitation generates a suboptimal allocation of resources for a number of reasons: most workers refuse such exploitative employment, causing a lower than normal supply of labour to the exploitative industries; the workers accepting such employment are not mobile and/ or do not have bargaining power (here, the case of women and children is referred to); a higher than normal profit rate in these industries maintains 'in business' 'incompetent or badly situated employers'; and the capital–labour ratio is lower than the optimal level (pp. 562–3).

After analysing these two general exceptions to fair wages, Pigou states that his discussion up to this point was of 'quite general application'. But he adds: 'there still remains a special problem arising out of *the relation between men's wages and women's wages*' (p. 564; his emphasis). For him, what makes the problem 'special' is that women cannot be treated as normal workers. The two categories of unfair wages reviewed so far cannot, therefore, provide an adequate analytical framework for their special case.

## 'Fair wages for women'
When he addresses the case of women's wages, the ground of Pigou's discussion of 'fair wages' shifts. The special category of 'fair wages for women', is fabricated by the economist. 'It may happen that women's wages in some place or occupation are fair relatively to women's wages in other places or occupations, but unfair relatively to men's wages in that place or occupation' (ibid.).

The definition of fair wages, which seemed to be universal up to this point – applying to 'workpeople in all places or occupations' – must in fact be understood as applying within specific, separate groups of workers – in this case working men and working women – each group commanding a different level of 'fair wages'.[7]

Pigou discusses the 'special problem' of men's and women's wages by focusing on the 'marginal occupations' in which men's and women's efficiencies have the same relation as their respective day wages. In these occupations, 'the efficiency wages of the two sexes are equal' which 'means, with certain allowances, equality of piece-wages' (p. 567).[8] However, this situation is not seen as 'fair' in all senses: women's wages are 'unfairly high' compared to women's wages elsewhere but fair compared to men's wages in the same occupation.

The 'play of economic forces' does not always bring about this outcome 'in real life'. Thus,

> in particular occupations employers may pay to women workers an efficiency wage, which, though fair relative to women's wages elsewhere, is less than the efficiency wage they are paying to men workers, and yet may still employ some men. They may do this either for a short time, while they are in process of substituting the one sex for the other; or for a long time, because trade union pressure or customs either compels the retention of some men, or vetoes the entry of more than a limited number of women. (pp. 568–9)[9]

When this is the case, Pigou asks: 'is the claim "equal pay for workers of equal efficiency" justified? In what way would interference to raise the women's efficiency wage to the level of the men's affect the national dividend?' (p. 569). Nothing will happen to the national dividend if 'neither the number of women attached to the occupation . . . nor the number of women employed there' changes. Pigou estimates that 'this, however, is a very improbable state of affairs'.

On the one hand, even if there is no change in the number of women employed in the occupation, more women, attracted by the higher wages, will acquire skills for – and hence become attached to – this occupation. These skills will be wasted and the national dividend will suffer from the misallocation of resources (p. 569).[10]

On the other hand, it is likely that employers will refrain from hiring more women into the occupation given the change in the comparative efficiency–wage ratio of the two sexes. The major incentive for employers, the financial advantage afforded by the hiring of women workers, will have disappeared.

> [T]o compel the payment to [women] of an efficiency wage equal to that paid to men in occupations which they are seeking to enter, and in which such a rate would give them higher earnings than similar women can obtain elsewhere, must obstruct their entry directly or indirectly by relaxing employers' efforts to break down the customs and rules that hinder it. (pp. 569–70)

Consequently, women lose employment opportunities.

Pigou extends this argument to the non-marginal occupations where women have an efficiency advantage. There, the payment to women of a wage reflecting their comparative efficiency would hinder their employment in these occupations and hence the national dividend. What he seems to suggest here is that employers would switch to relatively less efficient men. Pigou concludes that: 'interference designed to enforce the payment to them [women] of a "fair" wage, as compared with the wages paid to men, in circumstances where this means an unfairly high wage as compared with women's wages elsewhere, would injure the national dividend' (p. 570).[11]

The difference between the discussion of men's and women's wages and that of the two general cases of unfair wages reviewed earlier is striking. Indeed, Pigou does not specifically relate the two. He shifts the basis for determination of fairness and unfairness from the nature of the labour market in specific industries and occupations to the gender of the workers. Hence, instead of a single level of 'fair wages' for the workers in a particular industry or occupation, there is now one for each sex.

Pigou never refers to women's wages as simply 'unfair' – which would imply that the definitions established earlier apply – but always as 'unfair relative to men's wages', or 'unfairly high relative to women's wages elsewhere'. He also never addresses the question of whether 'exploitation' is involved in the case of women workers. This is curious because it is clear from his definition of exploitation that women who get lower wages than men when they display equal efficiency *are exploited* (whether the men themselves are paid a fair wage or not, women are paid *less*. Yet, no intervention is recommended. On the contrary, Pigou argues that a policy of equal wages for equal efficiency will in fact cause harm to the national dividend – an argument entirely inconsistent with his treatment of exploitation.

Pigou's argument against equal wages for equal efficiency is very weak. It is based entirely on his speculations on changes in the level of women's employment if their wages were raised to the level of men's. These speculations do not take into account the overall conditions of the supply of labour. Pigou also does not consider the negative impact on economic welfare of payments to factors below the value of their marginal product – something he is keen to point out in other instances. As well, he disregards the potential social and individual, short- and long-run, benefits of higher wage employment for women and only takes into account the short-run, supposedly negative, impact of an equal pay policy.[12] Finally, he limits his speculations on the impact of an equal pay policy to its implementation in a single industry or occupation, which, for obvious reasons, is inadequate.

But the most remarkable argument advanced by Pigou against equal pay is that in which he quotes Cannan, who asserts: 'the most powerful lever for increasing the opportunities of women is taken away if they are not allowed to do the work cheaper' (p. 569). Here, unequal pay for equal efficiency is seen as a necessary condition for women's entry into fields of employment from which, due to customs, traditions or trade union resistance, they have been excluded. The existence of these barriers is not questioned, so the perpetuation of a status quo of unequal pay is made to appear as beneficial to women. But the only benefit women derive from it is that of being exploited (in the Pigouvian sense) not just in the short run (upon entry in a particular industry), but for ever.

Pigou's conclusion is that keeping women's wages lower than men's is welfare maximizing. But one must ask: 'whose welfare is maximized?' We can be sure that the employers of women who reap perennially higher than normal profits benefit from this situation.

As noted earlier, Pigou ruled out the proposition that women's wages were lower than men's because of women's lower subsistence needs. He proposed instead that the value of their marginal product was the determinant of their wages. Yet his discussion of fair wages for men and women suggests that women's wages are not necessarily based on their marginal productivity. The question we must consider then is: how are women's wages determined in Pigou's economic theory?

For him, demand and supply factors 'together govern and determine the relation between the general level of wages per day paid to representative members of the two sexes' (p. 566). In focusing on 'day wages' paid to 'representative' men and women, Pigou departs from the concept of efficiency wage (based on individual marginal productivity), or individual fair wages. Day wages are market wages, and different equilibrium levels of day wages obtain for men and women. The determining factors for women's day wages are, on the demand side, women's productivity levels and the 'value of a woman' to employers, and on the supply side, the elements influencing the labour force participation of women.

**Productivity**
Pigou does not carry out a thorough investigation of women's productivity. Instead he consistently asserts that women are generally less productive than men and lists a number of reasons why he believes this to be true.

The type of work which women do is classified as unskilled, as in the case of 'simple sewing at home' (p. 607),[13] and women are concentrated in low-productivity trades or industries, 'in which even the normal so-called able-bodied workers are of an exceedingly low grade' (p. 607), and where work does not 'provide persons of average capacity in full employment . . . with fairly adequate earnings' (p. 723).

Pigou advances another reason for women's low productivity: their 'primary role' as housewives and mothers.[14] 'Women, *looking forward as they do*, to matrimony and a life in the home, are not trained to industry as men are, and do not devote to it that period of their lives when they are strongest and most capable' (p. 564; emphasis added). Here, Pigou blames women, '*who do not expect* to continue in industry after marriage' (p. 559), for their lack of training, their low productivity and their low wages. He implies that women simply choose home over employment and hence do not acquire the skills and training appropriate for better-paying jobs.

He identifies a specific life-cycle of labour force participation for women. They leave employment upon marriage; some may return to the labour force in the older age groups as a result of widowhood (p. 564). Like today's neoclassical economists, Pigou uses this pattern to 'explain', or rather justify, women's low productivity levels and low employment income. And, like them, he does not take into account the structural and economic factors which dictate this particular labour force behaviour to women.[15]

While he attributes this outcome to women's decisions, it is clear that Pigou does not disapprove of their behaviour. Women are, in his view, needed more by society in the home as reproducers than in the factories as producers, especially during 'that period of their lives when they are strongest and most capable' (ibid.).

Pigou concludes his observations on women's pattern of labour force behaviour as follows: 'In these circumstances, even though women's endowments of mind and muscle were equal to men, which, on the average they are not, it would be surprising if their day wages were not lower' (ibid.). This reveals that, for him, women's lack of continuous involvement in the labour force is secondary to what he sees as the real reason for women's lower productivity: they are inferior to men, not only in physical strength but also in mental ability. At no point does he advance proofs for this assertion.

This belief biases Pigou's analysis of wage differences between men and women. Here, he uses the argument of the *average* endowments and abilities of women relative to men to account for *universal* differences in wages between the two sexes. This allows him to incorporate commonplace prejudices on women's productive ability directly in his discussion. By building his 'analysis' of women's wages on the basis of the fictional 'average' or 'representative woman', he sets the stage for a justification of 'fair wages for women' which are universally lower than 'fair wages for men', his position being that they are determined on the basis of the presumed lower average level of productive efficiency of women compared to men, regardless of the individuals' own relative endowments and abilities. This, of course, contradicts Pigou's general definition of 'fair wages', which is based on the value of the individual worker's marginal product.

In the essay 'Men's and Women's Wages' (Pigou, 1952), which is based on Pigou's submission to the 1946 Royal Commission on Equal Pay, his bias on women's productivity becomes entrenched in the model he constructs to determine whether men and women ought to receive equal pay. At the start, Pigou advises the commissioners to consider

> only the relation between men's and women's wages – the significance for wage rates of maleness and femaleness as such. A method of approach is therefore, legitimate . . . the device, namely, of thinking away all differences save this particular difference . . . to construct for ourselves a model world in which all men are exactly alike and so are all women . . . in spite of the fact that the actual world is made up of a great variety of different sorts of men and different sorts of women. For it is only the differences between the sexes, not the differences within the sexes that concern us. (1952: 218)

Pigou then presents a model where, 'since all men . . . are exactly alike, men's weekly wages are the same in all centres where they are employed; and similarly women's wages are the same in all centres where they are employed' (ibid.: 219). Having assumed homogeneity of characteristics within each sex, a uniform wage rate for each sex follows axiomatically.

Hence, a model is constructed where the average is made universal, where all men are assumed to possess a particular level of skills and productivity and all women another – no doubt lower, since Pigou believes their endowments and abilities to be lower 'on the average' than men's. It is not surprising that Pigou should infer from such a model findings that precisely reproduce the bias inherent in the starting assumptions.[16]

This leads him to ignore those specific 'real world' cases (which may not be a negligible occurrence) which stand in direct contradiction to his model. In particular, since he never relaxes his 'simplifying' assumptions, Pigou avoids dealing analytically with the cases of women receiving lower wages than men while displaying equal or superior productivity. Pigou's approach brings him to the conclusion that women's lower wages are justified. But, rather than being based on realistic observation, it is the product of his biased caricature of reality.

His assumptions and the conclusions they inspire are apparently shared by employers who, it seems, judge the productive capacity of a prospective female employee and base hiring decisions and the determination of pay levels on the presumed average characteristics of women as opposed to the specific characteristics of the applicant herself.[17] Such apparent behaviour of employers is given credibility by Pigou's analysis, regardless of its merit. This is further enhanced when he adds another element to his theory of demand for women's labour: 'the value of a woman' to the employer.

**'The value of a woman to the employer'**
In *The Economics of Welfare*, employers' decisions to hire are, seemingly, solely based on the comparative efficiency of employees. The employer allegedly compares the ratio of men's and women's efficiencies to the ratio $W_M/W_F$ of the day wages of the 'representative men' and the 'representative women'.[18] Thus,

> men alone are employed in all occupations where the ratio of their efficiency to women's efficiency exceeds the ratio of their day wages to women's day wages; women alone in all occupations in opposite case; and men and women indifferently in the marginal occupations in which their respective efficiencies bear to one another the same ratio as their respective day wages. (1960: 567)[19]

While, according to Pigou's analysis, in these 'marginal occupations . . .

the efficiency wages of the two sexes are equal', he indicates that they may not be equal in practice. Consequently, he introduces some extra-economic elements to justify wage differences which are not based on productivity differences:

> In these marginal occupations . . . equality of efficiency wages means, with certain allowances, equality of piece wages. The principal allowances are, first, a small extra for men, because, since, at need, they can be put on night work and can be sworn at more comfortably, it is rather more convenient to employ them. (ibid.)[20]

Pigou does not make clear exactly how the 'bonus' men receive for being more 'convenient' employees than women is determined. It does seem that this bonus would set men's rate above the level called for by their marginal product, at a level where the employer's profit is not maximized. Alternatively, if men are being paid according to their marginal product, it signifies that women are being 'exploited'.

One may wonder here why Pigou so easily jettisons the short-run profit-maximizing criterion, cornerstone of employers' behaviour in marginalist theory, to shift to the extra-economic motive of 'convenience', and why he so readily accepts that men's and women's wages should differ, in spite of equal productivity.[21]

While extra-economic considerations by employers do not hold a prominent place in *The Economics of Welfare*, they are introduced in a direct manner in the essay, 'Men's and Women's Wages', under the form of a new concept, that of 'the value of a man' or 'the value of a woman' to the employer. The employer's hiring decision depends on $v$, the ratio of 'the value of a man . . . to the employer . . . divided by the value of a woman'. The employer is faced with a theoretical 'continuum' in the values of $v$:

> These values of $v$ will vary from occupations where a man is worth much more than a woman, say, coal heaving, so that $v$ is much larger than unity, through occupations in which their values are close together, to occupations, such as nursing and looking after young children, in which a woman is more valuable than a man, so that $v$ is much less than unity. (1952: 219)[22]

The employer compares $v$ to the ratio of male to female wages $W_m/W_f$. Men only are hired where $v > W_m/W_f$, women only where $v < W_m/W_f$, and men and women 'indifferently' where $v = W_m/W_f$ (ibid.).[23]

But while this could be equivalent to the comparison of the ratio of day wages to the ratio of efficiencies of men and women found in *The Economics of Welfare*, Pigou clarifies that 'these relative values to employers do not depend simply on the comparative capacities of men and women . . . to produce current physical output' (ibid.: 220). He goes as far as giving a series of examples of what may enter in the employer's 'evaluation' of a prospective employee:

> [The employer] may prefer a man because in some businesses it is an advantage to have a staff whose members give long service, and women are likely to leave on marriage . . . he may believe . . . that, though men and women are equally good workers in ordinary times, men are less likely to panic or become hysterical in a crisis; or that women will be absent from work more often than men through temporary ill-health; or that he is not so likely to find among women employees as among men people suitable for promotion to higher posts; or, maybe, because he and his foremen enjoy an occasional burst of swearing, and swearing is more enjoyable in male than in female company. . . . If in any occupation they value a woman worker less highly than a man because they believe that she would faint at the sight of a spider or a mouse, this opinion plays its part in the general wage set-up equally whether it is true or false. (ibid.: 220–1)

Most of these elements are the expression of social or individual prejudices against women, or, in some cases, far-fetched occurrences (fainting, hysteria) of which the frequency and actual impact on long-run productivity are not empirically documented,[24] or, in other cases, actions procuring 'enjoyment' to employers and foremen (swearing) without particular demonstrated effect on production.[25] Pigou gives them full credibility by tying them to employers' presumed calculations of long-run returns.

Thus, any irrational belief or irrelevant action of an otherwise presumed rational, profit-maximizing, capitalist employer gains, through the writing of the economist, the same status as rational marginal calculations.

It is indeed revealing that after this description of employers' behaviour, and his acknowledgement that it may not be 'reasonable or soundly based' (ibid.: 220), Pigou does not engage in a discussion of its potentially detrimental effect on market mechanisms, on the resulting suboptimal prices and resource allocation. Whether these elements may only be pretexts for segregating the workforce, paying women less, or reaping extra profits, they are readily accepted by Pigou and are seen to require no policy control. Instead, he argues that wider social considerations should transcend the 'narrow' economic focus on this matter and that economists should not interfere with the present state of things because it is 'outside their scope' (ibid.: 224–5).

**Labour market segregation**
The denial of employment opportunities to women is seen by Pigou as

having a negative impact on women's wages. In 'Men's and Women's Wages', he states that:

> pressures and contentions tending to exclude women from certain occupations . . . force them away from centres where their capacities relatively to men are larger and in centres where they are relatively smaller. Thus they . . . reduce the weekly wage rates of women relatively to those of men throughout the whole economy. (1952: 222)

To avoid this Pigou argues that women should be allowed to compete freely with men for all jobs in the labour market.[26] Yet, he holds the view that women's productivity level is such that they could not be hired in jobs presently held by men, except at a cost to economic efficiency. He maintains that 'there are industries which are properly women's industries' (ibid.), and that, even in the 'marginal occupations' held by both sexes (such as teaching) the women do not do *precisely the same job*' as the men (ibid.: 218). This amounts to a denial that competition for jobs between men and women on the labour market could really take place.

This view underlies the models Pigou constructs where the labour market is *de facto* structured into separate components and where occupations and industries are organized into a spectrum based on the perceived relative efficiency of the (average or representative) members of the two sexes (1960: 567).

In these models the argument of segregation in employment is used in support of Pigou's rationalization of unequal pay for men and women. At the same time, in a purely tautological manner, inequality in the 'fair wages' for the two sexes itself determines labour market segregation. As a result, women are paid women's wages in women's industries and occupations. New industries open up to women when the lower wage rates induce employers to switch from male to female employees. And, in the 'marginal occupations', the argument that women do not do 'precisely the same job' as men 'explains' pay differences between the sexes.

In addressing the question of unequal pay Pigou concentrates exclusively on discrimination in wages, while ignoring the fact that discrimination against women with respect to hiring or employment opportunities is relevant to the question as well. Accordingly, he argues that where employers substitute women for men in a particular field 'there will be no discrimination because no men are left there' (1952: 225). The question of whether this results from discrimination in pay, and whether it reinforces a situation where women receive lower pay than men across the board is not addressed by Pigou. Indeed, it appears from this passage that he would see no harm in a situation of completely segregated employment for men and women, as the thorny problem of unequal pay for the same work would not arise at all. In fact, his analysis would require such a situation.

## Women's labour supply

Pigou begins his analysis of women's labour supply by noting that the relative supply of men's and women's labour 'is determined partly by the physiological fact that male and female children survive in nearly equal numbers', a fact independent of the comparative wages paid to men and women (1960: 565). While, in itself, this physiological fact should lead to equal labour force participation by the two sexes, Pigou observes that this is not the case, but does not elaborate on the precise reasons for the discrepancy. Indeed, physiology is never mentioned again and one wonders why it was brought up in the first place.[27]

One obvious cause for lesser participation in the labour force by women, their other 'job' at home, is not mentioned at all in Pigou's discussion of female labour supply. Yet he is aware of a life-cycle pattern of labour force participation by women: they seek employment when they are young, leave it upon marriage, and return, if in need, when older. But he identifies this pattern only with reference to the effects on women's productivity which result from it. It is never used to develop an analysis of women's availability for employment.

Presuming that women's supply of labour is positively related to price, Pigou mentions 'women's wages' as a factor determining that supply. It is, however, a minor factor. What he sees as the major determinant of women's labour supply is their husband's labour income.

> The proportions, respectively of the men and women in existence who offer their work in industry depend, not only on the wages offered to members of either sex separately, but also, since women are less likely to work at industry the more money husbands are earning, on the aggregate amount of joint family income. (ibid.)

All women are presumed to be part of a nuclear family in which they are economically dependent on male household members. They are forced into the labour force only by financial need resulting from the male household member's absence or failure to earn a 'living wage'.[28]

The level of the husband's income is consistently identified by Pigou as the main determinant of women's (presumably married) labour supply (1960: 87n., 565–6, 600, 707; 1952: 221). In comparison, the level of wages that women can expect to receive in the labour market is mentioned only once as a supply factor. (1960: 565).

In a footnote on the mathematical formulation of labour supply and demand (p. 566), Pigou specifies the female labour supply as $f_1(w_1,w_2)$, a function of $w_1$, women's wage rate and $w_2$, men's wage rate. The first derivative with respect to men's wages,

$$\frac{\delta f_1(w_1,w_2)}{\delta w_2}$$

is described as negative, indicating a downward slope of women's labour supply when plotted against men's wages.[29] This function is not specified further. Nothing is said about the possibility of a perfectly elastic portion in that curve, where male income is nil.

With respect to women's wages, the first derivative of the supply function,

$$\frac{\delta f_1(w_1,w_2)}{\delta w_1}$$

is, according to Pigou, positive, which implies an upward-sloping supply curve for female labour. This is the only place where Pigou indicates how he perceives the relation between women's wages and their supply of labour which, he asserts, follows the standard 'law of supply'.

His assertion of an upward-sloping supply curve of women's labour is questionable, or, more correctly, it may be applicable only to women whose labour force participation is not necessitated by insufficient family income. It is possible, indeed likely, that married women would work for any wage when household income is below subsistence requirements, generating a perfectly elastic supply curve. It is possible too that they might increase their supply of labour in the face of a decrease in their wages to maintain their contribution to family income, which would make the supply curve downward sloping. And, more generally, women might decrease their labour force involvement as their wages increase.

While Pigou ignores these possibilities, his observation on women's labour force involvement, in a discussion on the effects of 'wage subsidies' ('poor rates') on the supply of labour, confirms them. He argues that subsidies do not lead workers to accept lower wages for their work, but, on the contrary, they help them to select better-paying jobs. One of the illustrations he offers in support of his argument is the example of women married to men who earn good incomes:

It is not the fact that the wife of a man in good work is likely to accept abnormally low wages. On the contrary, the woman who, for this or any other reason, can afford to 'stand out', is, in general, among those who resist such wages most strenuously. (pp. 707–8)

This observation is consistent with Pigou's overall view that what drives married women to the labour market is the insufficient incomes of their husbands. But what he does not explain here is why a well-off wife would want to work at all. Indeed, in Pigou's text there is no mention of any other motivation than family economic need for women's labour force participation.

In summary, for Pigou, women's labour supply is not determined by their individual needs, but by the needs of a collective entity: the family. As well, the major explanatory variable for their labour supply is not their own wages but someone else's wages – those of the male head of household. Women's labour supply is not self-determined, but derived.

Having looked at Pigou's treatment of the determinants of the demand and supply of women's labour, it is not obvious how precisely they 'together govern and determine the relation between the general level of wages paid to representative members of the two sexes' (p. 566). Indeed, it is not clear how Pigou's discussion of these factors offers the alternative explanation of the relative level of women's wages which he promised to provide at the beginning when he dismissed the subsistence-based explanation of men's and women's wages.

On the supply side, Pigou actually identifies the subsistence needs of the family as the major reason for women's labour force participation. On the demand side, he does not establish a straightforward relation between women's wages and their productivity levels. Instead, he constantly refers to the 'fair wages for women' or to their market-determined day wages as elements entering in the hiring decisions of employers. But the specific determination of these wages is never elucidated.

Pigou rationalizes below-productivity wages on the basis of the subjective values employers assign to women's labour. The range of factors that enter into this 'value' is so wide that it can point only to arbitrariness in employers' assessment of women's capacities and in their decisions on the hiring and remuneration of women. In particular, the wages offered can be abysmally low and bear little relationship to productivity if the employer knows that they do not have to provide for the full subsistence requirements of the worker.

**Subsidization of women's employers?**
Pigou rejects an argument, advanced in the *New Statesman*,[30] which

refers to employers whose labour costs are 'subsidised' by the fathers and husbands of their female employees:

> An industry, which uses up the human capital without replacing it, is not self supporting and does positive harm to the community. When therefore, a woman is partially maintained by some other source, such as by a father, husband, etc., the industry which employs her is being subsidised from these sources to the extent by which her wages fall short of proper maintenance. (p. 600)

Pigou does not deny that such 'subsidies' exist, that where employers pay wages below what a woman's subsistence would require, 'other sources' cover the difference. However, he does not see these occurrences as problematic as long as the women are paid at least as much as what they would earn elsewhere on the market, that is, as long as they are paid the so-called 'fair wages for women' (pp. 600–2). '[I]f they were not engaged in this industry,' reasons Pigou, 'they would still have to be "subsidised" to at least as great an extent' when taking employment elsewhere or when staying at home (p. 601).[31] He arrives at this conclusion by focusing on the subsidy *to the female workers* rather than *to their employers* by the male family members.

Whether women's subsistence needs are subsidized is irrelevant as long as their labour is not misallocated. A waste of productive power occurs only if women are employed at a wage below the market wage, or if they are not employed at all. The only 'true parasitism' Pigou acknowledges is where the employers profit from paying their workers 'less than they could and would earn elsewhere'. Accordingly, '[w]hen this is not happening, there is no parasitism even though workers are being paid much less than is required to maintain them in independent self-support' (ibid.).

Thus, Pigou begs the question posed by the *New Statesman*: whether it is economically justifiable that the labour costs of all the industries employing women should be subsidized by their workers' male relatives. He does not determine what the implication of such a situation is for the allocation of productive resources. He also ignores some of the implications of his position: for instance, why would women supply their labour to the market for less than a living wage and why is women's presumed productivity level consistently too low to earn them at least a full subsistence wage?[32] He is satisfied with the assertion that women are 'workpeople who are in fact worth, for all purposes, less than a living wage' (ibid.).

It is clear form Pigou's discussion that no market mechanism obliges employers to pay a living wage to their female workers. Moreover, women have insufficient bargaining power and organization to push their wages up. This situation allows employers to pay women a wage as low as they will accept (this level being determined by wages in alternative employment), regardless not only of the level required for their subsistence, but also of their productivity level.[33]

Pigou only acknowledges isolated instances of 'parasitism' when specific employers pay wages below the 'fair wages for women'. These arise only where employers enjoy specific market conditions (monopoly being one such case).[34] By seeing 'parasitism' as exceptional, Pigou avoids discussing the possibility of generalized parasitism when there is a common practice by employers of paying their female employees less than a subsistence wage, regardless of their marginal productivities.[35] Whether such a situation can actually be observed in the labour market is not addressed in Pigou's *Economics of Welfare*. However, in 'Men's and Women's Wages' he explicitly refers to employers' collusion with respect to women's wages, and asks: 'What of the effect of conventions and understandings among employers that lead to their offering lower rates of pay relatively to their worth to women than they offer to men?' (1952: 225), and recognizes that if such conventions spread 'over the generality of employment', women 'will have to suffer under-payment everywhere'.

Yet, whereas he does not deny that such a possibility exists, he claims that he cannot determine its actual existence and extent: 'Whether there is in fact a widespread anti-feminist convention of this kind and, if so, how large its effects are, I have no means of judging' (ibid.). Having identified the possibility of employers' collusion in the essay, and the rationale they can use to justify their actions in *The Economics of Welfare*, Pigou, surprisingly, stops short of putting the two elements together to develop an in-depth analysis of wage discrimination and exploitation of female workers.[36]

Instead, it seems that Pigou readily accepts his own rationalization for the inequality of men's and women's wages. He adopts as fact his own assumption about the low productivity level of women workers. He legitimizes the discriminatory behaviour of employers as a normal part of their economic decision-making. He does not question, from the point of view of economic welfare and the National Dividend, the implications of the low labour income earned by women. Indeed, it seems that he holds the belief that women's insufficient level of labour income does not bear any major economic or social consequence, since – in 'normal' circumstances – they derive their main source of livelihood, not from employment, but from economic dependence on men. He never ponders where that leaves 'self-supporting' single women.

The above considerations clarify the meaning of Pigou's concept of 'fair wages for women', which, he proffers, is the major guiding element in the determination of women's wages. The 'fair wages for women' do not seem to have any particular connection with the productivity of individual women workers. As a matter of fact, women who happen to receive a productivity wage higher than the 'fair wages for women' – perhaps because they are employed with men and get paid the same wages – are seen by Pigou to receive 'unfairly high' wages.[37] At best, if they are at all linked to productivity, the 'fair wages for women' are linked to the *average* productivity level of working women as a group.

Beside the presumption of the low average productivity of women, two other elements seem decisively to influence the determination of the 'fair wages for women'. On the part of the employers, the concept seems to be linked to their 'general understanding' that women do not need a full 'living wage', as they are presumed to be supported by husbands and fathers. On the part of the working women, the specific conditions of their labour supply (the requirement to provide for their family and their own subsistence needs), their lack of bargaining power *vis-à-vis* employers and their limited mobility would tend to generate acceptance of wages which stand below their own productivity levels and below their individual subsistence needs.

The concept of 'fair wages for women' reflects particular social assumptions on women's needs and how they are provided for, as well as the specific constraints women face in the labour market, rather than their actual, individual productivity levels. It yields a level of pay consistently below the subsistence requirements of a self-supporting woman. This is, in essence, the 'common idea' on women's wages that Pigou rejected as 'superficial'.

Far from producing a scientific explanation, Pigou merely accepts a dual system, a double standard of wage payment, with a 'living wage' or a 'family wage' for men and below-subsistence earnings for women. More significantly, the argument of separate 'fair wages' for the two sexes leads to the question of the applicability of marginalist theory to wage determination in general. Is marginalism applicable solely to the determination of men's wages? If so, what justifies women's exclusion from the scope of the theory? And how valid is marginalism if it applies only to a portion – though a majority – of the workforce, if it applies to it at all?

The implications of these questions for the neoclassical paradigm are indeed serious. Pigou's tortured discussion of the question of women's wages is a sign that he was probably aware of the problem. This is also reflected in the questions he excluded from consideration. He shuns consideration of the exploitation of women workers (on a grand scale). He does not investigate the extent of the 'abnormal' profits received by employers from the system of 'fair wages for women' and how such a system operates an effective redistribution of the product of industry from female workers to their capitalist employers. Furthermore, his assessment of the effects of this wage system on the National Dividend is incomplete and one-sided.

The neoclassical model coupled with Pigou's welfare economics approach, if rigorously applied to the question of women's wages, would normally lead to an indictment of employers' practices and to the recommendation of state intervention to ensure that women receive wages according to their marginal product. This, however, would threaten the position of women's employers on the market. It would also encourage women to enter the labour market. Pigou finds such an outcome undesirable, and says as much when he invokes the 'general' welfare of society as opposed to 'economic welfare'.[38]

> We must not assume that arrangements which are disadvantageous from an economic point of view are necessarily disadvantageous on the whole. 'Improvements' in the organisation of wages, if they divert women into industrial activity away from home-making, child-rearing and child-bearing may have implications which extend much beyond the sphere of economics and about which economists as such have no qualifications to speak. (1952: 224–5)

The implications of the present system for women workers are not taken into consideration in an approach where their exploitation by employers and their economic dependence on male family members are seen as optimal for society. In view of this, Pigou only makes a standard 'free market' recommendation to the Royal Commission on Equal Pay, which completely ignores his own demonstration that free market conditions are not present when it comes to women's work: 'It is, in general, safer to concentrate on removing barriers and taboos that obstruct the flow of women into industries suitable for them, leaving wage rates . . . to look after themselves' (ibid.: 226).

Given Pigou's position that, with respect to women, economic considerations come only second to social considerations, the questions arise of why he took the time to address the Royal Commission as an economist and why he claimed that economists have a better explanation for women's wages than the socially held 'common idea' he first rejected. It is clear that the objective effect of his intervention was to reinforce and legitimize 'unfair' treatment of women in the labour market.

# Notes

1. Pigou (1960). All quotations and page references are from the fourth edition unless otherwise mentioned.
2. 'When we have ascertained the effect of any cause on economic welfare, we may, unless, of course, there is evidence to the contrary, regard this effect as *probably* equivalent in direction, though not in magnitude, to the effect on total welfare' (p. 20).
3. It is paradoxical that, in this system, to maximize the national dividend, women are assigned to household production which does not enter into the calculations of that aggregate.
4. Pigou also quotes Marshall in his definition of the concept of 'fair wages': Wages in any occupation are fair when, 'allowances being made for the steadiness of the demand for labour, "they are about on a level with the payment made for labour in different tasks in other trades which are of equal difficulty and disagreeableness, which require equal natural abilities and an equally expensive training"' (p.549).
5. Pigou remarks that 'whether and how far . . . exploitation will actually take place, depends partly on the relative bargaining power of the employers and workpeople concerned . . . where the workpeople have been able to organise themselves in strong Trade Unions [. . . exploitation] is not even probable' (p. 559). So it seems that, as William Smart also remarked, trade unions are necessary to the optimal allocation of resources in capitalism, as they improve the workers' bargaining power without which, in most cases, wages could be set by employers below the value of the marginal net product of labour. See on this Persky and Tsang (1974). What is not clear is whether Pigou includes trade unions in the 'general tendency of economic forces' that equate wages with the value of marginal product. The concept of Pigouvian exploitation is based on the marginalist premises that the appropriate wage is equal to the value produced by the worker at the margin (VMNP). There is exploitation when the worker receives an inappropriate wage, inferior to this value. By contrast, in Marxian exploitation, the worker is assumed to receive an appropriate wage (equal to the value of his/her labour power) which is always inferior to the value he/she produces (Marx, 1967). In the remainder of this chapter, the terms 'exploited' and 'exploitation' are used in their Pigouvian sense.
6. The consequence of this 'exploitation' is to induce workers to work longer hours (a downward-sloping supply of labour?), which Pigou finds 'especially bad where the persons affected are women and younger persons, whose aggregate efficiency throughout life is liable to suffer greatly from over-strain in youth' (p. 467).
7. The definite implication of this is that a universal system of wage determination is threatened as soon as the working class is divided into separate groups.
8. Pigou calls these 'marginal occupations' because his evidence (gathered from the *Poor Law Commission Report*, S. and B. Webb's *Industrial Democracy*, and W. Smart's *Studies in Economics*) shows that there are very few of them (p. 567n.).
9. Pigou does not clarify how unequal wages could be paid to two separate individuals displaying equal efficiency. Also note that Pigou implies that this state of things is independent of the will of the employer – who, as a rational capitalist, would rather employ only women if they are paid a lower efficiency wage. The capitalist, far from being depicted as the source of discrimination against women, is presented as the progressive element in society, who attempts to 'break down the customs and rules that hinder' the hiring of women (p. 570). Nothing is said of the profit motive that pushes him/her to do so.
10. The father of welfare economics fails to address the fact that pre-existing low wages must have generated a misallocation of resources in the first place.
11. Pigou adds that even if the intention of an equal pay policy was actually to 'exclude women from industry', it still would be economically unsustainable for, beyond decreasing the number of women in industry, it would also generate a misallocation of the labour of the remaining women among different occupations.

12. In comparison, Marshall justified the Factory Acts on the basis of their long-run benefits exceeding their short-run costs; Pigou does not even address the question of the short-term costs of his own welfare proposals.

13. It is interesting to see how women's work such as 'simple sewing' is described as unskilled, and paid accordingly. Pigou here adopts the maxim that 'any woman can sew', and thus sees sewing as a natural, innate endowment, even if it takes lengthy training to acquire and perfect such a skill. Women's skills and trades have thus been systematically depreciated. If unskilled work is defined as work that can be decently performed with minimum (say a day's or even a week's) training, it is doubtful that even 'simple sewing' could be defined as such. Could Pigou have sewn as well as any cottage seamstress after such minimum training? See Phillips and Taylor (1980).

14. This argument is very similar to that developed more recently by adherents of the human capital school. There, women are depicted as having a choice between housework and market work and accordingly investing in their human capital. Women's 'lack of attachment to the labour force' is seen as a cause for low human capital investment and consequently low returns. See for instance Mincer (1962); Mincer and Polachek (1974, 1978); Mincer and Ofek (1979); Sandell and Shapiro (1978).

15. See Mincer (1962); Mincer and Polachek (1974, 1978); Mincer and Ofek (1979). Like them, Pigou does not propose solutions to the inadequate skill acquisition by women which results from this pattern. He never prescribes special training or education programmes. The only training he ever advocates for them is directed at improving their home-making skills.

16. The circularity, the unrealistic assumptions and the foregone conclusions of this model make it a perfect caricature of standard neoclassical economic modelling.

17. Such behaviour is also described as legitimate and further rationalized in 'statistical discrimination theories'. See Phelps (1972).

18. The day wages $W_M$ and $W_F$ are the outcome of the market: 'In equilibrium, there is one general rate of representative men's day wages and one general rate of representative women's day wages, the one or the other being higher according to the circumstances of supply, and according as the commodities demanded by the public are chiefly commodities for the manufacture of which the one or the other sex is especially well fitted' (p. 566).

19. Note here that W = VMNP for each worker (i.e. day wages = efficiency wages) is a sufficient condition for the equation

$$\frac{W_M}{W_F} = \frac{VMNP_M}{VMNP_F}$$

to obtain in any industry. If day wages were equal to the value of the workers' marginal product everywhere, all industries would belong to the 'marginal type'; marginal occupations would be the rule rather than the exception (p. 567n.).

20. A second type of allowance applies to the 'more skillful workers' of both sexes who occupy the machinery for a shorter period of time than the average workers.

21. Parallels can be drawn between Pigou's rationalization and Becker's (1971) 'taste for discrimination approach'.

22. Interestingly, Pigou uses the same examples as Cannan (see Chapter 3), yet in the essay he begs Cannan's question of why a children's nurse receives a lower wage than a coal heaver.

23. Note here that $W_m/W_f$ is a constant for all occupations as Pigou has derived a single wage rate for each sex from his assumption on intra-gender homogeneity. Given a presumed inequality of wages between the sexes, $v$ will have to be much greater than 1 for an employer to choose to hire a man. For instance, if $W_f = 60\%$ of $W_m$, $v$ will have to exceed $W_m/W_f = 1.67$. Hence, if employers keep hiring men in the

majority of jobs, one must deduce from Pigou's model that the 'comparative value of a man' must be amazingly high.

24. One should remember that this submission was made in 1946, after British women had proven their ability to attain and sustain high levels of productivity in the crises of two wars.

25. Pigou's argument on swearing appears in both texts. He could have argued that swearing is useful for maintaining or enhancing productivity when it is used on the shop floor to admonish workers to maintain workpace. Instead, on two separate occasions, he links swearing to the comfort, convenience and enjoyment of the employers and/or foremen. The use of this justification rationalizes industrial workspaces as the domain of men, which they can protect with behaviour offensive to women. A similar situation is created today with the posting of 'girlie pictures' on workplace walls and other forms of sexual harassment. Gary Becker has developed a similar rationale by setting such extra-economic elements as employers' and male (or white) workers' comfort and enjoyment in an economic framework and by arguing that employers are motivated by utility maximization rather than simple profit maximization when they satisfy their 'taste' for discrimination. In this latter approach, no disguises are needed; sexism or racism becomes accepted by economists as a normal component of the capitalist's decision-making process (Becker, 1971).

26. For Pigou, the main perpetrators of discrimination against women are male employees who fear being undercut by women and organize against allowing women into their trade. He contends that they would persevere in excluding women even if faced with an equal pay for equal work policy due to their fear that competition from women will generate lower overall wages as well as increased unemployment for men (1960: 508; 1952: 223). The possibility that employers may discriminate against women is not mentioned.

27. Perhaps this is linked to the lack of a real analysis of the labour supply in general by Pigou. The only definite statements he makes on its determination is that workpeople work and that the supply of labour increases 'through the addition to the number of workpeople or through an addition to their average capacity' (p. 664).

28. A 'living wage' is defined by Pigou as yielding 'a decent subsistence for the average worker', the concept of 'average worker' meaning a (male) worker with an average-sized family (pp. 597–8).

29. Curiously, the supply function of men's labour is specified in the same footnote as $f_2(w_1, w_2)$, with a negative first derivative with respect to women's wages,

$$\frac{\delta f_2(w_1, w_2)}{\delta w_1}.$$

Pigou does not explain anywhere in the footnote or in the text the reason for this formulation. At no point does he say that men's labour supply depends on women's wages. One can hypothesize that men's labour supply is specified in this fashion only for the sake of symmetry.

30. The date specified is 21 February 1914, but no author is indicated. No such article was found in this particular issue of the *New Statesman*. The argument of 'industrial parasitism' which Pigou addresses here was developed by the Webbs (1897).

31. Pigou's view that working women are subsidized by their husbands and their fathers regardless is curious in view of his treatment of women's labour supply where economic need – the need to complement or provide a 'living wage' for themselves and their families – is identified as the major determining factor.

32. It is striking that, in his whole discussion of women's wages, Pigou never reflects on the underlying proposition that, in industrial society, women's productivity level is consistently too low to earn them a full subsistence wage whereas men's productivity

level is consistently high enough to earn them a wage not only sufficient for their own subsistence, but also to provide partly or wholly for the support of a family.

33.  The belief (and the social reality) that women are supported by husbands/fathers is part of the reason for the weakness of women's bargaining power *vis-à-vis* their employers, and for employers' abuse of the situation.

34.  In one instance Pigou refers to a situation where a worker is willing to work for less than his subsistence requirements when 'confronted by an employer occupying towards him the position of a monopolist' (p. 707).

35.  Joan Robinson (1954: Ch. 26) developed the theory of monopsony-caused discrimination and applied it to specific groups in the labour market, such as women, who face distinctive conditions affecting their labour supply. More recently, Janice Madden (1975) has argued that labour market conditions faced by women can be analysed as a case of generalized monopsony.

36.  Pigou's submission to the Royal Commission on Equal Pay, which is the basis for the essay, 'Men's and Women's Wages', was delivered in 1946 while the fourth and last edition of *The Economics of Welfare* was published in 1932. Yet the discussion on the subsidy to women's subsistence which appears in *The Economics of Welfare* is not incuded in the essay.

37.  This expression seems a more appropriate reflection of the point of view of employers who may consider their situation 'unfair' compared to that of other employers who only have to pay the – lower – 'fair wages for women'.

38.  At the beginning of *The Economics of Welfare*, Pigou asserted that economic welfare was the measurable part of total welfare, and that 'the effect of any cause on economic welfare [. . . is] *probably* equivalent in direction, though not in magnitude, to the effect on total welfare' (p. 20). Here, however, he identifies a particular situation where an increase in economic welfare would – in his view – generate a decrease in total welfare.

# 10 The 'violent paradoxes' of A. C. Pigou: women in Pigou's welfare system

Pigou's treatment of the question of women's wages has to be situated within his overall approach to women's place in the economy. In *The Economics of Welfare*, he develops a blueprint for improvements in the efficiency of capitalist societies which includes an elaborate state-run welfare system. The major intent of this system is to rehabilitate the poorer portion of the working class and make it productive.

In this system, women are assigned to non-market reproductive work, a type of activity which is not recognized as contributing to the nation's economic welfare and which is not paid. Women must therefore rely on male family members' income and/or on state welfare payments for subsistence. Employed women are not guaranteed access to a living income, as Pigou rejects the concept of a minimum wage. He advocates a national human capital investment policy but restricts its scope to the improvement of male workers' skills. For him, the focus of women's education should be their domestic 'duties'.

## Women's work and the National Dividend

Pigou defines economic welfare as 'that part of social welfare that *can* be brought directly *or indirectly* into relation with the measuring rod of money' (Pigou, 1960: 11; emphasis added). While this definition could allow him to consider economic activities which are not strictly speaking monetary (so long as their outcome could be measured in money terms), he chooses to restrict his attention to economic activity which directly generates a monetary outcome. In particular, following Marshall and the British income tax commissioners, he excludes women's non-market work from inclusion in the National Dividend.

Pigou is aware of the inconsistency which this choice generates in his analysis:

> The bought and the unbought kinds [of services] do not differ from one another in any fundamental respect, and frequently an unbought service is transformed into a bought one and *vice-versa*. This leads to a number of violent paradoxes. . . . the services rendered by women enter into the dividend when they are rendered in exchange for wages, whether in the factory or in the home, but do not enter into it when they are rendered by mothers and wives gratuitously for their own families. Thus, if a man marries

*169*

his housekeeper or his cook, the national dividend is diminished. These things are paradoxes. (32–3)[1]

When women are barred from employment by the Poor Laws or by Factory legislation and 'diverted from factory work or paid home-work to unpaid home-work, in attendance of their children, preparation of family meals, repair of the family clothes, thoughtful expenditure of housekeeping money, and so on', activities Pigou obviously considers as work and as productive of utility, 'the national dividend suffers a loss against which there is to be set no compensating gain' (p. 33). When, in the opposite situation, a woman shifts from domestic to market work, the National Dividend increases. But in this case Pigou does not argue, as Marshall did, that the decrease in domestic production should be counted against the increase in the National Dividend.[2]

This difference between Marshall and Pigou is not an oversight on the latter's part. While Marshall could not decide whether housework was productive or, for that matter, what specific criteria should be used in making such a decision, Pigou 'resolved' the problem by linking the concept of productivity to the National Dividend. For him, the value of the marginal product of a given unit of a factor of production corresponds to its net contribution to the National Dividend (pp. 131–5). By this definition, housework, even though it is work, is not 'productive'.

Yet Pigou does not deny the 'economic' character of housework. This is apparent when he compares the productive efficiency of housework and market work: 'In occupations where commodities are produced, not for sale in the market, but for domestic consumption, and where, therefore, the competitive struggle is relaxed, the standard of competence tends, other things being equal, to be lowered' (pp. 754–5).[3]

He also recognizes the useful character of housework, particularly when it assumes specific forms: when it is performed by the mother, when it follows certain standards, and when it is the primary activity of women. One of his consistent positions is that women should not be prevented – in particular by economic need – from performing adequate amounts of domestic work. As a result he argues that impoverished women, especially if they are mothers, should receive state funds rather than having to seek employment to support themselves and their families. To bring the performance of housework to certain standards, Pigou advocates the expenditure of state funds on the 'training of the girls of the present generation to become competent mothers and housewives' (p. 100n.). He also rejects, when a mother is employed, the performance of child-rearing by other persons and, to justify this, asserts that 'a woman's work has a special personal value in respect to her own children' (p. 188n.).

Given that housework cannot be readily excluded from the realm of economic welfare, Pigou is hard pressed to find a rationale for his position that it should not enter into National Dividend calculations. Services rendered by housewives and mothers *can* be measured in money terms.[4] Yet Pigou insists on the need for a *precise* definition of the National Dividend. An unobjectionable definition, 'one that coincided in range with the whole annual flow of goods and services', is unacceptable to him as 'it would be tantamount to abandoning dependence upon the measuring rod of money', and 'would certainly arouse distrust even though it led to no confusion'.[5] A 'compromise' is required: 'It is only possible to define [the National Dividend] precisely by introducing an arbitrary line into the continuum presented by nature' (pp. 31–3). Here, in the name of *precision*, Pigou resorts to an *arbitrary* limitation of the field covered by his basic quantitative measure of aggregate economic welfare.[6]

After a lengthy justification of the need for such arbitrariness, Pigou declares that the 'arbitrary line' falls between 'the services that a man obtains from a house owned and inhabited by himself', which are somehow monetarily assessed and included in the National Dividend, and the services gratuitously rendered by women to their families, which are not included (pp. 33–4). Pigou concludes by asserting that, however unsatisfactory his compromise, 'nothing better appears to be available'.

**Economic welfare and women's work**

Pigou's major preoccupation in *The Economics of Welfare* being the enhancement of economic welfare, equated with the National Dividend, one might expect him to show little concern for domestic production, which he excluded from the aggregate, and to argue in favour of the expansion of women's activity in the labour market at the expense of their non-market activity. It is therefore surprising to see him advocate the restriction of women's market activity.

In his discussion of the effects of the length of the workday on workers' productivity and on the National Dividend, Pigou's immediate concern is not so much the welfare of the workers, their access to greater leisure for themselves, but the maximization of the National Dividend. Workers' leisure contributes to the National Dividend only indirectly and inasmuch as it is not spent 'in mere dissipation' but rather in activities which restore their productive powers.[7] The optimal length of the workday, then, is 'the exact length of the workday beyond which an increase would contract the national dividend' (p. 462).

In the case of women workers, a shorter workday is required to ensure that they have adequate time to perform 'their household duties'.

> children and women, and particularly women who, besides industrial work, have also the burden of looking after their homes can, in general, stand less than adult men. Further leisure for them yields a bigger return – for children in opportunities for healthy sleep and play, for women in opportunities for better care of their homes. (p. 463)[8]

Pigou does not mention who is the recipient of this 'bigger return'. Is it a benefit to the housewife that she should have more time to care for her home and family? Or does it rather benefit her family, the country as a whole (although it is not recorded in the National Dividend), or capital? Whereas the above statement acknowledges employed women's double workday and its negative impact on their productivity level, it exposes Pigou's position that domestic work should be their main activity.

His statement is very problematic from an orthodox economics point of view: he utilizes market-based economic concepts (returns, productivity) to direct women to non-market work. Hence Pigou's vagueness: having excluded housework from the realm of economic welfare and National Dividend calculations, he cannot provide a specific economic rationale for the reduction of women's workday in the labour market.

While the negative effect of an excessive workday on the National Dividend can be assessed (and controlled) in the case of male wage labourers who engage exclusively in market work, this cannot be done with female workers, who also perform domestic work. Changes in economic (and general) welfare caused by variations in women's wage workday will only partially be recorded in the changes in total commodity output.

Elsewhere, Pigou asserts that 'work done by women in factories, particularly during the periods immediately preceding and succeeding confinement' is a cause of higher infant mortality and is injurious to the health of mothers and children. Yet the only empirical evidence he possesses of a significantly lower rate of infant mortality in districts where women are employed is dismissed in the following fashion:

> The reality of this evil is not disproved by the low, and even negative, correlation which sometimes is found to exist between the factory work of mothers and the rate of infant mortality. For in districts where women's work of this kind prevails there is presumably – and this is the cause of women's

work – great poverty. This poverty, which is injurious to children's health, is likely, other things being equal, to be greater than elsewhere in families where the mother declines factory work, and it may be that the evil of the extra poverty is greater than that of the factory work. This consideration explains the statistical facts that are known. They therefore, militate in no way against the view that, *other things equal*, the factory work of mothers is injurious. (p. 187)

By 'other things equal', Pigou no doubt means that the variations in family income level caused by the employment or non-employment of mothers should be disregarded in the search for the causes of infant mortality. Pigou's sophistry has the effect of assigning the blame for infant mortality to the mothers – who 'insist' upon working when the family income is low – whereas, by so doing, they precisely attempt to remedy the poverty.

Having asserted that women's work was the cause of infant mortality 'other things equal', Pigou proposes a single solution: 'prohibition of such work' (ibid.). More humane than Marshall, he prescribes that this should be accompanied by state-funded compensation for lost income in the form of 'relief to those families whom the prohibition renders necessitous' (p. 188). He obviously did not imagine that these state funds could also be used to provide professional child care, improved medical care, or household help, alleviating the demands on women's time and leaving them free to decide between employment, partial employment or staying at home.

While he makes it clear that wage work should not interfere with women's household 'duties', Pigou is evasive on the question of whether women have a place in the labour market at all. His position seems to rest on the argument that women should not be *compelled* into the workforce by economic need, thereby being 'free' to give priority to their home and family.

Not only are 'financially secure' women able to choose whether to seek employment, they can also be selective in the type of employment they will take. Thus, 'in districts where men's wages are good, women only work at industry if they themselves can obtain well-paid jobs' (p. 87n.), and 'the woman who . . . can afford to "stand out" is, in general, among those who resist such [low] wages most strenuously' (p. 708). Pigou consistently assumes as normal that safeguard from economic need for women nominally requires reliance on men's incomes, or, failing that, on state welfare.

**Pigou's blueprint for a welfare state system**

A major portion of *The Economics of Welfare* is dedicated to the

elaboration of what Pigou sees as an ideal state-funded and administered welfare system with the purpose of correcting the imperfections
of the market, in particular with respect to income distribution and the
supply of labour factors on the market. The structure of Pigou's system
reflects his concern that the proposed welfare schemes should not distort
the market and negatively affect the country's economic welfare. Such
a system would attempt to provide a sufficient income level to shield
the working class from poverty and its negative impact on productivity
levels. It would also endeavour to enhance the productive capacity of
current and future workers.

In an elaborate, lengthy discussion, Pigou reviews all the possible
forms of state assistance to the poor to determine which type would
generate the greater increase to the National Dividend while minimizing
the 'idleness and the thriftlessness' of the recipients (p. 720). His
typology yields two 'desirable' categories of 'transferences'. The first
kind includes those which 'differentiate against idleness and thriftlessness' with payments conditional upon individuals making efforts to
provide for themselves or to maintain set levels of productivity, and
transfers which induce new needs among the recipients and thus
increase their willingness to work.

Specific examples of the latter are free medical treatment and free
education for children. These, Pigou speculates, will lead parents, and
particularly mothers, to take a more active interest in their children's
well-being and education (p. 727). However, it is clear that the effects
of these transfers on the National Dividend are only indirect and
realizable in the future since the increase in mothers' reproductive work
will not be counted in.

The effect of free but compulsory education for children is described
as follows:

> Since . . . their parents are deprived of the wages they might otherwise have
> obtained, it may be that, even when to free education free meals are added,
> there is no net lightening of the cost of living to parents, and, therefore, no
> diminution in the contribution of work and waiting which they find it
> profitable to make. In these circumstances the expectation of this variety of
> neutral transference will leave the size of the national dividend unaltered.
> (p. 726)

Indeed, the size of the National Dividend may actually increase if
parents end up 'contributing' more to make up the lost income and
satisfy the new needs created by their children's education.

The second type of desirable transfers involves those which Pigou
calls 'neutral' because they do not induce any change in the productivity

level and the willingness to work of the poor, and hence in the National Dividend. He argues that only *universal* transfer payments, those which are 'dependent on some condition, not capable of being varied by voluntary action in the economic sphere' (p. 722), fit this definition. Such payments must not be linked to income levels – which would induce the poor to stay poor (and unproductive), an effect achieved by the Poor Laws – but to 'conditions' such as motherhood, old age, widowhood, sickness, schooling age. Instances of such transfer payments are the 'universal endowment for motherhood' and universal old-age pensions.

In these, Pigou discovers the ideal compromise for liberal economists: state intervention to improve the poor's standard of living and productivity without the introduction of 'distortions' to the market. These transfers aim at increasing the supply, qualitative and quantitative, of poor people's labour without requiring an increase in the wages paid to them. If such transfers do not 'distort the market', they also do not distort the structure of income distribution since all, poor and rich alike, qualify for them. The 'work and waiting' of the rich is not distorted either.

The 'universal endowment for motherhood' (ibid.) is the specific form of state intervention proposed to restore working-class families' incomes to a 'living standard' when mothers are prohibited from work. Pigou justifies the need for this transfer on the basis of his own indictment of women's work 'in factories shortly before and shortly after confinement' (p. 760). In very strong terms, he advocates that the state should 'not remit the law and allow women to work, where legislation prohibits it'.[9]

What is curious here is that seemingly compassionate positions – an argument in favour of a minimum living standard for the poor and a case for compensatory payments to poor families when they lose income because of legislation – are used to justify a proposal for a *universal* transfer payment. The rationale of a compensation for lost income obscures the fact that the 'universal endowment of motherhood' would effectively be a payment for women's reproductive work, going to every mother, regardless of financial need or participation in the labour force.

Pigou's other justification of universal transfers – that they will not distort the market – does not seem to apply to the case of the endowment for motherhood. Indeed, the labour market would suffer distortions (a decrease in the labour supply) as a result of Pigou's proposal of a strict prohibition of employment for mothers. It is likely that the motherhood allowance would further reinforce these distortions by removing an incentive for mothers to work extra-legally.

Pigou shows particular concern for the case of widows who have children. He recognizes that

> whereas most of the regular trades followed by men provide persons of
> average capacity . . . with fairly adequate earnings, most women's trades do
> not do this. It is not at all obvious that a widow of ordinary ability, even
> without children, *can*, with reasonable hours . . . earn enough to 'maintain
> herself and provide for the ordinary vicissitudes of life'. (p. 723)

Nevertheless, they should not be allowed to work beyond the limits set
by the Factory Acts, or to send their children to work. This would
jeopardize the practical intent of these laws.

Here again, the remedy offered is not of specific welfare payments to
needy households, but 'universal' transfers: universal widows' and old-
age pensions, free education for all children along with the provision of
free meals at school.[10] Again it is likely that these universal transfer
payments would 'distort' the labour market by diverting women and
children from it.

Motherhood allowances and widows' pensions have, in addition, a
differential effect on men and women, inducing women and not men
(widowers, with or without children) to stay out of the labour market.
For rich and poor alike, such universal transfers tend to enforce on
women the roles of housebound wife and mother. They also force
working-class women to orient their activities towards the reproduction
of future generations of workers.

While Pigou goes much further than Marshall in his advocacy of
welfare-oriented reforms and government intervention, the intent and
the practical result of the programmes he advocates do not depart from
Marshall's own position relative to the 'upgrading' of the poor classes'
human capital and to the sexual division of labour and distribution of
income.

### A national minimum income?

Pigou discusses a further welfare proposition which is still the object of
debate among economists: the concept of a national minimum income,
or, in his words, 'the universal gift to everybody of a sum deemed
sufficient to furnish by itself the essential means of subsistence' (p. 722).

He adopts Marshall's insistence that the real income of working-class
families should be sufficient to provide for (physiological) subsistence.
However, he does not subscribe to Marshall's support for a 'family
wage' paid to male workers, since this would distort the market, put
excessive constraints on the employers who would be required to pay
such a wage, and lead to discrimination against married men with
families. He argues that such an artificial increase in wages would lead

employers to substitute other factors of production for labour. Hence, the opposite effect would be obtained: a higher rate of unemployment and lower real incomes in general, and among men with large families in particular.[11]

Pigou defines the minimum standard of real income 'below which [the state] refuses to allow any citizen in any circumstances to fall' (p. 759) as an 'objective minimum of conditions' rather than a 'subjective minimum of satisfaction'. That is, such standard is to be determined not by individual workers in relation to their self-defined and perceived needs and welfare, but by state authorities in relation to state-defined standards required for optimal population growth, labour productivity and overall 'improvement' of the labour force. Workers cannot be trusted to make use of transfer money income in the best way: 'it is idle to expect that resources transferred to poor persons in the form of general purchasing power will be employed by them exclusively in the openings that are likely to yield the largest return of capacity' (p. 756). Accordingly, Pigou does not define his minimum standard in terms of money, but in terms of goods and conditions required to maintain it: 'some defined quantity and quality of house accommodation, of medical care, of education, of food, of leisure, of the apparatus of sanitary convenience and safety where work is carried on, and so on' (p. 759).

Not only are these standards to be defined without the workers concerned, by the state, they are to be imposed upon them and strictly enforced.[12] As we found in Marshall, workers are not trusted to make the 'right' welfare-maximizing decisions, they are not even allowed access to independent, self-oriented welfare maximization. Beneath the dogma of liberal economics, the belief that, in capitalism, the working class exists only for capital is exposed.

Pigou is aware of the problem involved in his advocacy of state intervention:

> There is indeed, some danger in this policy. It is a very delicate matter for the state to determine authoritatively in what way poor people shall distribute scanty resources among various competing needs. . . . This danger must be recognised; but the public spirit of the time demands that it shall be faced. (pp. 759–60)

The interest of the country (and capital) are foremost in this matter.

The same authoritative prescriptions prevail, as we have seen, in the prohibition on women and children's work, but also in the education of 'the normal children of the poor', where Pigou advocates that children be taken away from their homes as it would be self-defeating to educate them 'while leaving them the prey of demoralising home conditions'

(p. 751). Curiously, the direct care of poor mothers for their own children does not have the 'special personal value' that characterizes that of other mothers.

Pigou even advocates coercing workers into the proper work attitudes and consumption patterns with threats of withdrawing state help from those unwilling to conform or to maintain employment or productivity (pp. 732–4). This could go as far as 'disciplinary measures . . . detention under control . . . long periods of detention in labour colonies' (p. 735).

While endorsing the need to establish and enforce a minimum standard of real income for the poor, Pigou rejects the concept of a minimum money income. It would give too much autonomy to poor people and risk the squandering of state funds. It might negatively affect the labour supply.[13] It also might generate political opposition from 'practical politicians' who dislike 'universalising grants to large categories of persons' (p. 730).

Pigou does not try to 'strike a balance between the conflicting considerations' involved or to determine the costs and benefits (in terms of the National Dividend) of a national minimum income scheme. Instead, he advocates a more 'practical' and 'politically prudent' approach to the objectives of ensuring a 'minimum standard of real income' for all: by 'enlarging the scope of neutral transferences' to the point where 'the elementary needs of practically all persons, whatever their income, are met through them' (p. 728).

In summary, Pigou's welfare system encompasses a threefold programme: (1) universal neutral transfer payments: pensions, motherhood endowment, free education, free school meals; (2) transfers in kind which ensure the satisfaction of some of the 'needs', as perceived by the state, of the poor,[14] while avoiding misdirected spending and squandering of state funds by them (p. 726); and (3) financial help associated with deterrent conditions (to avoid idleness) or outright coercion, for the remainder of the welfare cases.

Pigou describes the 'optimal' funding of such programmes. Rather than relying on the taxation of the rich, he suggests that the poor and the working class finance these programmes, imposed upon them without any input and defined by interests alien to their class, through a 'social insurance' system. He argues that workers will be less inclined to idleness if pensions, sickness benefits and unemployment insurance are financed out of their own income (pp. 730–1).

One thing which is left in the dark is the financing of the universal endowment for motherhood. Pigou remains very vague on the ways and means to practically implement and enforce it. For instance, he is silent on what the amount of transferences should be to fulfil the goal of providing a subsistence income.[15] He is also silent on how such a complex system could be made to work with the degree of precision he insists upon and meet 'the elementary needs of practically all persons' (p. 728).[16]

Notwithstanding such practical shortcomings, Pigou did develop a comprehensive proposal for a capitalist state welfare system, using as a starting point and justification the existence of poverty and the need to eradicate the resulting waste of productive resources. This 'optimal' arrangement includes: minimum taxation of the rich with the financing of the proposed welfare through income transfers within the working class; minimum disruption of the labour market; minimum injury to the National Dividend with programmes which do not distort the market and do not discourage the rich from investing; productivity incentives for the poor; and the enrolment (forceful or not) of a large portion of the 'parasite elements of society' in the workforce. Whereas Pigou emphasizes the positive aspects of his proposals, he does not investigate the impact of income redistribution, and in particular, of new taxes levied to finance the programmes, on the working class as a whole.

## Minimum income and minimum wage

One might expect to find that Pigou's proposed system of a 'national minimum standard of real income' for all would include a proposal for a minimum labour income which would then only require to be complemented by specific transfer payments for those who are not employed. A minimum labour income could ensure access to minimum subsistence for those who stand at the bottom of the labour force, in particular women, but also older, disabled or unskilled men.

However, Pigou specifically rejects the concept of a minimum wage system, arguing that his complex 'minimum standard of real income' provides a superior approach to a minimum subsistence for all, and for women in particular – who no doubt constitute a majority of the low-wage working class (p. 618). The actual wages received by women – which he recognizes as insufficient for the subsistence requirements of even a single person – should not be a concern for state welfare planners.

By proposing a welfare system focusing on family needs, he pre-supposes that all women are economically situated within a family and essentially dependent on a male income earner. Where this is not the case, he proposes the patriarchal substitute of a state-administered welfare system. Women's livelihood must not derive from employment, but from dependence on men and on the state.

Nevertheless, Pigou discusses extensively the question of a minimum wage. He states straightforwardly that the levels of subsistence incomes for men and women should differ, implying inherent differences in the needs and family responsibilities of the two sexes. His discussion of minimum wages follows his treatment of fair and unfair wages. He reviews various approaches to subsistence incomes: a 'living wage', a 'living income', and a 'minimum time-wage'.

### The 'living wage'

A 'living wage' is defined as yielding 'a decent subsistence to the average worker' (p. 597), with a distinction made between two categories of 'average worker': male and female. '[A] "decent subsistence" for the average man and the average woman respectively being interpreted in the light of the fact that the former has, and the latter has not, to support a family' (ibid.). As illustrations, Pigou lists instances of various states and countries where the concept of a differential living wage for male and female workers has been implemented. But, while he might have used these to investigate the impact of implementing a living wage policy on the level of employment of workers of both sexes and on the National Dividend,[17] he neglects this opportunity for 'empirical testing'.

Minimum wages' impact on economic welfare depends on the possibilities for reallocation of the workers affected within the labour market. Pigou assumes that living wage rates will be attached to specific occupations where 'low grade workers' have heretofore been employed. A raising of the wage rate (presumed 'fair' initially) to a living wage level would generate a redistribution of 'inferior workpeople away from the occupations in which they are specially privileged, leaving these occupations to be occupied exclusively by more capable men' (p. 602). As a result, the 'inferior' workers, shifted to other low-wage occupations, will not benefit from the policy. In such cases, the National Dividend will not suffer if all wages still reflect marginal productivity.

Where reallocation of workers between jobs cannot take place – which Pigou assumes to be the general case – the result of a living wage policy will be that 'some labour is ejected from employment . . . unless the demand for labour is inelastic' (ibid.). These workers will end up either unemployed or employed elsewhere, where 'the value of the net product of [their labour] is less than it was'. Suggesting that this would be the general case, Pigou concludes: 'The inference is that . . . to force up wages to a "living" standard in an industry where the fair wage is less than a living wage must injure the national dividend' (ibid.). Furthermore, the harm to the national dividend will increase as alternative employment for the 'ejected' labour becomes less readily available (p. 603).

Clearly, Pigou is here concerned with a very restricted type of living wage policy, one which is applied only to specific jobs where pay happens to be below the level of a living wage. What he calls 'evasion' of the policy can then occur. However, very specific conditions are necessary to allow such evasion: the existence of even lower 'grades' of employment not affected by the policy, to which the 'inferior' workers can be shifted, a situation of less than full employment, and an elastic supply of 'more capable men' to fill the jobs thus vacated. He ignores the fact that there may be difficulties in shifting men to women's jobs, where the pay rates have been set at the 'living wage for women' level. His main shortcoming is that he neglects to consider the effects of a policy where the living wage is not attached to specific areas of employment, but applies to the labour market as a whole.

### A 'living income'

A 'living wage', says Pigou, will not yield a 'good life' to a 'man with a family in excess of the average or subjected to an unusual amount of sickness'. In contrast, a 'living income' is defined as a level of pay geared to individual rather than average family requirements (p. 599). Levels of 'living income' required vary because, among other reasons, 'the wives of some workpeople contribute nothing towards the family income, while those of others contribute largely' (ibid.).

In the case of women workers, Pigou adds:

> the connection between living wage and living income is even more remote [than in the case of men], in view of the great differences between the positions of women mainly supported by their husbands, self-supporting women, and women who are themselves the principal breadwinners of a family. (pp. 599–600)

He suggests that the variations found in the personal situation of women is greater, and more 'extraordinary' than in the case of men, making a 'living income' policy more 'cumbersome' to establish.

A policy of providing a living income to all workers is rejected on the grounds that it would be inconvenient to implement and, if implemented, would generate discrimination between equally productive workers. The policy would create a situation where unemployment is 'concentrated upon men with large families' (p. 604), defeating its very purpose. Women would presumably retain employment along with bachelors, at the expense of men with large families to support.

It seems that the underlying purpose of Pigou's discussion of 'living income' policies is to make a case against 'living wage' policies. Given in particular the wide variation in levels of required 'living income' depending on the family situation of the individual worker, the case for a 'living wage' policy cannot be based on the rationale of providing adequate subsistence income for everyone: 'These various considerations . . . make it plain that the enforcement in any industry of a living wage, in any plausible sense of that term, would go a very little way towards ensuring a "living income" even to those workpeople who regularly receive it' (p. 600).

Having discarded the major argument advanced by reformers in support of a 'living wage' policy, he states that: 'The policy of forcing up wage rates in industries employing workpeople of such a low grade that fair rates . . . are less than living rates . . . has . . . to be considered on its own merits' (ibid.). With these words, the initial rationale for interference to raise wages where they are already fair (to provide for a subsistence income) is summarily dismissed. It is not surprising to find Pigou concluding that 'on its own merits', that is on purely economic grounds, such a policy is harmful to economic welfare as it 'injures the national dividend' (p. 602).

### A 'minimum time-wage'

The last minimum wage policy examined by Pigou is that of a 'minimum time wage', or 'national minimum day-wage below which no workman whatever can legally be engaged' (p. 613). If such a policy were implemented at the national level, Pigou warns that no fields of employment will be left 'into which low-grade workers can be pushed to be paid a derisory wage' (p. 614). As a consequence, Pigou predicts, 'the effect produced upon the national dividend may prove serious and substantial' (pp. 614–15).

But the expected effects on economic welfare are not entirely negative. Pigou foresees two areas of potential benefit. First, the policy 'will incidentally prevent the payment of certain low wages that are unfair, in the sense that they are the result of exploitation'. Consequently, the National Dividend will benefit from 'strengthening competent employers in their competition with incompetent rivals' (p. 615). Secondly, the policy could have positive effects where low wages are fair if higher wages generate higher productive capacity. But, here again, he attaches little significance to such positive consequences: 'obviously, however, these are mere incidents, by-products as it were, of the establishment of a minimum wage, and not the main consequence of it' (ibid.).

Pigou elaborates: the 'main consequence is the expulsion from private industry of a number of low-grade workers', this number being directly proportional to the size of the wage increase. The policy would thus generate 'considerable' unemployment among the low-grade workers, defeating its purpose (p. 616). He mentions that, in the long run, the damage might be alleviated by means of state policies to set up a 'well-organised system of care for the poor' alongside the provision 'in farm colonies or elsewhere, [of] an economic training of which they can afterwards make use'. But, '[t]he benefit to be looked for in this connection is more apparent than real. The establishment of a national minimum time-wage would accomplish very little more than would be accomplished without it' (pp. 616–17).

That is, the contribution to general economic welfare provided by a state programme of care and training for the poor does not have to be linked to a minimum wage policy: its positive achievements will occur whether such a policy is present or not. In short, Pigou favours state welfare programmes over minimum wage policies of any kind.

## Exempting women from minimum wage laws

The last argument Pigou advances against a minimum time-wage policy specifically concerns women (along with other types of, in his words, 'low-grade workers' such as 'old men' and 'state pensioners'). According to him, 'elderly women home workers and younger women workers in factories, who are of low capacity and are partly supported by husbands and fathers', will not be 'in a position to derive benefit from State training' (p. 617). No particular reason for this is given, but the consequence predicted is that a policy of minimum time-wage will drive 'these persons into idleness' and 'inflict definite and uncompensated damage upon the national dividend' (ibid.). Therefore, should a minimum time-wage policy be adopted, Pigou recommends as 'essential' that 'provisions . . . be made for excepting from its operation would be workers of the above type, whom there is no serious prospect of rendering more efficient by training'. He concludes:

> No doubt, in the absence of such a minimum a number of low-grade workers, particularly low-grade women workers with families, will be left in private industry with earnings insufficient to maintain a decent life. This evil . . . it is imperative to remedy. But the cure for it consists, not in establishing a minimum time-wage at a level that will drive low-grade women workers out of private industry altogether, but by the direct action of the State, in securing, for all families of its citizens . . . an adequate minimum standard in every department of life. (p. 618)

Pigou's biases, rather than facts or economic justice, seem to inform his position. By stating that women workers depend on economic support from husbands and fathers he denies any urgency to the proposition that they should receive a minimum subsistence wage. By insisting that women are 'low-grade workers', he implies that their level of productivity can seldom justify wages higher than those they already receive and that it cannot be improved.

Pigou also emphasizes the necessity to preserve areas of 'low-grade employment'. Underlying his apparent concern for women workers is a greater concern for the employers in the sweated industries.

Incidentally, Pigou does not consider the possibility that 'more capable' women workers might be attracted to industry by the implementation of a minimum wage policy, resulting in an increase in the National Dividend. His silence on this point makes one wonder whether he is attempting to prejudice the reader. One might surmise that he sees such a consequence of a minimum wage policy as 'undesirable', preferring women to be at home rather than in the workplace.

Pigou's whole discussion of the various minimum wage schemes reveals a strong bias against their implementation. He marshals selective 'economic' arguments to oppose them, ignoring or downplaying any positive impact on economic welfare that might result from them while emphasizing their potential negative impact on economic efficiency. Moreover, he strenuously advances the position that, even if such policies were implemented, they should not be made universal: 'low-grade workers', and women in particular, should be exempted from their scope.

Interestingly, Pigou does not apply the same arguments and approaches to the policy he favours. He is less worried about the 'inefficient allocation of resources' that a 'minimum standard of real income' might generate. He attempts to reassure his readers that inefficiencies will not arise because his scheme involves cross-subsidization among members of the working class as opposed to increased wages. Yet there can be little doubt that transfer payments to individuals and families would have an effect on the supply of labour, specifically, resulting in a sizeable exit of women from 'low-grade employment'. This should affect the sweated industries, possibly forcing them to recruit 'higher-grade, higher-wage' workers, or to find other (possibly less efficient) sources of cheap labour.

The impact Pigou's minimum standard of real income policy would have on the economic and social situation of women cannot be ignored. Women's roles as wives, housewives and mothers would be clearly reinforced as they are ideally prevented from having to seek employment. Older women and widows, by becoming the recipients of pensions, would not have to rely on employment. However, a pool of women would be left in the labour force: the young and childless, who would still be forced to seek employment to attempt to make a living, unless they could rely on the support of fathers, brothers or husbands. Nothing in Pigou's proposals ensures that they earn a living wage from employment. Indeed, the presumption of partial economic support from male relatives alleviates pressure on employers to pay their female workers anything remotely connected to an individual living wage. So one of the outcomes of Pigou's welfare proposals is to ensure the continued existence of a supply of low-wage female labour for the employers in the sweated industries.

Pigou's argument favouring welfare payment over subsistence labour incomes assigns women to involvement in the labour force at a low wage level when young, followed by marriage (no doubt motivated by the need for economic security), and from then on, attachment to house-work and the reproduction of family members with, if need be, financial support from the state. The absence of provisions in Pigou's welfare system which encourage women to develop skills for lifelong labour force participation comes as no surprise.

**Training and women's productivity**
In the course of his discussion on women's wages, Pigou repeatedly states that women's low employment income stems from their overall low productivity, their lower productive capacity, both physical and mental, or their concentration in unskilled jobs and low-productivity trades and industries. Yet he never proposes a remedy to upgrade women's productive efficiency, as if he believed their low productivity was gender specific and inevitable.

In particular, in his argument on minimum wage policies, he dismisses the idea that the marginal physical product of women workers could be brought up to the minimum wage level with a programme of state-sponsored and funded training. Two elements seem to enter into this judgement. First, Pigou asserts, the 'low capacity' of 'elderly women home workers and younger women workers in factories' will stand in the way of their willingness and ability to 'derive benefit from State training' (p. 616). Secondly, the dependent status of women, 'who . . . belong to families able and willing to support them', strips them of all motivation to improve their earning power (ibid.). Thus Pigou suggests that women consciously choose to remain employed in low-productivity, low-wage jobs because they rely on other sources of income for their subsistence.[18] Curiously, this contradicts his argument elsewhere (pp. 707–8) that subsidies to individuals' wages do not make them accept lower wages, but instead allow them to 'stand out' and look for better-paying work.

What is also curious is that Pigou states elsewhere his belief that most persons' (does he mean only male?) productive ability can be improved through state training and transfer payments. According to him, the exceptions 'constitute only a small part of the whole body of poor persons' (p. 746), whom he characterizes as 'morally, mentally or physically degenerate' (p. 745). Pigou implicitly lumps women with people who cannot be 'rehabilitated' for the purposes of capitalist production.

Indeed, the only place where Pigou addresses the question of the education of girls and women is where it has nothing to do with employment and everything to do with housework and reproductive activities. He advocates 'the expenditure of State funds upon training the girls of the present generation to become competent mothers and housewives' (p. 114n.). In spite of his observation that women spend a number of years in the labour force, he promotes the improvement of their 'human capital' only for the portion of their active life which is spent at home. For him, however great women's contribution to industry and the National Dividend, their sole social and economic usefulness is as reproducers, this role being the only one justifying state expenditure.

### The role of women in Pigou's human capital theory

The absence of recommendations on the improvement of women's productive capacity outside the home is striking, given the amount of space Pigou dedicates to policy proposals geared to developing the 'human capital' of the nation. Indeed, the major rationale for his welfare system is the improvement in the productive capacity of the people targeted by it.

In describing investment of capital in human productive capacity, Pigou employs the terminology developed by Marshall (1930): 559–79, 660–7).

> In a perfectly adjusted community capital would be invested in the nurture, education and training of different persons, no matter in what class they were born, in such wise that the values of the marginal net product yielded by it would be equal everywhere. (p. 746)

From a social point of view, equal attention should be given to investments in 'human' and in physical capital, the allocation of investment funds being directed by standard maximization rules.

Yet Pigou observes that investment in the 'human capital' of the poor has been less than an optimal allocation of capital funds would require, owing to the discrepancy between the social returns from this investment, including returns to the poor themselves, and the private returns to the investors, including employers (pp. 746–7). In light of this situation, which is detrimental to maximum economic welfare, Pigou calls for the transfer of a 'moderate amount of resources . . . from the relatively rich to the relatively poor', to be 'invested in poor persons with a single-eyed regard to rendering the poor in general as efficient as possible' (p. 747). Like Marshall, he insists that the benefits to national economic welfare resulting from such actions will be cumulative, being compounded with each successive generation.

In the course of his argument Pigou involves himself in the contemporary controversy on eugenics. The eugenicists argued that human capacity can be improved only through genetic selection, by suppressing reproduction between human beings of 'inferior stock' (which in their eyes included the poor) and encouraging reproduction among those of 'superior stock' (including the rich). Consequently, they opposed any economic or welfare policy which they thought would encourage population growth among the poor.

In defence of his welfare proposals, Pigou argued that 'environments and ideas' have an influence on people's capacity, and that this influence is cumulative over the successive generations, even if it is not genetically transmitted. He applies a version of evolutionary theory to social change and economic welfare, and maintains that the impact of such elements on 'human stock' are of equivalent strength:

> We conclude, then, that there is no fundamental difference . . . between causes operating on acquired, and causes operating on inborn, qualities. The two are of co-ordinate importance; and the students of neither have a right to belittle the work of those who study the other. (p. 116)

While stating that eugenic considerations are 'outside the sphere of economics' (p. 110), Pigou makes certain recommendations of eugenic inspiration in his welfare proposals:[19]

> there are certain classes of poor persons whom no transference of resource could render appreciably more efficient. . . . [S]ociety is faced with a certain number of incurables. For such persons . . . the utmost that can be done is to seclude them permanently from opportunities of parasitism upon others, of spreading their moral contagion, and of breeding offspring of like character to themselves. . . . our main effort must be, by education and, still more, by restricting propagation among the mentally and physically unfit, to cut off at the source this stream of tainted lives. Here . . . from the standpoint of investment, the soil is barren. (pp. 745–6)

Pigou seems to believe that, in some cases, poverty and low productive capacity are linked with 'inferior' genes, which are transmissible genetically. However, he also believes in the influence of environments on the development of human capacity and proposes severing children of the poor from their environment of origin:

> It is useless . . . to spend money on educating children while leaving them the prey of demoralising home conditions. If they are not properly looked after at home, a part of the transference to them must be utilised in boarding them out with carefully chosen families, or in sending them compulsorily to an institution or industrial school. (p. 751)[20]

For similar reasons, Pigou requisitions the time of working-class women, whom he assigns to the production of an appropriate environment, which requires their exclusion from industrial work to improve their delivery of reproductive services (pp. 463–4, 187).[21]

Women have to be trained to become good mothers and housewives.[22] To achieve this he advocates

> the expenditure of state funds upon training the girls of the present generation to become competent mothers and housewives, because, if only one generation were so taught, a family tradition would very probably become established and the knowledge given in the first instance at public cost would propagate itself through successive generations without any further cost to anybody. (p. 114n.)

Interestingly, Pigou scrupulously attempts to minimize the expenditure of state funds on women's education, even when he approves of its goal. This one-shot human capital investment is supposed to have a double return for society: appropriate nurture of families and human capital investment in the present generation, as well as training the mothers and housewives of the next generation, free of charge. This proposal is based on a blatant oversight of the costs borne by women (present mothers and future generations) in terms of denial or lost opportunities for alternative training and occupation, and the fact that they will not reap any personal benefit.

Pigou's social Darwinist tendencies also surface in his belief that improvements in the conditions of the present generation (its living environment, health, education, skills, leisure activities, and real income level) will partly or wholly be transmitted to the next generation with a cumulative effect.

> [T]he environment of one generation *can* produce a lasting result, because it can affect the environment of future generations. Environments, in short, as well as people, have children. . . . ideas, once produced or once accepted by a particular generation . . . may not only remodel from its very base the

environment which succeeding generations enjoy, but may also pave the way
for further advance. (pp. 113–14)

The impact of increased real income for the poor will also be
cumulative. Initiated by the means of transfer payments, whether
monetary or in kind, higher real income will generate increased productivity among the direct recipients of these transfers and among their
(male) children.[23] This, in turn, will lead to the ability to earn a higher
real income, generating further increases in productivity (pp. 609–10).

But the resources transferred by the state to poor families will be
wasted unless they are brought to fruition by the appropriate reproductive care of women. To generate such care, mothers must spend more
time at home and income must be raised 'so that the wife [is] less
burdened with work and worry' (p. 754).

To further support his call for the specialization of women in
housework and the development of their education in household
matters, Pigou cites W. O. Mitchell's argument that people – across the
whole class spectrum – have insufficiently developed 'the art of spending
money', in part due to the lack of market-like competition among
housewives. Housewives must be better trained as consumers (pp. 755–
6).

It is clear that Pigou's blueprint for the enhancement of human capital
reserves a specific, sex-determined, role for women. Only persons of
the male gender are to be recipients of productivity-oriented human
capital investment. Women are seen not as direct beneficiaries of human
capital investment but as instruments enabling the fruition of the
investment bestowed on the male producers, present and future. This
involves a redirection of women's activity from market work to housework and motherhood, as well as a redefinition of the education of
young women to reflect their predestined occupation. In this light, one
can see that the place of women in Pigou's *Economics of Welfare* forms
part of a logically consistent, although not necessarily economically
coherent, whole.

## Conclusion
Pigou's views on women were indistinguishable from the most
retrogressive Victorian ideology. He believed that women were weak
creatures, incapable of heavy work, with inferior 'natural endowments
of mind and muscle', and whose health would be damaged by 'unduly
long hours'. He presumed that his ideas were widely accepted:

> Nobody would seriously wish to have women working at the coal face or at
> iron puddling, even if they were good at these jobs and could earn high

weekly wages at them. The adverse reactions on their own health and general
well-being and on that of their families would far outweigh any narrow
economic advantage that there might be. (1952: 224)

He saw them as incapable of protecting themselves, of organizing to
build up their bargaining power and improve their working conditions
and pay.[24] He supported the Factory Acts, and felt that women would
be safer in the home, under the protection of a husband.[25]

Pigou saw women's reproductive functions as paramount. In his
mind, women ought to be mothers because they were endowed with
special nurturing abilities: 'a woman's work has a special personal value
in respect of her own children' (1960: 188n.).[26] He therefore assigned
women their 'natural' place: the home, where their reproductive
function could not be neglected and their reproductive health
threatened.

Pigou's treatment of women in *The Economics of Welfare* is grounded
in his adherence to an ideology where they are not seen as independent,
self-contained and self-determined human beings, but as entirely
subsumed in the family unit,[27] with indirect claims to economic support
from a husband or the state, contingent on their performance of
reproductive work.

Pigou's beliefs become explicit or implicit assumptions which are used
towards justifications and proposals reinforcing a status quo in the
sexual division of labour (women at home, men in the workplace) and
in women's conditions of employment (low wages, discrimination,
short-term participation). This ideology, while conveniently reinforcing
a given socioeconomic order, is integrated into his political economic
thought. Following in Marshall's tracks, Pigou solidly anchors his major
contribution – his welfare economics – in patriarchal Victorian values.
This ideological structure is retained and reasserted in the face of major
social change, well into the middle of this century, as attested by his
1946 essay, 'Men's and Women's Wages'.[28]

His beliefs lead him to approaches and proposals which conflict with
the principle of economic rationality, with the basic method of marginalist economics, and with the very goals of his system of economic
welfare. The strength of his credo makes him forcefully defend
proposals which radically contradict his own definition of optimum
economic welfare. This is the case with, for instance, his rationalization
of wages below the value of the marginal product of labour, the
maintenance of normally inefficient industries, or the denial of human
capital investment to women and girls. He can only attempt to defend

these untenable positions by appealing to a 'superior', yet unspecified, concept of social welfare.

It is striking that, in Pigou's system, women's economic activity presents the sole, albeit generalized, exception to his asserted conjunction of social and economic welfare. He attempts to obliterate this major inconsistency by systematic obfuscation with the help of seemingly scientific economic reasoning. This indeed is the 'violent paradox' of Pigou's system.

Historians of economic thought have characterized Pigou's work as a coherent, all-inclusive whole providing a comprehensive approach to the abnormalities of capitalism.[29] In it, public intervention is reconciled with the workings of the free market – in contrast to the Smithian tradition where intervention was anathema. Indeed, his proposals are always aimed, he pleads, at perfecting and correcting the market rather than at constraining it. The policies propounded attempt to fill the gap between private and social costs and benefits. His human capital approach aims at generating better levels of health, education and skills among people – the poor – who do not have a sufficient income to 'invest' in these items at a level necessary for individual and social optima. In another instance, restriction of employers' powers is advocated where employees lack bargaining power, resulting in suboptimal economic welfare situations.

In the treatment of women's economic activity, Pigou's coherent system falls apart. The state is not enjoined to 'invest' in women's human capital, or to correct the sexist barriers to the development of their abilities. Employers' profits take precedence over women's subsistence needs and over economic welfare optimization. The individual is replaced by a group – the family – as the basic unit for economic decision-making. Women's individual utility functions must not exist in Pigou's mind, for they are never mentioned. If they exist at all, they are subsumed under or traded off against the 'superior' utility functions of the family or of capitalist/patriarchal society as a whole.

The ideology Pigou subscribes to makes him assert the superiority of a social system which is at odds with the pursuit of economic optimum. The true economic nature of this social system is not analysed as Pigou declares himself incompetent, as economist, to dwell on social matters.[30] Furthermore, the question of why, in this particular case, social welfare is to take precedence over economic welfare is not debated.

One could excuse Pigou when he does not want to discuss matters that he sees as relevant to the social as opposed to the economic realm. But what is not excusable is the liberty he takes with matters that are relevant to the economic realm. Such is the case when the economic *individuality* of women is negated, when they are not seen as human beings who can, in their own right, engage in the economic decision-making process and the rational maximization of their own welfare, and, further to this, when they are *not allowed* access to these processes.

Furthermore, by defining women as dependants, Pigou makes inter-personal welfare comparisons and subjectively ranks the welfare functions of individuals in society. In this ranking, women are placed at the bottom (along with children and 'the unfit'). His assignment of women to domesticity and motherhood is contrary to the most basic hedonist principle. He does not even presume that there could be a conjunction between their individual interests and those of society or that they might get some satisfaction in the performance of their 'duties'. In his eyes, it is enough that their assigned purpose is 'good for the nation as a whole'.

As for the appropriate reward to women for these activities, it is not discussed. The conditions under which women supply their labour present enormous theoretical anomalies when analysed within the marginalist paradigm: in the labour market, they perform work even though the payment they receive should *not* induce them to supply their labour; in the home they perform work for no payment at all. These challenges to the consistency of the neoclassical paradigm and to its theorization of the basic *modus operandi* of the capitalist system are purposely ignored by Pigou, who chooses to defer to something beyond his purview.

In Pigou's welfare economics, the advance over the *laissez-faire* doctrine is the proposal of corrective intervention by the state in cases where individual welfare maximization impairs overall economic welfare and where economic power is imbalanced. These corrective interventions necessarily attempt to restrain the economic power, and the advantage and gain, of the powerful party and to generate greater benefits to the abused party. However, in the case of women, in spite of his ready acknowledgement that they are one of the groups in society with the least access to organization and economic power, which lends them to easy victimization by their employers' greed, Pigou forcefully opposes intervention.

His *Economics of Welfare* provided theoretical rationalizations for the new trends in post-World War I capitalism. In it a model of 'welfare capitalism' is elaborated where improvements in the outcome of unbridled capitalism are sought in particular with respect to income distribution, the reproduction of the workforce, and the pricing of production factors.[31] Whereas these policies appeared to be more humane towards the working class and the poor, they entrenched the domestic and reproductive roles of women.

Pigou's system includes a double standard in wage payments, where men receive 'fair wages' which somehow provide them with a family subsistence income, while women's wages are kept at an exploitative level. Pigou's rationalization of this inequality exposes his belief that women's labour income can only be supplementary to a man's 'family wage' and that a – by definition – dependent woman does not need an income which would make her economically self-sufficient. The state transfer payments proposed by Pigou complement this. Not merely intended to supplement male labour income, they are also meant to maintain the roles assigned to the sexes in a perfected capitalist social order.

The conjunction of low market wages and transfer payments in support of women's reproductive activities (the 'universal endowment for motherhood') are economic 'incentives' used to keep women in the family as dependent reproducers, while not altogether depriving employers of a cheap workforce. The economic nature of the coercion exerted on women is reinforced by social or ideological elements such as, for instance, the denial of women's access to education, except for the acquisition of domestic skills.

Pigou advocates the involvement of the state in the determination of income distribution, in particular by redistributing income to the poor, although not necessarily from the rich. At the same time he gives the state wide-ranging power to control the determination and use of household income. The state is hence directed to intervene, not only into the autonomy of market mechanisms, but also into the autonomy of individual decision-making by interfering in individuals' choice between employment and reproductive activities, their acquisition of human capital, their expenditure of income, and so on.

The justification for such intervention is of an altogether different nature to that used to justify interference in market mechanisms: in the neoclassical paradigm there is no such thing as a 'perfect' outcome of individual decision-making since such outcome results theoretically from autonomous individual utility functions, preferences and choices. An argument in favour of intervention in individual utility rankings and individual decision-making can only be informed by normative value judgements implying the negation of individual values and welfare maximization, in the name of what is pronounced to be a 'higher' order of values and welfare.

What informs this most serious deviation from the neoclassical paradigm on Pigou's part is his perception that autonomous utility functions and decision-making by the class which supplies productive labour and by the sex which supplies reproductive labour in capitalist society will not lead to a situation where individual welfare maximization is congruent with the interests of the capitalist class: the 'invisible hand' left to its own devices is unable to effect a reconciliation of the interests of workers, women and capitalists.

Pigou's definition of an optimum state of economic welfare for the country as a whole encompasses, beyond the maximization of the National Dividend, a set of conditions necessary to the reproduction of the working class. The maximization of 'capitalist welfare' requires conditions permitting population growth as well as human capital investment in the male working class and a reduction in the 'waste' of potential human capital presented by the unproductive poor. Crucial to this goal is the requisition of women's life activity. To that end, women are denied to a further degree than working-class men access to autonomous welfare maximization. Patriarchal values inform and determine the exact nature of 'capitalist welfare'.

Pigou's welfare economics have been interpreted as providing humane solutions to poverty and the most predatory aspects of the capitalist free market. Yet a careful study of his views and proposals relating to women's social role and economic activity has allowed us to throw some light on the particular intent of his reformism. Behind the humanitarian façade are hidden proposals that reinforce patriarchal values, the authority of the state, the power of capital and the lack of options for the working class, the poor and, particularly, women.

**Notes**

1.  It is strange that Pigou should declare 'paradoxes' phenomena created by his own definition. The work and life activity of the majority of women have been ritually dismissed in most economic textbooks and by most economic lecturers since Pigou by the means of a worn-out sexist joke. Samuelson, in a fit of tokenism, used role reversal to recycle the joke for the eleventh edition of his *Economics* (1980): 'When a woman marries her chef . . .'. Except where otherwise specified, all page numbers refer to Pigou (1960).

2.  In one instance, Pigou argues that the sudden influx of women into the labour force should be counted as a *net* contribution to the national dividend: during World War I, he asserts, such an influx did not generate a decrease in domestic production as (1) previously idle women went into the labour force; (2) previously idle women replaced domestic producers who went into the labour force; (3) the total amount of housework required decreased due to the absence of men from their homes (p. 33n.). Pigou does not recognize the double workday of women workers and its effect on their productivity. He also forgets to mention additions to the National Dividend from the provision of market or government-produced services (child care, cooking, laundry) during the war.

3.  In this argument, market work is the norm against which housework is measured. It is inspired by W. O. Mitchell (1912), who remarked that the lack of competition between housewives leads to inefficiencies in domestic production. Similarly, the

members of the home economics movement and economists such as Margaret Reid (1934) deplored the fact that specialization of labour and the techniques of scientific management and Taylorism could not be fully applied to housework. These views can be contrasted with those expressed by Mill and Taylor on the efficiency of the domestic work process (Mill, 1965: 127–8).

4. This he acknowledges when he states that 'the concept of economic welfare is essentially elastic. The same measure of elasticity belongs to the concept of the national dividend' (p. 31).

5. Pigou does not specify who would distrust a comprehensive definition of the National Dividend. Is the question of scientific measurement at stake? Or is it rather the inclusion of such 'trivial' economic activity as that performed by women at home that would discredit the economist?

6. Also to be noted is Pigou's dubious perception of a 'continuum' in nature where in fact, it is he, the economist as a would-be positive scientist (one who is not supposed to meddle with the object of inquiry), who rearranges nature and ranks its phenomena with respect to the measuring rod of money, from the measurable to the non-measurable, in a 'continuum'.

7. Following the marginalist maximizing logic, Pigou could have argued that the appropriate length for the workday is that at which the marginal change in income exactly balances the marginal change in the worker's disutility from work. But, like Marshall, Pigou is not interested in the workers' own welfare-maximizing choices.

8. He does not seem to be aware of the irony of his proposal that women fill the leisure time he wants them to have with work in the home. If domestic work is leisure, why are men so reluctant to engage in it? and why do the rich hire domestics to perform it?

9. Where the Factory Acts prohibit or restrict the employment of women and children, Pigou argues that the law should *not* be waived in specific cases to accommodate the income needs of workers and the labour force needs of employers. Nevertheless, he maintains that, as a result, present and future workers should not be left to starve. We can here again contrast Pigou's prescriptions with those of Marshall, who had no concern for the decreased working-class incomes resulting from the Acts.

10. The latter proposal is justified as a way to assist needy children while avoiding the 'social awkwardness . . . and also the practical difficulty of determining which parents can, and which cannot, afford to pay' (pp. 729–30).

11. See Pigou (603–6; 1924a). Note here that Pigou assumes that the family wage would be paid only to men with families, rather than to all men regardless of family status, which would have avoided the cause for discrimination by employers. He generally rejects all across-the-board wage increases as distorting the market.

12. Pigou states this three times, in forceful terms, in the same page: for example: 'the minimum is absolute [. . . the state] will not allow [a citizen] to save money for a carouse at the cost of living in a room unfit for human habitation' (p. 759).

13. Pigou does not explore the extent of such potential effects. For instance, in 'Some Aspects of the Housing Problem', he states that 'in view of the fact that good conditions of life undoubtably increase the efficiency of those who enjoy them, state assistance might . . . be given in considerable measure before . . . gravely injurious reactions [upon the production of wealth] were set up' (1924b: 123–4).

14. These include 'public parks for the collective use of the poor, or flowers for their private use' (p. 726).

15. The reason might be that their costs would be too high. Today, such payments as family allowances, state pensions, welfare and unemployment insurance have fallen far short of the required level of subsistence income Pigou argued they should provide.

16. This is tantamount to leaving it to an invisible hand to administer a multitude of state payments and programmes and wishing for a miraculous fulfilment of the goals set.

17. Later in the text he uses the limited size of industry in Australia to dismiss the evidence that little harm was done to the National Dividend in that country (p. 603).
18. This argument can be contrasted to that of the modern human capital school who see women *choosing* home over employment on account of their 'greater efficiency' in the former sphere (Mincer, 1962; Mincer and Ofek, 1979).
19. In his view, 'propagation among those afflicted with imbecility, idiocy, syphilis, or tuberculosis' should be prevented. 'Especially urgent' is the case of the 'mentally defective, on the account of the exceptionally high rate at which, if left to themselves, they tend to produce children'. He also notes that 'feeble-minded women often begin child-bearing at an exceptionally low age', causing 'generations to succeed one another with greater rapidity' among this group (pp. 108–9).
20. This authoritarian posture follows that of Marshall, who advocates the closing of homes and the 'limitation of the freedom of the parents' of poor children (1930: 714–15n.).
21. He states: 'under the term environment I include the physical circumstances of the mother before, and immediately after, childbirth' (p. 116).
22. It would be interesting to determine whether Pigou had any knowledge of the 'home economics' movement.
23. To reassure the eugenicists and other critics, Pigou speculates that such transfers will not immediately induce idleness among the poor: 'State assistance . . . might be given in large quantity before negative effects show up' (1924b). He also argues that transfers of funds to the poor will not increase their fertility rate, citing Brentano's argument that increased income generates a decrease in fertility. 'Hence, it would seem, an improvement in the distribution of the dividend may be expected actually to diminish the proportion of children born from inferior stock' (pp. 212, 766–7).
24. It is amazing that Pigou failed to notice that women could successfully organize as attested by the Women's Suffrage Movement, to mention only the best known and documented organizational attempt by women.
25. He was obviously unaware that the home is not a safe place for women, even though his predecessor, John Stuart Mill, had repeatedly denounced the physical and sexual abuse women suffer at the hand of their fathers and husbands (Mill, 1965: 761).
26. He never reconciles this assertion with his remark that mothers neglect their children when they take up factory work and with his recommendation to sever poor children from their natural families.
27. In his essay, 'Report of the Royal Commission on Income Tax', Pigou strongly supports taxation of the household as a unit and opposes the feminist demand that wives be allowed to file for their income tax separately. He describes this demand as 'plainly unreasonable' (1924c: 129). In the essay, 'Eugenics and Some Wage Problems', he states his support for systems of income and taxation which 'encourage family building' (1924a: 89).
28. Pigou witnessed such changes as women's suffrage, their increased involvement in the workforce, especially during the two world wars, and reforms in their property rights. He was no doubt a witness to the ongoing feminist and progressive demands for a complete overhaul of the social and economic situation of women.
29. See for instance H. W. Spiegel: 'Pigou's welfare economics . . . offered, in fact, a systematic treatment of such instances [where "the pursuit of private gain did not redound to the welfare of society" . . .]. It opened up a wide range of opportunities for public policy and constituted an early attempt at developing a principled theory of such a policy' (1983: 574).
30. This does not prevent him, throughout, from incorporating in his approach a number of normative assumptions of a social character.
31. Between World War I and the late 1940s, major reforms establishing the 'welfare state' were enacted in western capitalist countries. Most of these find a theoretical rationale in Pigou's work. Exceptions are his opposition to policies of minimum wages for all workers, or particularly for women, and to minimum money incomes ('family wage' or 'living wage').

# CONCLUSION

In this study, we have been able to gain some insight into the patriarchal bias which informs neoclassical economic theory and determines the specific treatment given to women by economists. The neoclassical paradigm is based on a point of view which excludes women from the sphere of economic rationality: they are construed as not belonging in the market sphere and as unmotivated by self-interest. The treatment of women is rationalized by an ideology of femininity which excludes them from the strife of the market under the guise of protecting them. The principles of economic efficiency are thus not seen as applicable to them. Yet, as providers of reproductive services essential to the nature of capitalist production and social relations, and as (unwelcome) participants in some of the production processes, their exclusion from the realm of economic rationality yields contradictory situations.

The resolution of these contradictions by the early neoclassical economists involves the subscription to, and integration into economic writings of, the dominant (bourgeois patriarchal Victorian) ideology of sex roles. This resolution explicitly calls for the restriction of women's 'economic' activity (as defined by the economists), under the guise of 'protecting' women and the family/home against the harshness of the market, and for the safeguard of the supply by women of qualitatively appropriate reproductive labour. Ideology is used to control the economic status of women and to ensure their participation in a specific economic order where their own contributions are declared uneconomic while being unambiguously seen as necessary to the overall economy.

Going back to Adam Smith allowed us to ascertain that the division between the public and the private sphere and the attendant neglect of economic activities, productive and reproductive, performed by women in the private sphere inscribe themselves within the ideological tradi-tions initiated by the eighteenth-century political philosophers. The entrenchment of women's invisibility by the classical economists was insufficiently challenged by John Stuart Mill and Harriet Taylor. This attempt was flawed due to Mill's adherence to liberal Victorian views of women and to Mill and Taylor's class bias. Notwithstanding these limitations, it is clear that their feminism, and that of the late nine-teenth-century and early twentieth-century feminist writers, failed to acquire even a semblance of legitimacy within the orthodox economics discourse.

It is indeed remarkable that none of the feminist writers reviewed were participants in the neoclassical paradigm. Rather, they belonged to the classical school and to early manifestations of today's institu-tional and radical economics paradigms. Here one must contrast the non-neoclassical paradigms' relative openness to feminist views with the consistently regressive positions and anti-feminist reactions that characterize neoclassicalism, old and new.

The review of the debate on equal pay brings to light a shift, on the part of male economists, from an initial bona fide interest in the issue, involving a sincere attempt at theoretical developments and policy propositions, to the mystifying apologetic exercise of Edgeworth. While initially taken earnestly into consideration, the feminist positions, which prove the most developed and sensible approaches, are either ignored or derided by Edgeworth. It is noteworthy that the debate seems to be cut off once Edgeworth has stated his position that men's rights to a family wage and to employment supersede women's right to equality. Clearly he used his power as editor of the *Economic Journal*, and as the recognized 'expert' on economic matters, to close the debate.

The writings of Marshall and Pigou reveal that economists' treatment of women is informed by their belief that women do not belong in what they call the economic sphere. With no demonstration of whether that proposition maximizes economic or social welfare, women are assigned to the home. Both writers forcefully assert that women 'contribute more' as unpaid reproducers and as nurturers of 'human capital'. Not only are women denied any freedom of choice, but precisely because they have no choice the provision of economic rewards or incentives for their 'contribution' is viewed as totally unnecessary by the economists.

A singular theme therefore emerges in the history of main/male-stream economic thought: women belong in the private sphere and should, as much as possible, stay out of the market sphere – their presence there being allowed only in so far as it does not endanger their reproductive abilities and threaten their assigned nurturing role. The reason for this position, contrary to appearances, has nothing to do with women's actual productive capacity or with their ability to behave as rational economic beings. Instead it stems from the patriarchal beliefs of the male economic or political theorists, which reflect the economic reality of designated sex roles in a patriarchal capitalist society, and which, in turn, led them to construct and entrench the sexual division of labour in their theory. From Smith to Pigou, women are required to stay home to raise 'able workers and good citizens' (Marshall, 1930: 721) and to provide there the congenial moral environment necessary to the fruitfulness of what the economists define as the 'human' part of capital.

As women are not encouraged to participate in capitalist production, and as they are construed as dependants, they are not seen to require appropriate remuneration. Feminist demands for equal pay and equal treatment in the market sphere are dismissed. In turn, the ideology informing the rejection of feminist claims serves to reinforce the status quo: as economic dependants, women are not seen to require alternative sources of income or economic incentive to provide reproductive services in the home. Meanwhile, starvation wages and the lack of employment opportunities provide strong dissuasion to employment. With no viable alternative to domesticity and dependency, dependence can be further maintained by non-recognition and non-remuneration of domestic production and reproduction. The fine interaction of the ideology and reality of women's position in patriarchal capitalism provides a stable equilibrium of female oppression and exploitation.

Women are thus completely excluded from the sphere of economic rationality,[1] not on the basis of their physical or mental make-up, but because they are socially and ideologically defined outside this sphere. At the same time, the private sphere is defined as non-economic. In short, it is not that women are not economic beings, they just are not allowed to be. Their access to self-interest, to economic maximization, to free choice would threaten the whole economic and social structure, as is intimated by Edgeworth, Marshall and Pigou. This explains these economists' candid and forceful opposition to women's attempt to achieve recognition of their economic status.[2] Unfortunately for the neoclassical claim to scientificity, their ideological stance is in the way of a coherent and universal application of the 'laws' they have constructed.

Attempts have been made in the 'new home economics' to eliminate this problem. Women's economic position is analysed in the context of their involvement in both housework and market work. It is asserted that economic efficiency and joint utility maximization in the household require women's continued 'specialization' in the home-making role. Their individual utility and preferences are subordinated to collective needs and decisions. On the flip side, modern 'human capital' theory rationalizes women's labour market position on the basis of their 'captive' status in the household. These approaches again require a scrutiny of the treatment of women's access to individual, rational decision-making. As in the writings of Marshall, Pigou and Edgeworth, the methodological flaws and the sexist assumptions which prevail in later neoclassical theory are not accidental or unintentional, but deliberate exercises in ideology.

In this study we have observed the evolution of the definition of women's role in the history of mainstream economic thought in relation to the development of a feminist challenge to women's place in society. In the classical times, before the emergence of a consistent and

202 Feminism and Anti-Feminism in Early Economic Thought

analytical questioning by feminists of women's economic position, it was sufficient to appeal to an idealized vision of women and the home, a vision which even Mill adhered to in spite of his feminism. By World War I this vision no longer sufficed and the early neoclassical economists had to resort to a forceful expression of patriarchal ideology. However, as this position could not be sustained within the logic and methodology of the paradigm, it required purposefully confusing exercises in ratiocination and modelling.

The 'economy of women'[3] issue lay dormant until rekindled by the second women's movement, with its renewed demands for equal pay, along with demands for 'wages for housework' and analyses of the articulation of housework to capitalist production, among other challenges to the status quo. The mainstream economics reaction has taken the shape of the 'new home economics' and the Beckerian version of human capital theory. In the latter, the marginal productivity theory of wages is reasserted, and women's level of pay and their limited range of occupations are rationalized. In the former, neoclassical economics 'moves into' the household to 'demonstrate' the economic efficiency of the traditional sexual division of labour.[4] The feminist analysis of the construction of these new theoretical developments and of their implications is presently unfolding,[5] but is beyond the scope of the present study.

It is not clear whether the new inroads of neoclassical economics into the previously non-economic sphere (which, by the way, still does not gain full economic status in spite of the new attention it receives) allows women entry into the world of rationality. The discipline's traditional exclusion of women from this sphere, along with the denial of their individuality and the subsumption of their interest into that of the larger socioeconomic units of the family or the national economy, poses interesting questions. Since no specific reason is given by the economists, one can only conclude that rationality comes with the job, that is, from direct contact with the world of money and capital, a world from which women have traditionally been excluded. But, given the conditions of reproduction of the capitalist system, one must ask: is the rationality of the market sphere based on and dependent upon the irrationality of the private sphere?[6] Can self-interest be pursued in the market only under the condition that benevolence prevail at home? And, if benevolence/altruism are 'natural', if mothering is what 'women do best', why wouldn't self-interest (and the invisible hand) work for them? why the need for economic and ideological coercion? This questioning exposes male bias in the construct of the concept of economic rationality, and the necessity, in patriarchal capitalism, of such an ideological construct to obtain specific behaviour from women. We are thus brought to the realization that both the rationality of the market sphere and the non-rationality of the private sphere are but ideological constructions grounded in masculinist epistemology and patriarchal capitalist interests (Hartsock, 1985).

One certainty emerges from this epistemological questioning. In the economist's eye, conditions of reproduction of the capitalist system would not obtain if left to the free play of women's self-interest ('irrationality' for the economist). This certainty is reinforced when we go beneath the surface of appearances, bolstered by the mystifying magic of money in capitalism and the tales of the illusionist economists, to answer the question of who *really* depends on whom in the patriarchal capitalist organization of production and reproduction.[7]

This study further demonstrates the need for a feminist epistemology in the social sciences, for continued feminist critiques of malestream economic theory and for the building of a feminist economics. It shows that the process of building these also involves the documenting and recognition of a past history of feminist challenges to patriarchal economic theory. It stresses the need to reject limiting ideological concepts such as 'economic rationality' from theory and to base theory in the material reality of women's lives. And, beyond this, it requires that a feminist economics be intrinsically linked to the reality of women's freeing themselves from the material and ideological strait-jacket cum chastity belt which has maintained us as prisoners in the 'sphere' of benevolence.

**Notes**
1. Economic rationality can be defined as the pursuit of self-interest; see Folbre and Hartmann (1988: 4–11).
2. Mill offers the sole exception to the ideological stance of the profession when he proposes that women should be allowed the choice, albeit only once in their lifetime, between employment and marriage.
3. 'Economy/economics of women': see Vandelac (1986).
4. The 'new home economics' signifies a complete about-face of economic theorizing which had so far kept its distance from what goes on within the household. As noted by Folbre and Hartmann (1988: 5–6), Smith's division between public and private spheres allowed economists conveniently to dismiss what went on in the home as not-economics, as relevant to the realm of morality and benevolence. Beckerians now claim this domain as part of the economists' terrain. Altruism (Smith's benevolence) itself becomes the object of economic theorizing. The joint utility function is the sophisticated formalization of James Mill's concept that women receive protection within the family in exchange for their benevolence. Yet not much has changed: now as before power relations between the sexes are ignored.
5. See Cohen (1982); Folbre (1988); Folbre and Hartmann (1988); MacDonald (1984); Sawhill (1980) and White (1984).
6. Or is it the economists themselves who run out of theoretical rationality when they discuss the situation of women, when they impose on them 'choices' which go against

individual and social economic welfare maximization, when their famed logic makes way to unsophisticated acrobatic sophistry, when their ideologically inspired policy prescriptions contradict their own theoretical bases?

7.  See for instance Leghorn and Parker (1981); Ferguson and Folbre (1981); Vandelac (1986) and Vandelac *et al.* (1985).

# Bibliography

Arrow, Kenneth (1963), *Social Choice and Individual Values*, New Haven: Yale University Press.

Arrow, Kenneth (1976), 'Comment I', *Signs, Journal of Women in Culture and Society*, **1**, (3), Part 2, Spring: 233–7.

Banks, Olive (1981), *Faces of Feminism*, Oxford: Martin Robertson.

Banks, Olive (1986), *Becoming a Feminist*, Athens: University of Georgia Press.

Barrett, Michèle and McIntosh, Mary (1980), 'The "Family Wage": Some Problems for Socialists and Feminists', *Capital and Class*, **11**, (Summer): 51–72.

Barrett, Michèle and McIntosh, Mary (1982), *The Anti-Social Family*, London: Verso.

Becker, Gary S. (1964), *Human Capital*, New York: Columbia University Press.

Becker, Gary S. (1971), *Economics of Discrimination*, (1957), Chicago: University of Chicago Press.

Becker, Gary S. (1973), 'A Theory of Marriage: Part I', *Journal of Political Economy*, July/August: 813–46.

Becker, Gary (1976), 'Altruism, Egoism and Genetic Fitness: Economics and Sociobiology', *Journal of Economic Literature*, **14**, (3): 817–26.

Becker, Gary (1981a), 'Altruism in the Family and Selfishness in the Market Place', *Economica*, **48**: 1–15.

Becker, Gary S. (1981b), *Treatise on the Family*, Cambridge, Mass.: Harvard University Press.

Bell, Susan Groag, and Offen, Karen M. (eds) (1983), *Women, the Family, and Freedom, the Debate in Documents*, Vol. I, Stanford: Stanford University Press.

Benham, Lee (1974), 'Benefits of Women's Education within Marriage', in T. W. Schultz (ed.), *Economics of the Family*, Chicago: University of Chicago Press, pp. 375–89.

Bergmann, Barbara (1986), *The Economic Emergence of Women*, New York: Basic Books.

Bergmann, Barbara (1987), 'The Task of a Feminist Economics: A More Equitable Future', in Christie Farnham (ed.), *The Impact of*

*Feminist Research in the Academy*, Bloomington: Indiana University Press, pp. 131–47.

Bladen, V. W. (1965), 'Introduction', in J. M. Robson (ed.), *Collected Works of John Stuart Mill*, Vol. II, Toronto: University of Toronto Press.

Blaug, M. (1962), *Economic Theory in Retrospect*, Homewood, Ill.: Richard D. Irwin.

Block, Walter (1982), 'Economic Intervention, Discrimination and Unforeseen Consequences', in W. E. Block and M. A. Walker (eds), *Discrimination, Affirmative Action and Equal Opportunity*, Vancouver: Fraser Institute.

Bodichon, Barbara Leigh Smith (1859), *Women and Work*, Introduction by Catharine M. Sedgwick, New York: C. S. Francis. First published by Bosworth & Harrison, London, 1857.

Bodichon, Barbara Leigh Smith (1987), *Women and Work* (1857), in Candida Ann Lacey (ed.), *Barbara Leigh Smith Bodichon and the Langham Place Group*, London and New York: Routledge & Kegan Paul.

Boland, Lawrence (1979), 'A Critique of Friedman's Critics', *Journal of Economic Literature*, 17, (June): 503–22.

Bonar, James (1926), 'Memories of F. Y. Edgeworth', *Economic Journal*, 36, (Dec.): 647–53.

Bowley, Arthur L. (1934), 'Francis Ysidro Edgeworth', *Econometrica*, 2, (April): 113–24.

Cadbury, Edward, Matheson, M. Cecile and Shann, George (1907), *Women's Work and Wages, A Phase of Life in an Industrial City*, (1906), Chicago: University of Chicago Press.

Canadian Research Institute on the Advancement of Women (1984), *Knowledge Reconsidered: A Feminist Overview*, Ottawa.

Cannan, Edwin (1914), *Wealth, A Brief Explanation of the Causes of Economic Welfare*, London: P. S. King.

Chafe, William H. (1972), *The American Woman, Her Changing Social, Economic and Political Role, 1920–1970*, New York: Oxford University Press.

Chiplin, Brian and Sloane, Peter J. (1980), 'Sexual Discrimination in the Labour Market', in A. Amsden (ed.), *The Economics of Women and Work*, New York: St Martin's Press, pp. 283–321.

Clark, Alice (1919), *Working Life of Women in the 17th Century*, London: George Routledge & Sons, Ltd.

Clark, Lorenne M. G., and Lange, Lynda (eds) (1979), *The Sexism of Social and Political Theory*, Toronto: University of Toronto Press.

Cohen, Marjorie (1982), 'The Problem of Studying "Economic Man" ', in Angela Miles and Geraldine Finn (eds), *Feminism in Canada, from Pressure to Politics*, Montreal: Black Rose Books.

Dalla Costa, Mariarosa and James, Selma (1972), *The Power of Women and the Subversion of the Community*, Bristol: Falling Wall Press.

Dobb, Maurice (1973), *Theories of Value and Distribution since Adam Smith: Ideology and Economic Theory*, Cambridge: Cambridge University Press.

Doeringer, Peter B. (1967), 'Determinants of the Structure of Industrial Type Labor Markets', *Industrial and Labor Relations Review*, **20**, (2): 206–20.

Doeringer, Peter B. and Piore, M. (1971), *Internal Labor Markets and Manpower Analysis*, Lexington, Mass.: D. C. Heath.

Dolecki, Joseph (1984), 'Vulgar Marxism in the Critique of Neoclassical Economics', unpublished paper, Dept of Economics, Brandon University, Brandon, Manitoba.

Driscoll, Kathy and McFarland, Joan (1989), 'The Impact of a Feminist Perspective on Research Methodologies: Social Sciences', in Winnie Tomm (ed.), *The Effects of Feminist Approaches on Research Methodologies*, Waterloo, Ont.: Wilfrid Laurier University Press, pp. 185–203.

Edgeworth, Francis Y. (1893), 'Review of William Smart's "Women's Wages" ', *Economic Journal*, **3**, (March): 118–19.

Edgeworth, Francis Y. (1917), 'Review of *After War Problems*', *Economic Journal*, **27**, (Sept.): 404–6.

Edgeworth, Francis Y. (1922), 'Equal Pay to Men and Women for Equal Work', *Economic Journal*, **32**, (Dec.): 431–57.

Edgeworth, Francis Y. (1923), 'Women's Wages in Relation to Economic Welfare', *Economic Journal*, **33**, (Dec.): 487–95.

Edgeworth, Francis Y. (1925), *Papers Relating to Political Economy*, London: Royal Economic Society/Macmillan.

Edwards, R. C., Reich, M. and Gordon, D. (eds) (1975), *Labor Market Segmentation*, Lexington, Mass.: D. C. Heath.

Ehrenreich, Barbara and English, Deirdre (1975), 'The Manufacture of Housework', *Socialist Revolution*, **26**, (Oct.–Dec.): 5–40.

Eichler, Margrit and Lapointe, Jeanne (1985), *On the Treatment of the Sexes in Research*, Ottawa: Social Sciences and Humanities Research Council.

Eisenstein, Zillah (1981), *The Radical Future of Liberal Feminism*, Boston: Northeastern University Press.

Elshtain, Jean Bethke (1981), *Public Man, Private Woman: Women in Social and Political Thought*, Princeton, NJ: Princeton University Press.

Elshtain, Jean Bethke (ed.) (1982), *The Family in Political Thought*, Amherst: University of Massachusetts Press.

Fawcett, Henry and Fawcett, Millicent Garrett (1872), *Essays and Lectures on Social and Political Subjects*, London: Macmillan.

Fawcett, Millicent Garrett (1870), *Political Economy for Beginners*, London: Macmillan.

Fawcett, Millicent Garrett (1892), 'Mr. Sidney Webb's Article on Women's Wages', *Economic Journal*, **2**, (March): 173–6.

Fawcett, Millicent Garrett (1904), Review of *Women in the Printing Trades*, ed. J. Ramsay MacDonald, *Economic Journal*, **14**, (June): 295–9.

Fawcett, Millicent Garrett (1916), 'The Position of Women in Economic Life', in W. H. Dawson (ed.), *After-War Problems*, by the Earl of Cromer, Viscount Haldane, the Bishop of Exeter, Alfred Marshall and others, London: Allen & Unwin.

Fawcett, Millicent Garrett (1918), 'Equal Pay for Equal Work', *Economic Journal*, **28**, (March): 1–6.

Ferber, Marianne A. and Teiman, Michelle L. (1981), 'The Oldest, the Most Established, the Most Quantitative of the Social Sciences – and the Most Dominated by Men: the Impact of Feminism on Economics', in Dale Spender (ed.), *Men's Studies Modified, The Impact of Feminism on the Academic Disciplines*, New York: Pergamon Press, pp. 125–39.

Ferguson, Ann and Folbre, Nancy (1981), 'The Unhappy Marriage of Patriarchy and Capitalism', in Lydia Sargent (ed.), *Women and Revolution*, Montreal: Black Rose Books, pp. 313–38.

Folbre, Nancy (1984), 'Household Production in the Philippines: A Non-Neoclassical Approach', *Economic Development and Cultural Change*, **32**, (2): 303–30.

Folbre, Nancy (1988), 'The Black Four of Hearts: Towards a New Paradigm of Household Economics', in Judith Bruce and Daisy Dwyer (eds), *A Home Divided: Women and Income in the Third World*, Stanford: Stanford University Press.

Folbre, Nancy (1989), 'The Forms of the Family Wage', unpublished paper, Dept of Economics, University of Massachusetts, Amherst, Mass.

Folbre, Nancy and Hartmann, Heidi (1988), 'The Rhetoric of Self Interest: Ideology and Gender in Economic Theory', in Arjo Klamer, Donald McCloskey and Robert Solow (eds), *Consequences of Economic Rhetoric*, Cambridge: Cambridge University Press.

Friedman, Milton (1953), *Essays in Positive Economics*, Chicago: University of Chicago Press.

Galbraith, John Kenneth (1973), *Economics and the Public Purpose*, Boston: Houghton Mifflin.

Gilman, Charlotte Perkins (1962), *Women and Economics* (1898), reprinted with an introduction by Carl Degler, New York: Harper & Row.

Godelier, Maurice (1972), *Rationality and Irrationality in Economics*, New York: Monthly Review Press.

Gronau, Ruben (1973), 'The Intrafamily Allocation of Time: the Value of Housewives', *American Economic Review*, **63**, (4): 634–51.

Harding, Sandra (ed.) (1987), *Feminism and Methodology*, Bloomington: Indiana University Press; Milton Keynes: Open University Press.

Hartmann, Heidi (1976), 'Capitalism, Patriarchy, and Job Segregation by Sex', *Signs, Journal of Women in Culture and Society*, **1**, (3), Part 2: 137–70.

Hartmann, Heidi (1981), 'The Family as the Locus of Gender, Class and Political Struggle: the Example of Housework', *Signs*, **6**, (3): 366–94.

Hartmann, Heidi and Markusen, Ann (1980), 'Contemporary Marxist Theory and Practice', *Review of Radical Political Economics*, **12**, (2): 87–94.

Hartsock, Nancy (1985), *Money, Sex and Power: Toward a Feminist Historical Materialism*, Boston: Northeastern University Press.

Heather-Bigg, Ada (1894), 'The Wife's Contribution to Family Income', *Economic Journal*, **4**, (March): 51–8.

Hildebrand, George (1980), 'The Market System', in E. R. Livernash (ed.), *Comparable Worth: Issues and Alternatives*, Washington, DC: Equal Employment Advisory Council.

Hill, Georgiana (1896), *Women in English Life from Medieval to Modern Times*, London: R. Bentley.

Himmelfarb, Gertrude (1974), *On Liberty and Liberalism*, New York: A. A. Knopf.

Hogg, M. H. (1921), 'Dependants on Women Wage Earners', *Economica*, **Jan.**: 69–86.

Holton, Sandra (1986), *Feminism and Democracy, Women's Suffrage and Reform Politics in Britain, 1900–1918*, Cambridge: Cambridge University Press.

Humphries, Jane (1975), 'The Working Class Family, Women's Liberation and Class Struggle: the Case of Nineteenth Century British History', *Review of Radical Political Economics*, **9**, (3): 25–41.

Humphries, Jane (1977), 'Class Struggle and the Persistence of the

Working Class Family', *Cambridge Journal of Economics*, **1**, (3): 241–58.

Hunt, E. K. (1979), *History of Economic Thought, a Critical Perspective*, Belmont, Calif.: Wadsworth.

Hunt, E. K. and Schwartz, J. (eds) (1972), *A Critique of Economic Theory*, Harmondsworth and Baltimore: Penguin Books.

Hutchins, Elizabeth Leigh (1915), *Women in Modern Industry*, London: G. Bell.

Hutchins, Elizabeth Leigh and Harrison, A. (1903), *A History of Factory Legislation*, Westminster: P. S. King.

Jeffreys, Sheila (1985), *The Spinster and her Enemies, Feminism and Sexuality 1880–1930*, London: Pandora Press.

Jones, Thomas (1916), 'Biographical Sketch', introducing William Smart's *Second Thoughts of an Economist*, London: Macmillan.

Kennedy, Ellen and Mendus, Susan (1987), *Women in Western Political Philosophy*, Brighton: Wheatsheaf Books.

Keynes, John Maynard (1926), 'Obituary, Francis Ysidro Edgeworth, 1845–1926', *Economic Journal*, **36**, (March): 140–53.

Keynes, John Maynard (1944), 'Obituary, Mary Paley Marshall', *Economic Journal*, **54**, (June–Sept.): 268–84.

Killingsworth, Mark R. (1985), 'The Economics of Comparable Worth: Analytical, Empirical and Policy Questions', in H. Hartmann (ed.), *Comparable Worth: New Directions for Research*, Washington, DC: National Research Council, pp. 86–115.

Krouse, Richard W. (1982), 'Patriarchal Liberalism and Beyond: from John Stuart Mill to Harriet Taylor', in J. Bethke Elshtain (ed.), *The Family in Political Thought*, Amherst: University of Massachusetts Press, pp. 145–72.

Krouse, Richard W. (1983), 'Mill and Marx on Marriage, Divorce, and the Family', *Social Concept*, **1**, (1): 36–76.

Lacey, Candida Ann (ed.) (1987), *Barbara Bodichon and the Langham Place Group*, New York and London: Routledge & Kegan Paul.

Land, Hilary (1980), 'The Family Wage', Eleanor Rathbone Memorial Lecture for 1979, Liverpool: Liverpool University Press.

Lazonick, William (1978), 'The Subjugation of Labor to Capital: The Rise of the Capitalist System', *Review of Radical Political Economy*, **10**, (1): 1–31.

Lebowitz, Michael (1973–4), 'The Current Crisis of Economic Theory', *Science and Society*, **37**, (4): 385–403.

Leghorn, Lisa and Parker, Katherine (1981), *Woman's Worth, Sexual Economics and the World of Women*, Boston: Routledge & Kegan Paul.

Leibowitz, Arlene (1974), 'Education and Home Production', *American Economic Review*, **64**, (2): 243–50.

Lewis, Jane (1975), 'Beyond Suffrage: English Feminism in the 1920s', *Maryland Historian*, **6**: 1–17.

Lloyd, Cynthia B. (ed.) (1975), *Sex, Discrimination, and the Division of Labor*, New York: Columbia University Press.

MacDonald, Martha (1982), 'Implications for Understanding Women in the Labour Force of Labour Market Segmentation Analysis – the Unanswered Questions', in Naomi Hersom and Dorothy E. Smith (eds), *Women and the Canadian Labour Force*, Ottawa: Supply and Services Canada, pp. 167–207.

MacDonald, Martha (1984), 'Economism and Feminism, The Dismal Science', *Studies in Political Economy*, **15**, (Fall): 151–78.

Madden, Janice F. (1972), 'The Development of Economic Thought on the "Woman Problem" ', *Review of Radical Political Economics*, **4**, (3): 21–38.

Madden, Janice F. (1975), 'Discrimination – A Manifestation of Male Market Power?', in Cynthia B. Lloyd (ed.), *Sex, Discrimination and the Division of Labor*, New York: Columbia University Press.

Malthus, Thomas R. (1964), *Principles of Political Economy*, 2nd edn (1836), New York: Augustus M. Kelley.

Malthus, Thomas R. (1970), *An Essay on the Principle of Population and a Summary View of the Principles of Population*, (1798), Harmondsworth and Baltimore: Penguin Books.

Marglin, Stephen (1974/1975), 'What Do Bosses Do?', *Review of Radical Political Economy*, **6**, (2): 60–112 and **7**, (1): 20–37.

Markusen, Ann (1977), 'Feminist Notes on Introductory Economics', *Review of Radical Political Economy*, **9**, (3): 1–6.

Marsden, Lorna (1981), ' "The Labour Force" is an Ideological Structure: A Guiding Note to the Labour Economists', *Atlantis*, **7**, (1): 57–64.

Marshall, Alfred (1907), 'The Social Possibilities of Economic Chivalry', *Economic Journal*, **17**, (March): 7–29.

Marshall, Alfred (1930), *Principles of Economics*, repr. of 8th edition, London: Macmillan; Guillebaud edition, London: Macmillan, 1961.

Marshall, Alfred and Marshall, Mary Paley (1881), *The Economics of Industry*, 2nd edn, London: Macmillan.

Martineau, Harriet (1855), *The Factory Controversy; a Warning Against 'Meddling Legislation'*, Manchester: National Association of Factory Occupiers.

Marx, Karl (1967), *Capital*, Vol. I, New York: International Publishers.

Matthews, Jacquie (1983), 'Barbara Bodichon: Integrity and Diversity', in Dale Spender (ed.), *Feminist Theorists, Three Centuries of Key Women Thinkers*, New York: Pantheon Books.

McCrate, Elaine (1987), 'Trade, Merger and Employment: Economic Metaphors for Marriage', *Review of Radical Political Economy*, **19**, (Spring): 73–9.

McCrate, Elaine (1988), 'Gender Difference: the Role of Endogenous Preferences and Collective Action', *American Economic Review*, **78**, (2): 235–9.

McFarland, Joan (1976), 'A Critique of the Scope of Traditional Analysis and Research', *Atlantis*, **1**, (2): 26–41.

Mies, Maria (1986), *Patriarchy and Accumulation on a World Scale*, London, Zed Books.

Mill, James (1965), *Elements of Political Economy*, repr. of 3rd edn (1844), New York: Kelley.

Mill, James (1983), *Article on Government*, (1814), in Susan Groag Bell and Karen M. Offen (eds), *Women, the Family, and Freedom, the Debate in Documents*, Vol. I, Stanford, Stanford University Press, p. 122.

Mill, John Stuart (1935), *Autobiography* (1873), Oxford: Oxford University Press.

Mill, John Stuart (1965), *Principles of Political Economy, with some of their Applications to Social Philosophy*, Vols II and III of the *Collected Works of John Stuart Mill*, ed. J. M. Robson, Toronto: University of Toronto Press.

Mill, John Stuart (1970a), *The Subjection of Women*, in Alice S. Rossi (ed.), *Essays on Sex Equality*, Chicago: University of Chicago Press.

Mill, John Stuart (1970b), 'Early Essays', in Alice S. Rossi (ed.), *Essays on Sex Equality*, Chicago: University of Chicago Press.

Mill, John Stuart (1983), 'Speech before the House of Commons, 20 May 1867', in Susan Groag Bell and Karen M. Offen (eds), *Women, the Family, and Freedom, the Debate in Documents*, Vol. I., Stanford: Stanford University Press, pp. 482–8.

Mincer, Jacob (1962), 'Labor Force Participation of Married Women: a Study of Labor Supply', in *Aspects of Labor Economics*, Princeton, NJ: National Bureau of Economic Research.

Mincer, Jacob and Ofek, H. (1979), 'The Distribution of Lifetime Labor Force Participation of Married Women', *Journal of Political Economy*, **87**, (1): 197–201.

Mincer, Jacob and Polachek, S. (1974), 'Family Investment in Human Capital and the Earnings of Women', *Journal of Political Economy*, **82**, (2), Part 2: S76–S108.

Mincer, Jacob and Polachek, S. (1978), 'Women's Earnings Reexamined', *Journal of Human Resources*, **13**, (1), 118–34.

Mini, Piero (1974), *Philosophy and Economics*, Gainesville: University of Florida Press.

Mitchell, W. O. (1912), 'The Backward Art of Spending Money', *American Economic Review*, **2**: 269–81.

O'Brien, Mary (1981), *The Politics of Reproduction*, Boston: Routledge & Kegan Paul.

Okin, Susan Moller (1979), *Women in Western Political Thought*, Princeton, NJ: Princeton University Press.

Oser, Jacob (1970), *The Evolution of Economic Thought*, 2nd edn, San Diego: Harcourt, Brace & World.

Persky, Joseph and Tsang, Herbert (1974), 'Pigouvian Exploitation of Labor', *Review of Economics and Statistics*, **56**, (1): 52–7.

Phelps, Edmund S. (1972), 'The Statistical Theory of Discrimination', *American Economic Review*, **62**, (4): 659–61.

Phillips, Anne and Taylor, Barbara (1980), 'Sex and Skill: Notes towards a Feminist Economics', *Feminist Review*, **6**: 79–88.

Pigou, A. C. (1924a), 'Eugenics and some Wage Problems', in *Essays in Applied Economics*, London: P. S. King.

Pigou, A. C. (1924b), 'Some Aspects of the Housing Problem', in *Essays in Applied Economics*, London: P. S. King.

Pigou, A. C. (1924c), 'Report of the Royal Commission on Income Tax', in *Essays in Applied Economics*, London: P. S. King.

Pigou, A. C. (1952), 'Men's and Women's Wages', in *Essays in Economics*, London: Macmillan, pp. 217–26.

Pigou, A. C. (ed.) (1956), *Memorials of Alfred Marshall* (1925), New York: Kelley & Millman.

Pigou, A. C. (1960), *The Economics of Welfare*, London, Macmillan; 2nd edition, 1924; 4th edition, 1932.

Pujol, Michèle (1984), 'Gender and Class in Marshall's *Principles of Economics*', *Cambridge Journal of Economics*, **8**, (3): 217–34.

Rathbone, Eleanor (1913), 'Report on the Conditions of Widows Under the Poor Laws in Liverpool' presented to the Liverpool Women's Industrial Council, 64pp.

Rathbone, Eleanor (1917), 'The Remuneration of Women's Services', *Economic Journal*, **27**, (March): 55–68.

Rathbone, Eleanor (1924), *The Disinherited Family, A Plea for the Endowment of the Family*, London: Edward Arnold.

Rathbone, Eleanor (1940), *The Case for Family Allowances*, London: Penguin Books.

Reich, M., Gordon, D. M. and Edwards, R. C. (1973), 'A Theory of Labor Market Segmentation', *American Economic Review*, **63**, (2): 359–65.

Reid, Margaret (1934), *Economics of Household Production*, New York: John Wiley.

Rendall, Jane (1987), 'Virtue and Commerce: Women in the Making of Adam Smith's Political Economy', in Ellen Kennedy and Susan Mendus (eds), *Women in Western Political Philosophy, Kant to Nietzsche*, Brighton: Wheatsheaf Books.

Ricardo, David (1962), *The Principles of Political Economy and Taxation* (3rd edn 1821), London: Dent.

Robinson, Joan (1954), *The Economics of Imperfect Competition*, London: Macmillan.

Rossi, Alice (1970), 'Introduction', in *Essays on Sex Equality*, Chicago: University of Chicago Press.

Rossi, Alice (ed.) (1973), *The Feminist Papers, From Adams to de Beauvoir*, New York: Columbia University Press.

Rowntree, B. Seebohm and Stuart, Frank D. (1921), *The Responsibility of Women Workers for Dependants*, Oxford: Clarendon Press.

Rowthorn, Robert (1974), 'Neo-classicism, Neo-Ricardianism, and Marxism', *New Left Review*, **86**, (July/Aug.): 63–87.

*Royal Commission on the Poor Laws and Relief of Distress* (1909).

Salama, Pierre (1975), *Sur la valeur*, Paris: Maspero.

Samuelson, Paul (1980), *Economics*, 11th edition, Montreal: McGraw-Hill.

Sandell, S. H. and Shapiro, D. (1978), 'An Exchange: the Theory of Human Capital and the Earnings of Women: A Reexamination of the Evidence', *Journal of Human Resources*, **13**, (1): 103–17.

Sawhill, Isabel (1980), 'Economic Perspectives on the Family', in Alice Amsden (ed.), *The Economics of Women and Work*, New York: St Martin's Press, pp. 125–39.

Schreiner, Olive (1978), *Women and Labour* (1911), London: Virago.

Schultz, Theodore W. (ed.) (1974), *Economics of the Family, Marriage, Children and Human Capital*, Chicago: University of Chicago Press.

Scott, Joan and Tilly, Louise (1978), *Women, Work and the Family*, New York: Holt Rinehart & Winston.

Smart, William (1892), 'Women's Wages', *Proceedings of the Philosophical Society of Glasgow*, 1891–2, **23**: 87–105. Glasgow: John Smith & Son.

Smart, William (1895), *Studies in Economics*, London: Macmillan.

Smith, Adam (1976: *WN*), *An Inquiry into the Nature and Causes of the Wealth of Nations* (1776), Oxford: Clarendon Press.

Smith, Adam (1976: *TMS*), *The Theory of Moral Sentiments* (1759; 6th and final edition, 1790), Oxford: Clarendon Press.

Smith, Ellen (1915), *Wage-earning Women and their Dependants*, On behalf of the Executive Committee of the Fabian Women's Group, London: The Fabian Society.

Spender, Dale (ed.) (1983), *Feminist Theorists, Three Centuries of Women's Intellectual Traditions*, London: Women's Press.

Spender, Dale (1985), *For the Record: The Making and Meaning of Feminist Knowledge*, London: Women's Press.

Spiegel, Henry W. (1983), *The Growth of Economic Thought* (rev. and expanded edn), Durham, NC: Duke University Press.

Steuart, James (Sir) (1967), *Inquiry into the Principles of Political Oeconomy: Being an Essay on the Science of Domestic Policy in Free Nations* (1767; Reprints in Economic Classics), New York: Augustus M. Kelley.

Stocks, Mary (1950), *Eleanor Rathbone*, London: Victor Gollancz.

Strachey, Ray (1969), *The Cause* (1928), Port Washington, NY: Kennikat Press.

Taylor, Harriet (1970), *The Enfranchisement of Women*, in Alice S. Rossi (ed.), *Essays on Sex Equality*, Chicago: University of Chicago Press.

Thomson, Dorothy Lampen (1973), *Adam Smith's Daughters*, New York: Exposition Press.

Uglow, Jenny (1983), 'Josephine Butler: From Sympathy to Theory', in Dale Spender (ed.), *Feminist Theorists*, London: Women's Press, pp. 146–64.

Vandelac, Louise (1986), 'L'économie des femmes?', *Cahiers de recherche sociologique*, **4**, (1): 15–32.

Vandelac, Louise, with Diane Belisle, Anne Gauthier and Yolande Pinard (1985), *Du travail et de l'amour, les dessous de la production domestique*, Montreal: Editions Saint Martin.

Veblen, Thorstein (1902), *The Theory of the Leisure Class* (1899), New York: Macmillan.

Vickers, Jill McCalla (1984), *Taking Sex into Account: the Policy Consequences of Sexist Research*, Ottawa: Carleton University Press.

Walker, Francis (1906), *The Wages Question: A Treatise on Wages and the Wages Class*, London: Macmillan.

War Cabinet Committee on Women in Industry (1919), *Report*, Cmd 167.

Waring, Marilyn (1988), *If Women Counted*, San Francisco: Harper & Row.

Webb, Beatrice Potter (1914), 'Personal Rights and the Woman's Movement, v. Equal Remuneration for Men and Women', *The New Statesman*, 1 August: 525–7.

Webb, Beatrice Potter (1919), 'Minority Report', *War Cabinet Committee on Women in Industry*, Cmd 167.

Webb, Sidney (1891), 'The Alleged Differences in the Wages Paid to Men and Women for Similar Work', *Economic Journal*, **1**, (4): 639–58.

Webb, Sidney and Webb, Beatrice (1897), *Industrial Democracy*, 2 vols, London: Longmans, Green.

White, Margaret A. (1984), 'Breaking the Circular Hold: Taking on the Patriarchal and Ideological Biases in Traditional Economic Theory', Occasional Papers in Social Policy Analysis No. 7, Department of Sociology in Education, Ontario Institute for Studies in Education, Toronto.

Woolf, Virginia (1982), *Three Guineas* (1938), Harmondsworth: Penguin Books.

# Name index

Arrow, Kenneth 94

Becker, Gary 2–4, 7
Bergmann, Barbara R. 2, 4
Bodichon, Barbara Leigh Smith 9, 15, 37–42, 44$n$23, 51, 94

Cadbury, Edward 68–70, 72, 108, 115–16
Cannan, Edwin 98, 116, 151, 166$n$22

Edgeworth, Francis Y. 4, 9, 72, 78, 94–112, 114–18, 200–201
Eisenstein, Zillah 44$n$21

Fawcett, Henry 58
Fawcett, Millicent Garrett 9, 26, 57–60, 63, 67, 75–8, 80–84, 94, 101, 115–16
Folbre, Nancy 203$n$4
Friedman, Milton 11$n$17

Gilman, Charlotte Perkins 46$n$37

Hartmann, Heidi 52, 92$n$12, 203$n$4
Hartsock, Nancy 11$n$19, 47$n$55
Heather–Bigg, Ada 60–61, 72, 115–16
Himmelfarb, Gertrude 44$n$20
Hogg, M. H. 110$n$9

Key, Ellen 109
Keynes, John Maynard 140$n$10, 141$n$12

Madden, Janice F. 1, 168$n$35
Malthus, Thomas 23
Marshall, Alfred 9–10, 53, 69, 72, 96, 170, 121–43, 177, 186–7, 190, 200–201
Marshall, Mary Paley 53, 69, 129
Martineau, Harriet 141$n$16

Marx, Karl 165$n$5
Mill, James 23, 203$n$4
Mill, John Stuart 9, 15, 21, 23–37, 42, 94, 96, 98–9, 141$n$16, 195$n$3, 196$n$25, 199, 203$n$2
Mincer, Jacob 166$n$14
Mitchell, W. O. 189

O'Brien, Mary 11$n$20

Pigou, Arthur Cecil 4, 9–10, 72, 78, 121, 142$n$18, 144–96, 200–201

Rathbone, Eleanor 9, 75–85, 100, 102, 109, 114–17
Reid, Margaret 195$n$3
Rendall, Jane 16, 22, 43$n$2
Ricardo, David 23
Robinson, Joan 168$n$35
Rowntree, B. Seebohm 101

Schreiner, Olive 104–5, 109
Senior, Nassau 60–61, 141$n$16
Smart, William 62–8, 71–2, 108, 116, 165$n$5
Smith, Adam 9, 15–23, 28, 36, 42, 60–61, 133, 199, 203$n$4

Taylor, Harriet 9, 15, 23–37, 40, 42, 195$n$3, 199

Vandelac, Louise 4, 5, 10$n$11, 11$n$14, $n$15
Veblen, Thorstein 131

Walker, Francis 96, 105
Webb, Beatrice Potter 9, 75, 84–92, 108–9, 114–17
Webb, Sidney 53–60, 62, 64, 71–2, 114–16
Woolf, Virginia 47$n$52

# Subject index

absenteeism 55, 78, 156
allocation of resources 6, 76, 142n23,
   148, 156
  and trade unions 97
  and welfare policies 184–5
allocation of labour 161
  and minimum wage 96, 180
  women's 139
altruism 29, 35, 125, 140n8, 202–3
anti-feminism 2, 162, 200–201
apprenticeship *see* training
assumptions 3, 4, 7, 97, 103, 107–8,
  162, 190
  biased 57, 63, 154, 183–4, 201

bargaining power of women workers
  56–8, 65, 78, 116, 129, 148, 162,
  192
barriers to entry 25–6, 71, 76–7, 85–6,
  89, 95, 105, 108, 114, 164
battered wives 25, 45n27, 129, 196n25
benevolence *see* altruism
birth control 33
Boards of Trade 27
budget, household 127–8, 132, 135,
  139

Cambridge University 121, 141n12
capital
  accumulation 136
  'fixed' 18
  –labour ratio 148
  physical 186
  subsidization of 138
capitalism 6, 15, 33, 36, 82–3, 98, 113,
  177, 191
  reform of 23–4, 75, 83, 106–7, 109
capitalists 65–7, 101, 107, 136, 194
child care 70, 77, 126–7, 134–5, 155,
  173
child labour 102
childrearing 77, 79, 139, 171, 188
  and poverty 20

state control of 124
children 24, 132
  'human capital' investment in 4,
    20–21, 124–8, 137, 139
  and labour force participation of
    women 79, 126–7
  and poverty 20–21
  removal from poor families 124, 188
  support of 83, 88–9, 101–2, 109
  value of 21, 101
  and welfare 83, 89
chivalry 25, 105–6, 111n20, 129
choices, of women 25, 40, 100, 106,
  203
class (in capitalism) 44n18, 129,
  140n6, 143n33
  and domestic work 133
  and 'human capital' 135–8
class bias 4, 34, 46n34, 134–5
clerical work 55–6
coal
  heaving 70, 155
  mining 98–9
collective bargaining 85–9
collusion, of employers 116, 162
commodities markets and women's
  pay 56–9, 63–4, 66, 71
comparable worth 70, 72, 80
competition
  and minimum wage 69, 182
  perfect 3, 62, 69, 95, 98, 103–4, 114
  women and 35, 65–6, 70, 77–8, 80,
    86, 95, 103, 105, 108, 114, 129
consumption 107, 123, 131, 189
consumers 64, 66, 69, 71, 79, 189
contraception *see* birth control
countervailing power *see* bargaining
  power of women workers
cost of living adjustment 88–9, 117
crowding 26, 37–8, 59–62, 71, 76, 79,
  81, 97–8, 105, 114
  theory 8, 94, 97
custom 17, 25–6, 65, 99, 129, 149, 151

piece- 68, 99, 149, 155
and poverty 123–4
and productivity 53–4, 95, 114, 124, 162
reasons for women's low 17, 25–7, 37–8, 53–8, 76–7, 81–2, 89, 115, 128
remedies for women's low 56, 66, 69, 71, 89, 102, 116
as rent 26
standard rate 85–8, 115
subsidies 68, 159
subsistence 26, 63–9, 78–83, 101–2, 114–17, 130–32, 146
subsistence theory of 6, 8, 101–2, 114, 161–2
time- 93*n*13, 98–9, 129
unfair 146–9
and welfare maximization 95–6, 103–7, 132
of widows 65, 176
women's 6, 8, 17–18, 25–7, 37–8, 40, 51, 53–118, 128–9, 145, 149–54, 185
and women's labour supply 158–9
*see also* 'family wage'; income; minimum wage
wages for housework 47*n*51, 83, 202
war, and women's work 75–7, 81, 84, 88, 106, 194*n*2
War Cabinet Committee on Women in Industry 75, 84
welfare
  capitalism 89, 192
  economic 8, 66, 94, 103–9, 114, 144–5, 162, 169, 178, 182, 191
  economics 6, 8, 94–5, 103–9, 121, 164, 169–96
  and eugenics 187–9
  and the family 107–8, 179
  'general' 144–5, 164, 190–91
  and 'human capital' 171–6
  interpersonal comparison of 104, 111*n*11, 192
  and market mechanisms 122, 174–6
  maximization of 6, 66, 96, 104–7, 132, 151, 177, 191
  optimum 96, 104–9, 122
  payments 169–70, 173

and the sexual division of labour 107, 186
state 10, 89, 121, 169, 173–89
and taxes 178–9
widows 21, 147
and employment 63, 65, 152, 175–6
pensions 176
and welfare 184
wives 3
battered 25, 45*n*27, 129
contribution to family income 16, 39, 60–63, 104, 108, 181
duties of 19, 30, 35–6, 131, 189
employment of 16, 19, 29–31, 35–6, 39–41, 60–61
and housework 16, 29–31, 38–9, 169
income of 60–61, 108
and welfare 169–76, 184, 189
*see also* housewives; married women
women
abilities of 24, 27–9, 37, 54, 70, 75, 78, 81, 87, 153–4, 183, 189
autonomy of 35–6, 85, 90–91, 101, 106
as breadwinners 37–8, 61, 63, 76, 181
and class 19–20, 134–5
contribution to family income by 29–30, 63
contribution to the National Dividend by 17, 21, 40, 186
economic dependence of 3, 17, 24–31, 37–41, 56, 61, 68–9, 77, 80, 106, 108, 139, 162, 173, 179, 183, 185, 190–93, 200
economic individuality of 1, 24, 30–33, 40–41, 61, 69, 83, 139, 192, 201, 203
education of 18–19, 28, 34, 57, 114, 127, 141*n*17, 186–9
efficiency of 26–8, 64, 75, 81–2, 89, 98, 102
employment opportunities of 8, 16–17, 25, 29–31, 36–41, 77, 84, 95, 102, 105–6, 150–51, 157, 189, 201–2
exclusion from industry 25, 76–8, 85, 87, 188, 200